Burnt House
Beams
Coopers
Barnets
Hooks T.
Gotham
Bucks
M. H.
Smiths
Ellicotts upper
Furley
BALTIMORE
Red
iths
Stoney Hill
Saw Mill
Ellicotts
Mendenhalls
Canton
Golsuch Pt.
M. M. House
Cornthwaits
Balt. C.
Clapham Pt.
Bear C.
Martins
Dorseys
Norwoods
Ridgely of Wm.
PATAPSCO
Kelsos
Sparrows Pt.
Dorseys
Hockley
Selby
Hammonds
Cromwells
Curtiss C.
Dorseys
Deep Run
Elkridge Lan.
Plummers
Deep C.
Rock C.
Rock Pt.
DEL
Chapel Rock
Bodkin
Urquharts
Magothy R.
Severn Run
Wallaces
Ston
Snowdens
COUNTY
Porters Br.
Indian Spring Methodist
Snowdens
Urquharts
Hammonds
Severn R.
Hammonds Chapel
Baldwins
in Yard
Jones's Falls
Whetstone Pt.
Ferry
Deep Run

Best Wishes,
Jutta Cramm
1988

Christmas 1988

Dear Geigers.

Here is a history of your roots — some established by living, some by birth and growing up.

Remember, although your roots were transplanted over the ocean for three years, your real roots are deep within yourselves.

S- C -

In Appreciation to:

A. G. Parrott Co.
Brantly Development Corporation
Mr. and Mrs. Howard Harrison III
Security Development Corporation
The Columbia Foundation

For Their Support to

Howard County
A Pictorial History

Howard County
A Pictorial History

by Joetta M. Cramm

Francis Asbury, an itinerant preacher, visited Elkridge and presided over services for a congregation as early as 1772. Melville Methodist Church was formed from these early days and has celebrated its bicentennial. This brick house of worship was built in 1834. Later a frame church was built in 1885, which was moved onto a basement to enlarge the space available to the congregation. The exterior was veneered with brick and is the current home for the active Methodist congregation. The church is located on Furnace Avenue. Maryland State Archives, Robert G. Merrick Archives of Maryland Historical Photographs, Md. HR-G 6581

Designed By
Patrick S. Smith

THE
DONNING COMPANY
PUBLISHERS
NORFOLK/VIRGINIA BEACH

The Donning Company/Publishers
5659 Virginia Beach Boulevard
Norfolk, Virginia 23502

Edited by Amy E. M. Kouba and Richard A. Horwege

Library of Congress Cataloging-in-Publication Data

Cramm, Joetta, 1932-
   Howard County: a pictorial history.

   Includes index.
   1. Howard County (Md.)—History-Pictorial works.
2. Howard County (Md.)—Description and travel—Views.
I. Title.
F187.H8C73   1987   975.2'81   87-6661
ISBN 0-89865-539-0 (lim. ed.)

Printed in the United States of America

"Cheaper by the dozen" fits this parade of cousins at a birthday party in the nineteenth century. The family is that of Albert G. Warfield, Sr., and the setting is Oakdale. The home in the background is the way Oakdale appeared before Edwin Warfield, later the governor, enlarged it.

He added a grand front entrance with large white pillars and steps. These may be some of the governor's children and those of his brothers and sisters. Notice the two babies to the right. Maryland Historical Society

To my sons

Table of Contents

Foreword 6

Acknowledgments 7

Introduction:
Forming a New County 9

Chapter I:
Settling the New World, Lord Baltimore Style 17

Chapter II:
The Beginnings at Elk Ridge, a Community Grows 25

Chapter III:
Arrival of the Ellicotts and Other Millers 43

Chapter IV:
People of the Nineteenth Century 63

Chapter V:
Communities 99

Chapter VI:
Growing into the County Seat, Ellicott City Matures 123

Chapter VII:
Flourishing of Churches and Schools 145

Chapter VIII:
Entering the Twentieth Century Quietly 167

Chapter IX:
New Ways, New People, New Town 193

Bibliography 221

Index 222

About the Author 224

Foreword

The Howard County Historical Society is delighted there is a new publication detailing the history of our county. Howard County which has grown so quickly and changed so rapidly in recent years has a rich heritage. It is important to know that the story of the county's beginnings and growth, of its places and people will be available in an attractive pictorial format.

We are in the unique position of being a young county, formed from one of the oldest counties in the state. Ms. Cramm has captured our history from its beginnings in upper Anne Arundel County and carried it through the centuries. Integrating the past with the later half of the twentieth century; she details events which have catapulted Howard County into the modern world.

The Historical Society was pleased to open its files and collections to the author for a mutual sharing of information. This book should be a useful and important resource to long time residents as well as those who are newly developing roots in the Howard communities.

To the businesses and citizens of Howard County inspired by this work, we extend an invitation to join the Howard County Historical Society in its continuing efforts to collect and disseminate evidence of our colorful history.

C. Edward Walter
President, 1985-1986
Howard County Historical Society

Acknowledgments

Sincere appreciation goes to many people and organizations for their advice, assistance, support, encouragement, suggestions and forbearance during the process of writing and preparing this history. The initial suggestion that Howard County should have such a publication came from Dr. Larry Madaras, after he saw the Prince George's county book. My regret is that he was too involved at Howard Community College to co-author the publication.

The heart and soul of this book are its pictures and the text. The Bibliography credits many of the sources. However, old copies of the *Ellicott City Times* which repose at the Enoch Pratt Free library or on microfilm provided extensive information for the late nineteenth and early twentieth century periods.

Many pictures came from the Maryland Room of the Pratt library and its staff was extremely helpful and cooperative in sharing their rich resources. Dean Krimmel at the Peale Museum gave assistance and advice. Mame Warren with the Hall of Records offered its collection. The Maryland Historical Society staff provided cooperation. The volunteers at the Howard County Historical Society, particularly Anita Cushing and Doris Chickering, were always supportive, Shirlene Bauman of the Elkridge Heritage Society shared the Society's collection. Alice Cornelison, who labored over her own project of black history, was more than generous.

Once we located photos, it became necessary to reproduce them. Quentin Kardos of Howard Community College tackled the assiduous task of copying and printing hundreds of photos. Their excellent quality is the result of his skill and caring. Leigh Wachter also contributed to the collection.

Robert Vogel of the Smithsonian provided a wealth of information about the bridges and mills. James M. Coram and Dr. Gary Browne were helpful with editing comments.

Many families and individuals shared from their photo collections and are credited in the book. My heartfelt thanks goes to all of the people, named and unnamed who tolerated my immersion in this project, especially my close friend, Roy D. Bailey, Jr.

A seal was adopted in 1840 by Howard District. This county seal kept some elements of the first District seal. Edward Stabler, a well-known designer, was commissioned to produce the original seal. He incorporated the agricultural elements that were representative of the county: a shock of wheat, tobacco plants, a plow, and the rolling fields. In 1973 the present seal was adopted by the county. From the author's collection

John Eager Howard, for whom this county was named, was one of Maryland's most prominent citizens. A revolutionary war hero, governor, and a United States senator, he owned property in upper Anne Arundel county but did not live there. There are streets named for him in Baltimore, for each of his three names and a statue of him mounted on a horse in Mount Vernon Square, which was a part of his large estate. Howard's Park once covered much of the heart of Baltimore, from Federal Hill to Biddle Street and from the Jones's Falls to Eutaw Street. Howard was born in Baltimore County, in the area of Pikesville. His eldest brother had no children and four other brothers died bachelors. He married Peggy Chew of Philadelphia. Peggy was the sister of Harriet Chew, wife of Charles Carroll of Carrollton's only son. The Carrolls lived at Homewood, off Charles Street not far from the Howard's estate. The Howards had two daughters and six sons, one of whom, George, lived in Howard County. Enoch Pratt Free Library collection, reproduced by permission

Introduction:
Forming A New County

There's a delightful quality of life in Howard County. Columbia offers a well-planned cosmopolitan community. Ellicott City, the county seat, presents the contrast of the nineteenth century. The rolling, tree-lined, country roads transport you through a rural environment of old barns, log cabins, Victorian homes, and fields of corn and grains changing colors with the seasons.

You still can find that settled quality that has pervaded this county for centuries. A quiet contentment was nudged gently into the second half of the twentieth century by suburban growth. More accelerated growth continued with the advent of Columbia.

We welcome this opportunity to journey through the history of Howard County. For every family, home or event you will find in this book there are twice as many not included that were just as important. We have selected a broad representation to help tell our county's story.

Maryland's third-youngest county was named for Col. John Eager Howard, revolutionary war hero, wealthy Baltimore merchant and philanthropist. Would we have been named for Charles Carroll of Carrollton if our neighboring county to the north had not been formed in 1836? Although John Eager Howard owned property in this county, he did not live here, but Charles Carroll did.

Howard's illustrious military service earned him a prominent place in Maryland's history as he started that career as a captain at age twenty-four. His role in the defeat of the British at the Battle of Cowpens highlighted his distinguished record. As a civilian he served as the Governor of Maryland, a state senator and as a United States senator. Howard donated the land for the Washington Monument in Baltimore, a part of the estate he had inherited from his mother's family, the Eagers. Such a prominent citizen deserved to have his name remembered when a new county came to be named and that county proudly bears the name of Howard.

Situated in the heart of Maryland, Howard is the state's second-smallest county, containing 251 square miles. Only Calvert County is smaller. Originally, the lands were a part of Anne Arundel County; but the assembly placed them in Baltimore County from 1659 to 1726. Returned to Anne Arundel County in 1726, they remained there until becoming Howard District of Anne Arundel in 1839. Finally in 1851, Howard became an independent jurisdiction, making it the third-youngest county in Maryland.

Belvidere was the home in Baltimore of John Eager Howard, located in a park-like setting known as Howard's Park. Although often spelled, Belvedere, *Howard himself always spelled it* Belvidere. *The construction of the mansion was started in 1786 and required eight years to finish. A description from 1879 identified a central room of octagon shape with windows opening on a view of the town and county, the Patapsco River and the Chesapeake Bay. Baltimore citizens visited Howard's Park for parades, military exercises, picnics, and even duels. The house stood diagonally across present-day Calvert Street, just south of Chase Street. It did not survive even 100 years for it was torn down in 1876 for the extension of Calvert Street. Enoch Pratt Free Library collection, reproduced by permission*

John Eager Howard sent this letter to Mr. James Frost at Waverly in 1818. Frost was the manager of the farm for Howard, until George and Prudence Howard were married and moved to the property. The letter read as follows: "Sir I will purchase your pork, say a thousand pounds, at $10 a hundred. I wish the hogs to weigh from 140 to 160 lbs. It will not answer well to have them this week for to come on saturday nothing can be done with them till monday—I think to kill them on monday and send them down on tuesdays will answer best, provided the weather suits, but do not send them in wet weather nor when it is too warm—I am your obed'serv.^t J. E. Howard— Tuesday, December 8th 1818, Mr. James Frost—P.S. If you have a few hundred pounds more you may send it—" Courtesy of Tracy Stackhouse, great-grandson of James Frost

Dr. William W. Watkins, a delegate from Anne Arundel County and resident of Richland along Shepherd's Lane, led the successful effort to form Howard District in the late 1830s. Speaker Charles Sterrett Ridgely gave his support to the legislation despite opposition from members representing St. Mary's, Somerset and Worcester counties, according to Dr. Nicholas Varga of the Howard County Historical Society. Amendments had been offered that would have made it difficult to form Howard into a separate county at a later date. With successful passage of the proposed bill without the damaging amendments, Howard District was formed. Dr. Varga comments that members of the legislature did not want new jurisdictions formed for fear they would dilute the strength of the current members and their interests in slavery and the building of the railroad. The growing population in the northern and western areas of the state had different—and some felt hostile—views.

During the 1840s Judge Thomas Beale Dorsey and Thomas Donaldson played important roles in the creation of the new county. The act establishing Howard County was approved in 1850 by the Constitutional Convention and the new constitution was approved by a vote of the people in 1851. It became effective on July 4.

The majority of this county lies in the Piedmont Plateau, which is rich farmland that encourages intensive agriculture. Only a small area along the southeastern edge in the vicinity of U.S. 1 is part of the Coastal Plain, a sandy, less fertile soil.

Howard is the only Maryland county totally surrounded by other Maryland counties. Located between the two large metropolitan areas of Baltimore and Washington, it attracts people who work in either locale.

Four men who resided in what became Howard County have served the state of Maryland as governor. The names of these men have been memorialized in the naming of the four county office buildings located on Courthouse Drive in Ellicott City: George Howard, T. Watkins Ligon, John Lee Carroll, and Edwin Warfield.

Changes came slowly in Howard County, but in the 1960s decisions were made that led the county into new ways of doing things. At this time the county government changed from the commissioner form to that of charter government providing for the election of a county executive and council members. There are no incorporated cities in the county, so one government controls all services, taxes, and laws, which are normally within the jurisdiction of local government. There is one public school system, one police force, one fire service, one government to determine the county's direction and future. We take this opportunity to enjoy the history of a small but exciting county.

George Howard, son of John Eager Howard, served as governor from July 1831 to January 1833, reluctantly. At the sudden death of Gov. Daniel Martin, Howard was named to finish that term and re-elected for an additional one-year term. He viewed his task as one to carry forth his predecessor's goals. His term could be called uneventful. He was a foe of lotteries, which were being used to build churches, colleges and monuments. As a large slaveholder he supported legislation that would secure the owner of bondsmen the full enjoyment of their property, although he did support the colonization movement. Generally following his term in office, he participated very little in public life. One exception was when he served as presidential elector in 1836 and 1849 in support of Benjamin Harrison. George Howard received his education through a tutor at the family home, Belvidere, in Baltimore. Due to his father's influence he was a member of the Federalist party. He married Prudence Gough Ridgely and lived at Waverly where they raised a large family. Enoch Pratt Free Library collection, reproduced by permission

Thomas Watkins Ligon, a resident of Howard County, served as the chief executive of the state from 1854 to 1858. He was elected to the state legislature in 1843 and to Congress the next year where he remained until 1849. As a Democratic candidate for governor in 1853 he ran against the Know-Nothing party candidate, Richard Bowie from Montgomery County. It was a difficult and close election, in which Ligon was elected by a small majority. The opposition party won in both branches of state government. In spite of the difficult position that this put him in, Ligon worked on reform movements against crime in politics. He also worked to warn the citizenry of the dangers of politics based on race or sect. The Know-Nothings exhibited these prejudices against those not of native birth and all Roman Catholics. Elections were hostile, with many injuries and deaths. Ligon was a native of Virginia and was educated at Hampden-Sydney College, the University of Virginia and the Yale Law School. At twenty-one he came to Baltimore looking for a promising location in which to practice law. In 1840 he married Sallie Dorsey. After her early death he married her sister, Mary Tolley Dorsey. Enoch Pratt Free Library collection, reproduced by permission

11

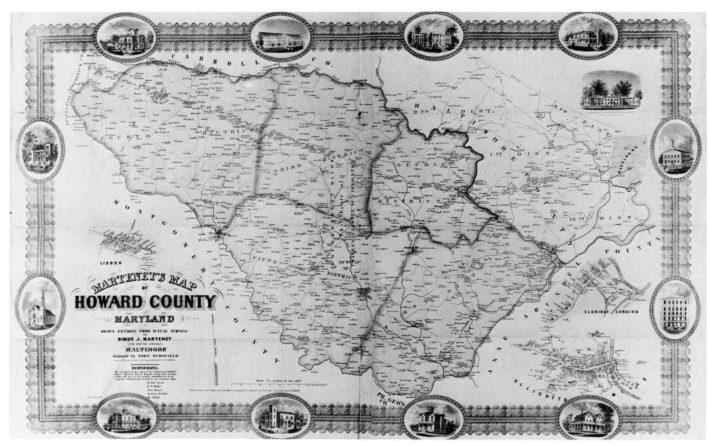

Martenet's Map of 1860 is the earliest detailed map drawn of Howard County. Around the border are impressive buildings. Starting left of center, on the top border, and moving counterclockwise, St. Charles College, Chatham, Alhambra, St. John's Episcopal Church, Elmonte,

Glenelg, Temora, Claremont, New Town Hall, Courthouse, Wilton, and the Patapsco Female Institute. In the upper right hand corner is Doughoregan Manor. Inserts of towns include Lisbon, Elkridge Landing, and Ellicotts Mills. Four of the buildings are no longer standing, St.

Charles College, Chatham, Wilton, and the Patapsco Female Institute. Fire destroyed the college and Wilton. The new town hall was owned by John Schofield, who published the map at his place of business in the town hall. Maryland Historical Society

Chatham was the home of Thomas Watkins Ligon and his wife Mary Tolley Dorsey, daughter of Charles Worthington Dorsey. Dorsey was in the process of building this home for his daughter Comfort who was married to James McCubbin. Before the home was completed, she died. It then became the home of his daughter Mary. This home was the work, architecturally, of Nathan Starkwether who also designed Temora, El Monte, and Wilton, all of the Italian villa style and all built by members of the Dorsey family. The Ligon descendants sold the property to Joseph Natwick, a lumberman. After he cut the trees from the property he declared that he was "Dunloggin." He then developed the Dunloggin Dairy Farm by constructing modern barns in the 1920s and 1930s. His herd of Holsteins were prize winning. These animals were sold in the late 1940s

and the entire herd brought $384,000. "Woodmaster" was the outstanding sire of the herd. He with his three sons sold

for $266,800. Eventually Chatham was torn down. Courtesy of Howard County Historical Society

Waverly was the home of George Howard and his wife Prudence Gough Ridgely. The couple married in 1811 and received the property as a wedding gift from George's father, John Eager Howard. Howard had bought the property in 1786 and rented it to the Frosts, whose own property was across the Old Frederick Road. George and Prudence named their home after the novel by the same name, which was very popular in America. The original land was patented and call The Mistake by Daniel Carroll. He sold it to John Dorsey who gave it to his youngest son, Nathan. Nathan built the main section in the mid-1700s. After Nathan had years of financial problems, two of his brothers came to his rescue and Edward Dorsey became the sole owner. It was this Dorsey who sold it to Howard. The Howards modernized the house and added the hyphen and servants' wing.

Prudence Ridgely was the daughter of Charles Carnan Ridgely of Hampton, one of the wealthiest families in Maryland. The property has recently been renovated by the owners, Preserva-tion Maryland, and it is available for rental. Waverly is located at Maryland 99 and Marriottsville Road. From the author's collection

John Lee Carroll served as governor of Maryland from 1876 to 1880. His election followed a bitter contest when he opposed J. Morrison Harris, a prominent member of the Know-Nothing party, who used the fact of Mr. Carroll's Roman Catholicism as a matter of great criticism. However, Carroll won the election by 10,000 votes. The handling of the B & O strike in July 1877 was the outstanding accomplishment of his term. Due to a downturn in the economy, the railroad stated that they were reducing wages ten percent for all workers making one dollar a day or more. The workers went on strike and other workers were hired, which resulted in violent activities. The governor ordered the National Guard to Cumberland where the strikers were doing the greatest damage. Those sympathetic to the strikers tried to detain the military at the Camden station,

Doughoregan Manor was the home of Gov. John Lee Carroll. It is located off Maryland 144 and remains in the Carroll family. This interesting photo shows palm trees landscaping the front of the house. The original portion of the house is the center, which was built in the 1730s by the Signer's father. The struc-ture was one and a half stories. Before the Signer's death, he had started the addition to the left and extended it to the original section. His grandson completed

which resulted in riots before the troops could leave. Carroll was able to quell the riots and settle the matter peacefully. He was the great-grandson of Charles Carroll of Carrollton and of Thomas Sim Lee, once a Maryland governor. Born at Homewood in Baltimore in 1830, he moved to Doughoregan at age three. He was educated by tutors, at Mount St. Mary's College at Emmittsburg, George-town University, St. Mary's College in Baltimore, and Harvard Law School. He traveled extensively in Europe before returning to practice law in 1854. He

the home in the 1830s, raising the center portion to two full stories and connecting it to the chapel, on the right, making a 300-foot-long structure. A brick house, it is painted yellow to help seal the bricks from moisture. This was Charles Carroll of Carrollton's country home, where he relaxed and enjoyed his family and friends. Entertaining was casual and visitors were always welcome in his days. Enoch Pratt Free Library collection, reproduced by permission

married Anita Phelps of New York and moved there. He returned to Maryland at the advent of the Civil War when his father developed a serious illness. In 1876, he purchased Doughoregan Manor from his brother, Charles, and in the same year his wife died, leaving five sons and four daughters. These children received their education in schools in France. In 1877, he re-married. He and Mary Carter Thompson of Virginia had one child. Enoch Pratt Free Library collection, reproduced by permission

Edwin Warfield of Howard County served as the state's governor from 1904 to 1908. He started his political career in 1874 as the register of wills for Howard County and was elected in 1881 to fill the unexpired term of Senator Arthur Pue Gorman. He served a full term, 1883-1887, and returned by choice to Ellicott City to practice law. He owned and edited the Ellicott City Times from 1882 to 1886. As reward for his participation in the campaign and election of Grover Cleveland as president, he was appointed

surveyor of the port of Baltimore, 1886 to 1890. Warfield founded the Fidelity and Deposit Company of Baltimore. He expressed his interest in serving as governor but was defeated in his first attempt. His second campaign was successful. He was responsible for the restoration of the chamber in the State House where Washington resigned his commission. He married in 1886 and raised a family. Enoch Pratt Free Library collection, reproduced by permission

Oakdale was the home of Gov. Edwin Warfield and is located off Ed Warfield Road in Daisy. The original part of the house was built in 1838 by Albert Gallatin Warfield, the governor's father. The house has been enlarged considerably, including the imposing pillared front hiding the original simple facade. It is no longer in the Warfield family but is an elegant home in excellent condition. Enoch Pratt Free Library collection, reproduced by permission

The Warfield Building houses the Police Department. It quickly outgrew its original facilities and a large addition was added in the early 1980s, as the demand for an increased police force came from the citizens. In 1958 the county had ten police officers. More than that join the police force each year as classes of recruits are trained and added to the department. Gov. Edwin Warfield gave his name to this facility. From the author's collection

As the county grew, the operation of the county government grew with it. No longer could the courthouse provide the space needed for the offices to run the government. In June 1967, new buildings were opened to house the county employees. Today the Carroll Building provides space to many branches of county services, including the Department of Social Services, Employment, Office on Aging, Purchasing, and Consumer Protection. The building is named for Gov. John Lee Carroll. From the author's collection

The Ligon Building, named for Gov. Thomas Watkins Ligon, is connected to the Carroll Building and was opened in 1967. Today it houses the Department of Health and the services that they offer county residents. Data processing services also operate here. From the author's collection

The George Howard Building was opened in 1976, barely ten years after the first new county office building (now the Carroll Building) was occupied. The offices of the county executive and the council are here. Many of the departments, Public Works, Recreation and Parks, Planning and Zoning, Law, Personnel, and Finance are located in the Howard Building. The Banneker hearing room, where public hearings are held, is in the left foreground. Office of Public Information, Howard County

The first Lord Baltimore looked to his grant from King Charles I as the means to increase the wealth of the Calverts. He and his heirs were given all the land in the colony "in free and common socage" with power to dispose of the land in any manner. By the time the Charter was granted, it fell to the second Lord Baltimore, Cecilius Calvert, to find an effective means to settle these broad lands. Such land grants, he hoped, would assure the Calvert family a vast and continuing fortune.

Land Grants

Lord Baltimore's land agent was responsible for the granting of the land, the recording of such transactions and the collection of fees. A settler paid the purchase price, or "caution money," and received a warrant for a piece of land. The next step would be for the surveyor to determine the desired piece of ground and produce a description of the boundaries, known as the "certificate of survey." Once this was produced the settler would receive a patent, or title, to the land. The new patentee would then choose a name for his property, which would be recorded along with the warrant, certificate and patent. Early patent information survives and is available at the Hall of Records in Annapolis. It was here where Dr. Caleb Dorsey researched over a period of years and produced a map of the original land grants of Howard County in 1968.

The new land owner had certain liabilities, including a "quitrent," a semiannual tax or rent.

Dr. Dorsey's monumental work has made available considerable information about the land grants of Howard County. In the first quarter of the eighteenth century, 69 patents were granted to settlers. The fastest growth came between 1725 and 1750, with 157 parcels claimed by the early planters. The two decades before the start of the revolutionary war saw 84 patents assigned by the land agent. Very few patents came after the war. The largest land grant entirely in the county was called Doughoregan, seven thousand acres patented by Charles Carroll, July 22, 1702, and the smallest was called Find It If You Can, one acre patented by Charles Welsh on May 23, 1767.

The original patent is the first that appears in the records on a certain property. Lands could be resurveyed and repatented as happened with Doughoregan in 1711 to include two patents, and a total of ten thousand acres. Often the original patent was enlarged and there would be a new patent name, such as Addition to Troy or Athol Enlarged. Or a settler might purchase a portion of a larger grant and rename it.

Interpreting the meaning of patent names provides an entertaining exercise. Batchelor's Choice, Ben's Delight, and Rebecca's Lot are easy. What was the Ranter's Ridge or The Mistake, Lost by Neglect, Left Out, Grog, Break Neck Hill, or Hard to Get Dear Paid For?

A patent on the land did not necessarily indicate when the land was inhabited or farmed; and likewise, property could be occupied for many years before a patent was secured. Property could be patented by someone seeking to expand his holdings many years before it became occupied. That appears to be the case with Doughoregan, which was patented in 1702, repatented in 1711 and probably not settled for another decade or two.

From studying the information available from Dr. Dorsey's map, it appears that the size of patents were generally small. Only 11 patents were over two thousand acres, while 115 of a total 359 original patents were under one hundred acres.

Some of these early patent names appear in the new town of Columbia: Long Reach, Phelps His Luck, Stevens Forest, and Hickory Ridge.

The patents granted before 1700 were generally in that part of the county south of today's U.S. 40 and east of U.S. 29 and were not contiguous. By 1725 parcels were patented throughout the eastern two-thirds of the county, and by 1750 a majority of the land east of Maryland 32 was claimed by an owner.

Early Planters

The majority of the early settlers were planters and not large land holders. They were true pioneers who worked hard to survive. At first the term plantation referred to the colony itself. However, the settlers came to use that term for the cleared, planted area of their farm, at first a few acres surrounded by the woodlands. It was a heroic effort to clear the land, erect the buildings, develop the roads, plant orchards and to accomplish all of these needed improvements literally through sweat, blood, and tears.

The settler that succeeded and profited the greatest was the one who combined the use of mind and muscle. The merchant-planter sold goods from his store on credit and settled accounts when tobacco was ready for market. These "book debts" as the statutes called them, enabled some planters to get a foothold in the growing economy. State records show that one skillful merchant died in 1676 leaving a fortune of over 800 pounds. But most men who died in the 1698 era had an estate of about fifteen pounds, mainly livestock and a crop of tobacco.

In 1710, 84 percent of the settlers were poor and 15 percent in a better class; but by 1750 only 67 percent remained poor and 31 percent were classified as "good to affluent," showing economic progress.

Where Were the Indians?

Indians roamed this area that became Howard County, Maryland. Indeed, there were Indians living in Maryland when the first settlers came. Unfortunately, we know very little about these early people. Archaeologists reveal that the earliest inhabitants of Maryland descended from Asian emigrants who entered North America by way of Alaska at least 12,000 years ago. The Paleoindian period (12,000 to 8000 B.C.) and the Archaic period (8000 to 1000 B.C.) left some remnants that modern day man has located.

The Woodland period existed at the time of settlement by the Europeans. It was Indians of this period who greeted those pioneers who disembarked from the Ark and the Dove in 1634.

Maryland's Indians were of the Algonquian stock, the largest tribal stock on the seaboard, stretching from what is now Maine to Virginia. The other linguistic stock was the Iroquoian to which the Susquahannocks belonged.

These Susquahannocks from along the Pennsylvania border greatly impressed John Smith on his 1608 journey up the Susquehanna River. His description included:

Such great and well-proportioned men as are seldom seen, for they seemed like Giants to the English, yeah, and to their neighbors, yet seemed of an honest and simple disposition . . . The strongest people of all both in language and attire, for their language it well beseems their proportions, sounding from them as a voice in a vault . . . The calf of the greatest of the Werowances (chiefs) was three-quarters of a yard around, the rest of his limbs in proportion. The goodliest man that ever was beheld.

According to John Hoffman, an authority on Indians, the Maryland Indians of the Algonquian stock, were the Piscataway, Pocomoke, Assateague, and Nanticoke. The Piscataway nation was located in southern Maryland. Other tribes were included which bore names such as Anacostans, Potomac, Potopacs, and Chopticans.

The Pocomoke-Assateagues were two loosely aligned tribal units. The Pocomokes resided above the Wicomico River in the county of the same name. The Assateagues lived closer to the ocean.

The Nanticokes were fairly numerous and considered warlike. They liked fishing and trapping better than hunting and that probably accounts for their settling on a river, which today bears their name.

The main Indian population lived in the tidewater region of the Chesapeake Bay. Food was plentiful and the weather moderate. Water was available for many uses, including transportation.

This region of the Tidewater is known as the Costal Plain, mostly flat with sandy soil. Fruits were available, persimmon, mulberries, huckleberries, strawberries, raspberries, gooseberries, cherries, and wild plums. Game was plentiful. Deer were bountiful and elk were to be found, along with black bears, and cougars. The bay provided immense treasures including clams, oysters, blue crab, rock/striped bass and perch. Their homes were wigwams, round huts with bark over a framework of green saplings. Their villages were in the lowlands along rivers and creeks, near the good soils. These Indians of the late woodland period also developed the use of agriculture. Their cultivated crops included tobacco, corn, pumpkins and beans.

Much evidence exists that indicates the Indians roamed Howard's lands. Many families have collected arrowheads and other relics. Archaeologists have located sites that identify these early inhabitants. Since the permanent settlements were along the Chesapeake Bay, it is thought that temporary hunting parties roamed inland and lived for a time away from the bay.

Although there is little information about the pre-historic Indians of Maryland, archeological exploration in Howard County has uncovered artifacts from these very early periods. The Middle Patuxent Archeological Group, directed by Lee Preston, performed a dig at the Wallace site near the Triadelphia Reservoir during a period of dry weather when the bottom land was exposed. Projectiles, commonly called "arrowheads," were found at this site by the thousands. They can be dated to the early Archaic period as far back as 8000 B.C. From the left are the Palmer, Kirk and LeCroy points, which were attached to a shaft to be shot or thrust in hunting and fishing. They were also used as knives and scrapers. Other stone tools used by these early Indians were axes, adzes and celts for woodworking, hammerstones for flaking stone tools, and grinding stones for processing grains and nuts. Courtesy of Lee Preston

The principal villages of the Indians in the Chesapeake region were usually stockaded. Indians lived in small houses covered with bark and rush mats. This is a Susquehannock village to the north but Piscataway villages were similar. The palms and cattle depicted are not accurate. *Library of Congress, Prints and Photographs Division*

Early Indians made a dugout canoe by burning the inside of the felled log. They would also burn the base of the tree prior to chopping it down. The colonists learned these skills from the Indians and adopted them as their own. From Theodor de Bry's America. *Library of Congress, Prints and Photographs Division*

The earliest map to show details of the development of upper Anne Arundel County was made in 1795 by Dennis Griffith. The names with asterisks denoted the location of mills. The bordering rivers as well as inland locations were dotted with mills. Red House and Blacks are shown on the Old Frederick Road with symbols for taverns. Spurriers Tavern is shown on the Washington Road (U.S. 1) at the Old Annapolis Road (Maryland 175). Whites Mill was approximately where Savage is today. Poplar Spring and Hilton were villages. Hilton is extinct, having been located on the Columbia Pike near Maryland 103. Maryland Historical Society

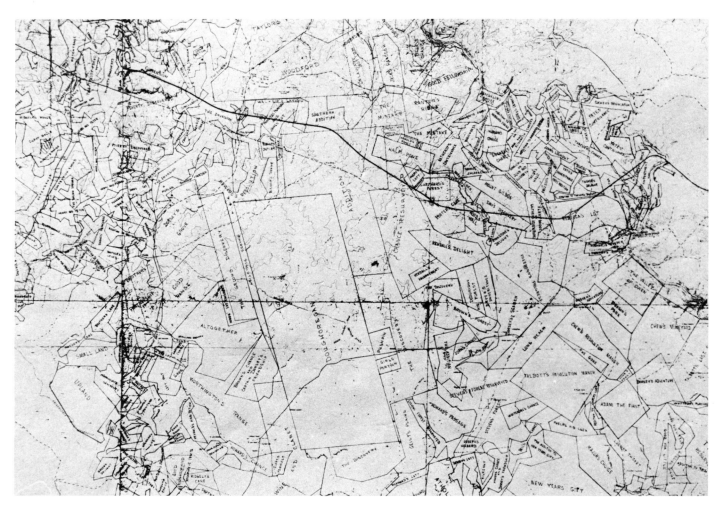

Dr. Caleb Dorsey completed his map of Howard County's original land grants in 1968 after nine years of commuting to Annapolis for research of the original patents to these lands. This portion of the map shows the central section of the county with the large Carroll patent, Doughoregan, and the other Carroll patents, Addition and Chance Resurveyed, on which the manor house and buildings are located. They totaled about twelve thousand acres. Maryland 108 runs through the large patent near the 'D'. U.S. 40 is visible meeting with U.S. 29 in the middle of Rebecca's Lot. Long Reach lies along the eastern edge of U.S. 29. Steven's Forest and Phelps His Luck are identifiable, as are many other patent names. These were the first patents, many dating before 1700, such as Adam the First, which is located on Maryland 108, formerly called Waterloo Road. From the author's collection

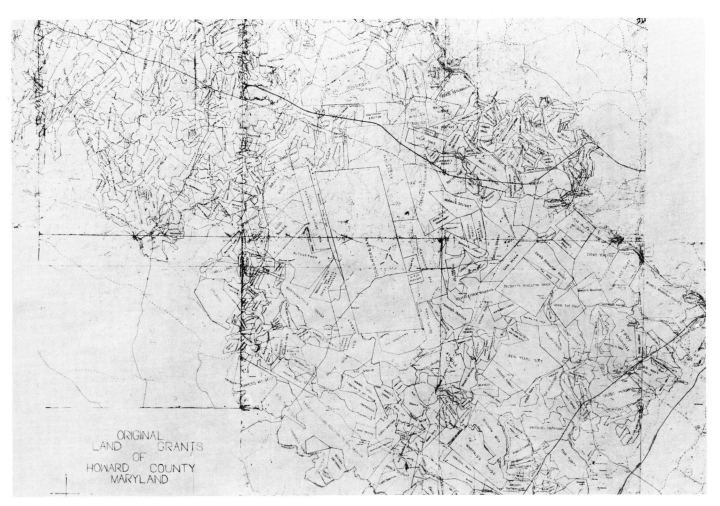

A three hundred-year-old jig-saw puzzle came together in 1968 when Dr. Caleb Dorsey completed the Original Land Grant Map of Howard County. Dr. Dorsey incorporated into his map the first patents which were made to these lands in upper Anne Arundel County starting with the late 1600s. In the lower right hand corner are the B&O Railroad and U.S. 1. The roads shown are modern roads, to help locate the parcels of land. Dr. Dorsey started his task with a marker designating a boundary of Doughoregan, Pushpin, and Girls Portion and worked from that point. From the author's collection

Elkridge Landing may have resembled this modern day sketch of a port along a busy waterway. The River ran nearly fourteen feet deep, allowing large ships to come up the Patapsco from the Chesapeake Bay to the busy landing. Here the tobacco hogsheads and the pig iron were loaded for shipment to England in colonial days. The river silted and after the revolutionary war, the port of Baltimore attracted the major shippers. The surprise is that no early sketches of the landing have survived. John H. B. Latrobe from Lawyer's Hill sketched extensively and left books of his European travels. However, it appears that he overlooked his own community. A. Aubrey Bodine, talented Sunpapers photographer, was raised on Augustine Avenue in Elkridge but did not photograph the area widely. Painting by Mrs. Joan Hull, Clear Springs, Maryland

Chapter  2

The Beginnings at Elk Ridge, A Community Grows

Elkridge qualifies as the oldest settlement in the county. Its location on the Patapsco River was an important key to its early growth. Additionally, tobacco exports, iron manufacturing, and the building of the railroad all helped Elkridge to grow.

Initially, Elk Ridge Landing developed as a place where planters brought their tobacco to load aboard large vessels going overseas to England. In many parts of Maryland each planter had his own wharf along the river, but as the land became more densely settled it became necessary to designate a landing for community use.

At Elk Ridge the tidewater of the Chesapeake Bay was navigable. Beyond this landing the mighty falls of the Patapsco River, plus the dangers of smaller falls and rocky gorges limited navigation.

By 1750 the iron industry had started at the landing with the establishment of the Elk Ridge Furnace and the Dorsey Forge. They provided employment for the settlers.

After decades of prosperity that lasted through the American Revolution, the iron industry flattened in the early 1800s. The Ellicott family purchased these related properties and with growing technology kept the industry alive.

An even greater boost to the prosperity of Elk Ridge was the coming of the railroad. It brought employment, ease of transportation—especially to the nation's capital—and an opening to the West.

The population grew at the landing and along the Ridge of Elk, but the boundaries were never clearly defined. Elk Ridge Landing referred to the concentrated population along the Patapsco River where the shipping occurred. The name Elk Ridge was for the large area created by the ridge line that stretched at least as far west as Doughoregan Manor and as far south as Oakland Mills.

The name of this oldest settlement has been written both as two words or as a single word, throughout the centuries. The choice related to the whims of the writer, with the two words, Elk Ridge, appealing to the romanticist or the historian.

Hockley was identified on the Caleb Dorsey land grant map as the earliest land grant in Howard County. It was patented in 1670, 100 acres to William Ebden. Moore's Morning Choice is probably the best known grant in the eastern part of the county, since it became the home of Caleb Dorsey, Jr., the ironmaster. The home is now called Belmont. Mordecai Moore patented his choice in 1695 to include 1,368 acres.

Hanover, a 1737 patent to Charles Carroll and John Lawson for 679 acres along the Deep Run, gave its name to a still existing community. Earlier patents on this land were named Cussacks Forrest, Cussacks Welfare, and Foster's Fancy, but they appear to have never been settled by the original patentee and reverted to the Calverts.

In 1733, the Maryland General Assembly passed a law to erect a town at Elk Ridge Landing near the head of the Patapsco River in Anne Arundel County. To be called Jansen Town, it was to consist of forty lots laid out on a tract of thirty acres. The town was settled and thrived, but the name Jansen Town never used.

Shown in a 1700s plat drawn in 1933 by J. E. Dempster, a village stood east of today's Main Street in Elkridge. Elk Ridge Street was shown where the Old Post Road ran, near Railroad Avenue today. Furnace Avenue was Market Street with Fish and Hill streets running parallel to it. More than fifty lots were laid out with Patrick MacGill, Joshua Griffith, John and Joshua Dorsey, Philip Hammond, and Charles Carroll the largest property holders.

Many of the oldest buildings at the landing were destroyed in a fire recorded in the *Niles Register* in May 1825. The blaze destroyed nine of the ten houses in the small village.

Raising Tobacco

Tobacco was the money crop of these early planters. For a long time the land remained productive. The farmer loaded his crop into hogsheads (shaped like, but larger than barrels and weighing as much as nine hundred pounds when filled) and rolled them, with the help of slaves, mules, or oxen to the wharves at the landing.

Annapolis was a major Maryland port in the 1700s, but Elk Ridge Landing rivaled it for tobacco exports. In 1763, 1,695 hogsheads were shipped from its wharves, nearly one-half of the crop that had been raised in all of Anne Arundel County. Baltimore was still a sleepy little town that did not offer competition as a port until after the revolutionary war. The 1790 population of Anne Arundel County totaled 22,598. There were 10,130 slaves and 804 free blacks—making the black population nearly one-half of the total number of people.

A public warehouse was established at Elk Ridge in 1763, on the land of the late Philip Hammond, for the inspection of tobacco. Records show that a ship, the

Dolphin, with Dougall McDougall as master, sailed from the landing in 1763 with its tobacco cargo. The ship and cargo were lost in a storm, but the tobacco was insured for six pounds sterling per hogshead. Ships would return to the landing with a variety of goods including furniture, materials, and dishes to be sold at public auction.

The fateful flood of 1868 put an end to nautical travel into Elkridge but problems had begun more than a century earlier. In 1753 the assembly of the province passed a law prohibiting the throwing or dumping of earth, sand, or dirt, which would cause the channel to fill up and injure the navigation of the river. This dumping had occurred when the ships needed to get rid of sand ballast before loading the heavy hogsheads being shipped to England. Digging into the banks of the river for iron ore also contributed to the problem.

Iron Industry

Second in importance to tobacco at Elk Ridge was the iron industry. When Capt. John Smith first ventured up the Chesapeake Bay and Patapsco River in 1608, he noted the red clay in the hills along the river. This iron ore was the basis for the establishment of the Elk Ridge Furnace by Caleb Dorsey in 1755.

In 1719, the General Assembly of Maryland encouraged manufacturing within the province by providing that one person could acquire one hundred acres of land along a river if the land was not being cultivated. The grantee, after paying for the acquired land, must have begun a mill within six months and finished it within four years. A series of furnaces and forges were erected in Maryland during the next thirty years. These crude operations used bellows and waterwheels with very little machinery. The furnaces produced pig iron to be exported to England.

After 1761, the Dorseys built their forge on the opposite shore in Baltimore County. Caleb Dorsey, the ironmaster, saw his fortune grow from his iron works, which passed to his sons in 1772 at his death. The early ironmasters copied the slave labor system from the tobacco plantations. Much of the labor of the early furnaces and forges came from these slaves. Dorsey's forge and furnace employed skilled and unskilled slave labor, including the blacksmith, collier, founder, and forgeman. Many ironmasters encouraged maximum production from their slaves by rewarding them with alcohol, although the practice was illegal.

Additionally, slaves at the furnace who worked overtime chopping wood would be paid two shillings a cord. In 1764, Joe, owned by Thomas Dorsey, earned nearly eight pounds for cutting seventy-six cords of wood, according to Michael Morgan, writing for the Sunpapers. Other work that slaves could do to earn extra money was hauling charcoal to the storage bins at the furnace. As the slaves developed skills and made outside contacts, they found it possible to escape, often into Baltimore. Owners would advertise for such runaways. By the early 1800s, the Ellicotts, descendants of the founders of Ellicott City, bought the Dorsey Forge and expanded it. In 1822, the Avalon Company was chartered and further developed the factory. Modernized and rebuilt in 1856, it produced forty-four thousand kegs of nails that year. The flood of 1868 totally destroyed this early iron factory.

The Elk Ridge Furnace at Elk Ridge Landing was located along Furance Avenue at Race Road. Ruins stood until the early 1900s. Developed by the Dorseys and Alexander Lawson, it too was purchased by the Ellicotts in the 1820s.

They built the millrace running from Deep Run to the furnace to expand its operation. By 1850, due to the inconsistency of tariff acts in the United States, the iron industry was suffering from competition abroad. The Ellicotts declared bankruptcy in the furnace operation.

The Great Falls Iron Works was the final name of the furnace operation. Damaged by the 1868 flood, it operated into the 1870s nevertheless. Following the dissolution of these works the unused land along Deep Run was cultivated into willow groves. These willows provided a new industry when they were harvested and woven into baskets. When the millrace was no longer needed, it was filled and became Race Road.

Ledger books from stores and businesses at the landing reveal the amounts of iron shipped by the Elk Ridge Company in the 1750s and credited to the accounts of the owners, Alexander Lawson and Caleb and Edward Dorsey.

These same books record that Miss Helen Owings, in 1762, received from the company store two-and-a-half yards of linen for five shillings; a silk handkerchief for seven shillings eight pence; a chest lock for one shilling three pence; and one-half pound of tea for four shillings six pence.

Expenses of the Furnace in 1766 included labor of the cooper (barrel maker) from the Patuxent Quarter for twelve days' work, one pound sixteen shillings; purchase of seventy-five quills, four shillings six pence; eight days ironing completed by Mary Legate for S. Dorsey; and bought from S. Dorsey, six bushels of oysters.

Other Mills Around Elk Ridge

Other mills also operated in the Elk Ridge area. In 1760, the Carrolls, Dulanys, and B. Tasker, Jr., patented one hundred acres on the main falls of the Patapsco at the place between Baltimore and Anne Arundel counties, which seems to have become the Hockley Forge, near the latter-day Thomas Viaduct. It was completed in 1766 and listed in 1798 as the property of Christopher Johnson and Company.

At that date, Hockley included a gristmill, slitting mill, blacksmith shop, nail factory, storehouse, and granary. This may have become Hockley Mill, later Levering Mill. The Hockley Mill Road is currently Levering Avenue. Scenes and maps from the 1830s locate a mill on the west side of Thomas Viaduct.

At the time of the 1868 flood, the *Common Sense* newspaper account relates that Mr. Robert's Hockley Mills were "considerably injured." The *Hopkins Atlas* of 1878 places the Hockley Grist Mill east of the viaduct on property of Thomas W. Levering, who had purchased the land in 1852.

Selby's gristmill, later Williams's, was located along Deep Run. A paper mill was shown on an 1833 Latrobe map of the projected railroad to Washington, near Deep Run at Budds Run. This could have been the Elk Ridge Paper Mill founded in 1776 by James Dorset. A partnership was dissolved in 1778, according to the *Maryland Journal*. The new owners, William and Mary Katherine Goddard, advertised in the *Maryland Gazette* on May 26, 1780, for old rags for their mill. In the 1850s, records show that William Lamborne owned the "Paper mille tract."

A mahogany saw mill was operated by Thomas Stowe as early as 1844. The 1850 census listed the veneering mill of Mr. Stowe and Sons with five thousand dollars capital, water power, two employees, and an annual output of 200,000 feet of veneering worth twenty thousand dollars made from one thousand mahogany logs. The Mahogany Mill Run is now Rockburn Branch. According to the *Howard Gazette* of July 27, 1850, a terrible storm at Elk Ridge Landing destroyed the dam of Mr. Stowe's saw and veneering mill on the branch opposite the Avalon iron works.

Transportation, Village Changes

Originally, to cross the Patapsco, traffic would ford it at a shallow spot. About 1777, Robert Long of Baltimore County built a ferry to run to the landing. The operation was described as a large scow connected across the river by a fixed rope.

By 1784 the ferry business was assumed by Edward and Samuel Norwood, who called it the Patapsco Upper Ferry. Through a Chancery Court case that arose from a disagreement between the Norwood brothers, it is learned that rates to use the ferry ran three pence per person on foot, six pence on horseback, two shilling six pence for a two-wheeled carriage, and three shillings nine pence for a four-wheeled carriage.

The court case in 1800 occurred when Samuel attempted to organize a second ferry operation. Testimony showed that on extremely good days, such as when cockfights were being held at the landing, income could reach fifteen pounds a day or other times, drop as low as eighteen pence. The ferry would be halted for as long as a month when the river was frozen.

With the construction of a turnpike in the early 1800s, a bridge soon replaced the ferry. The new turnpike road also relocated the center of the village, as buildings sprang up along the dirt road, now Main Street. Shop keepers lived above their stores.

The Temperance Hall was significant evidence that

the citizens of Elkridge were caught up in the lively temperance movement in America in the 1840s and 1850s. Triumphant Division, No. 38, of the Sons of the Temperance was formed in the middle 1840s at the landing. In 1850, officers were Joseph Weaver, Nicholas Thompson, Thomas Newton, Dr. H. P. Worthington, Edward Earp, John Y. Worthington, Caleb Stewart, Abraham Short, and Joseph Cole. Their magnificent temple, according to the *Howard Gazette*, was dedicated in November 1849, with Robert A. Griffith, a member, giving the dedicatory address. The *State Gazette* of 1871 lists thirty-seven merchants and craftsmen at Elk Ridge Landing. The physicians were Dr. Joseph Craggs, Dr. Samuel H. Henry, and Dr. Edward John. General stores were run by Margaret Hagerman, George Hobbs, Marshall McCauley, Edward and Richard Phelps and Nancy Soper. There were four millers, four blacksmiths, and more than fifty farmers.

The B & O Railroad

In 1830 the Baltimore and Ohio Railroad trains ran along the river opposite Elk Ridge Landing. Those first cars were horsedrawn vehicles similar in style to the stage coach. The thirteen miles from Baltimore to Ellicott's Mills was too great for one horse to complete in good time. Hence, the mid-way point at which horses were changed became Relay Station. From January to September 1831, 7,042 passengers boarded the train paying revenue of $1,821.56, reflecting the great interest in this new mode of transportation. In the next year of operation, from October 1831 to September 1832, there were 6,956 passengers.

Immediately, the railroad started plans to extend the line to Washington. Benjamin H. Latrobe, Jr., assistant to the chief engineer, made a detailed study and proposal for the extension, the Washington Branch. Two routes were considered at the point of crossing the Patapsco—by Smith's bridge or by Hockley Mills.

According to a railroad map of 1831, the Washington Turnpike crossed the river at D. A. Smith's bridge. The Hockley Mills site was chosen because it was shorter, there would be less earth to move, and repairs to adjacent property as well as yearly route maintenance would cost less.

Thus, in 1833, construction was begun on the large stone Thomas Viaduct. This 700-foot-long structure of eight elliptical arches—each 60 feet wide and 65 feet above the level of the river—cost approximately $150,000. It was named for Philip E. Thomas, the first president of the B & O.

Following two years of labor, the tremendous task was completed on July 4, 1835, by contractor John McCartney. A simple monument, said to have been built by McCartney in honor of his construction crew, stands at the Baltimore County end of the viaduct.

When the telegraph was developed and the wire extended from Baltimore to Washington, it crossed the river via the Thomas Viaduct. Not only did that famous first message, "What hath God wrought?" pass over this wire, but also the second—a personal greeting sent from Dolly

Madison to her friend, Mrs. John Wethered, wife of a Baltimore congressman and daughter of Philip E. Thomas.

The independence of Elkridge residents was displayed in 1849 when a group of citizens sent a petition to the state legislature and asked that, in the event Howard District was created a separate county, Elkridge Landing be included in Anne Arundel County. The correspondent from the landing to the *Howard Gazette* wrote that a strong counter-petition was being prepared. The majority of the Elkridge residents acknowledged that the Howard district commissioners neglected their community, particularly in the matter of road repairs. Finally the original petitioners admitted that they had acted in haste. All agreed that Elkridge should be included in the formation of a new county with the expression of hope that the commissioners would mend their neglectful ways.

During the Civil War

During the Civil War, sentiments were mixed among Lawyers' Hill residents. The war was not discussed. Judge Dobbin's daughter recalled when part of General Lee's army was not far from their home her parents shared their resources with the hungry men. Gen. Benjamin threatened to cut down all of the Lawn's trees to make room to move his guns.

The Thomas Donaldson family at Edgewood, with strong Northern sentiments, never betrayed their friends' activities. The Dobbin family was also known to help young men "go South" by night to join the Confederate army. Mr. Donaldson used his influence in the Republican party to protect henhouses and meathouses of his neighbors from foraging parties of hungry Union soldiers.

John H. B. Latrobe built his first Fairy Knowe as a summer home. A handsome and many-talented young man, John was the brother of Benjamin H. Latrobe, the architect for the Thomas Viaduct. Both were sons of the famous B. H. Latrobe, Sr., architect of the Basilica on Cathedral Street in Baltimore and portions of the nation's capitol in Washington.

When John Latrobe's first home burned, he immediately cleared the rubble and within a week started construction on a larger, ornate, Victorian home, encumbered with "gingerbread," but graced with statuary gardens. A life-long attorney for the B & O, John was also an artist and writer. This second Fairy Knowe burned in the 1900s.

Following the rigors of the Civil War, the nearly one dozen families on Lawyer's Hill started having social activities in their homes. Customarily they assembled at 8:00 p.m. and left by 11:00 p.m. Some form of entertainment followed by refreshments such as tea, coffee, sandwiches, or ice cream with fruit or cake, would add to the enjoyment.

Records show these home entertainments were being held in the summer of 1869, but by November 1870, the Elkridge Assembly Room had been completed.

To help finance the thousand-dollar structure, families bought shares in the Elkridge Assembly Room, which also provided space for a school room. A grand inaugural ball was held on November 8, 1870, with an amateur theatrical production of *The Rivals* held on November 11.

Performances were scheduled to coincide with the railroad schedule since many people, often as many as one hundred, would attend from Baltimore. The performances were presented by the Elk Ridge Amateur Dramatic Association, residents of Lawyers' Hill.

On May 26, 1871, the children performed *Beauty and the Beast* for a twenty-five-cent admission charge. For the adult presentation of *Merchant of Venice* during the same year, however, tickets brought one dollar apiece. In August 1871, a reading was given to benefit the Elk Ridge Baseball Club, and proceeds totaled thirteen dollars.

Dances at which gentlemen were charged fifty cents and ladies were admitted free were held. Receipts from such events helped maintain the building, but by 1878 a debt still remained, and each stockholder was assessed twenty-

five-cents per share. Records are incomplete, but the theatricals continued past the turn of the century.

Where were the early schools for the Elkridge children?

The Dobbins spoke of having tutors. Later the Elk Ridge Assembly Room housed a classroom. In the village, a school once stood near the Methodist cemetery, across the road from a white double house, which also served as a primary school. In 1860, Primary School No. 1 was described along the Washington Turnpike.

Young men or women who wanted an education beyond the elementary grades traveled into Ellicott City or Baltimore to attend private institutions. The Elkridge High School was opened in 1922 and became a four-year school in 1927. Now apartments, it continued to be used as a primary school when the new brick high school was completed across Old Washington Road in 1936.

An eighteenth century scene from an old map records life as it appeared at the Colonial ports. The planter is seated and talking with other businessmen while the slaves served them and tended to the hogsheads of tobacco. It was important that the planter receive credit for his crop as it was inspected and stored at ware-
houses or loaded onto a waiting vessel. These hogsheads held the dried tobacco leaves, the cash crop for the planter. The hogsheads were brought across the rolling roads enroute to the landing. None of the Howard County roads have retained the name; however, Baltimore County still has a Rolling Road. Later many
landings disappeared as the rivers silted in and other ports developed. Trade changed and after the revolutionary war, many of the smaller landings served no purpose. Library of Congress, Geography and Map Division

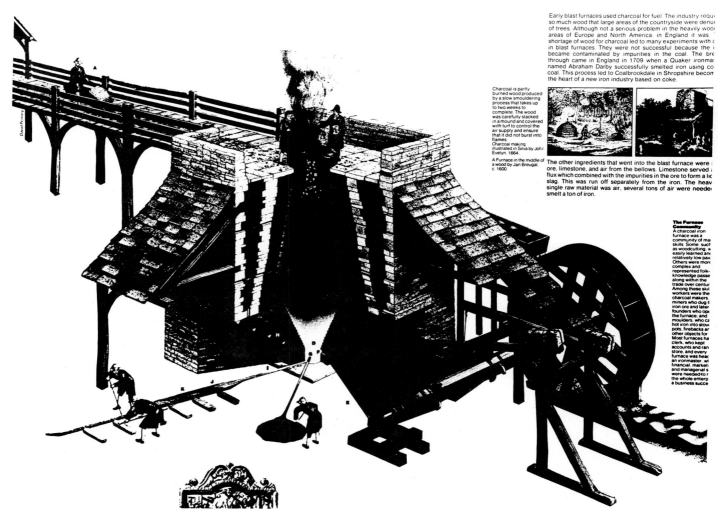

Early blast furnaces used charcoal for fuel. The industry requi[red] so much wood that large areas of the countryside were denu[ded] of trees. Although not a serious problem in the heavily woo[ded] areas of Europe and North America, in England it was [a] shortage of wood for charcoal led to many experiments with c[oal] in blast furnaces. They were not successful because the i[ron] became contaminated by impurities in the coal. The bre[ak] through came in England in 1709 when a Quaker ironma[ster] named Abraham Darby successfully smelted iron using co[ke] coal. This process led to Coalbrookdale in Shropshire becom[ing] the heart of a new iron industry based on coke.

Charcoal is partly burned wood produced by a slow smouldering process that takes up to two weeks to complete. The wood was carefully stacked in a mound and covered with turf to control the air supply and ensure that it did not burst into flames. Charcoal making illustrated in Silva by John Evelyn. 1664.

A Furnace in the middle of a wood by Jan Breugal. c. 1600.

The other ingredients that went into the blast furnace were [iron] ore, limestone, and air from the bellows. Limestone served [as a] flux which combined with the impurities in the ore to form a li[quid] slag. This was run off separately from the iron. The heav[iest] single raw material was air, several tons of air were neede[d to] smelt a ton of iron.

The Furnace Community
A charcoal iron furnace was a community of ma[ny] skills. Some such as woodcutting, w[ere] easily learned and relatively low pa[id.] Others were more complex and represented folk-knowledge passe[d] along within the trade over centur[ies.] Among these ski[lled] workers were the charcoal makers, miners who dug t[he] iron ore and later the furnace, and moulders, who ca[st] hot iron into stov[e] pots, firebacks a[nd] other objects for [...] Most furnaces ha[d a] clerk, who kept accounts and ran [the] store, and every furnace was hea[ded by] an ironmaster. w[hose] financial, marketi[ng] and managerial s[kills] were needed to r[un] the whole enterp[rise] a business succe[ss.]

The blast furnace industry developed through Maryland in the eighteenth century. Since Elkridge possessed the iron ore and limestone necessary for the making of iron a furnace was located there. Limestone served as a flux, which combined with the impurities in the ore to form a liquid slag. Air was another necessity and several tons were needed to smelt a ton of iron. Charcoal was also necessary and there were sufficient trees to produce it. Wood was carefully stacked in a mound, covered with turf and burned by a slow smouldering process that took up to two weeks to complete. The product of the blast furnace was cast iron or pig iron. Cast iron formed objects such as cannons, firebacks and grave-slabs cast directly from the furnace into molds. Pig iron was converted into wrought iron in a finery. Cannon and firebacks were cast with molten iron straight from the furnace into molds. In the 1850s and 1860s the industry was changing and after the 1870s the steel industry was using the open hearth process, using wrought iron for structural purposes.

Working the furnace. This drawing shows the principles common to all cold-blast furnaces. Men and boys on the charging bridge (A) tip raw materials from baskets and barrows into the blast furnace. The furnace works continuously, with iron ore and charcoal gradually descending through the stack (B). In the upper part, moisture and gases are driven off, and in the lower part the ore is reduced to metallic iron. At the top of the boshes (C) the earthy impurities (fused into slag) and iron are funneled down into the hearth (D), where the slag floats on top of the denser metal. The water-powered bellows (E) blow air into the hearth through the tuyere (F). At intervals, the slag is drawn off through the slag notch (G) at one side of the fore-arch (H). When sufficient iron accumulates in the bottom of the hearth, the clay plug in the tap hole (I) is broken and molten iron flows out into a channel to the pig bed (J). The main channel is called the sow (K). The iron in the branch channels solidifies to form pigs. The furnace was manned day and night during a campaign, which might last anywhere from two to ten months. The furnace was usually tapped twice a day. Courtesy of the National Park Service

Caleb Dorsey's furnace leaves little evidence or remains along the Patapsco River at Elkridge. The Maryland Geological Survey recorded these ruins about eighty years ago. Most of the chimney was gone, leaving only the base with some recognizable furnace features, in this photo. The furnace operation was begun about 1751 and existed well over one hundred years. The flooding of the river—but more importantly the changing of technology for the production of steel—spelled the end to this early industry. The raw pig iron was exported from Elk Ridge Landing to England or it was worked into tools, nails, etc. at local forges. Enoch Pratt Free Library collection, reproduced by permission

The Great Falls Iron Co. owned this property on Furnace Avenue, Elkridge in the mid-1800s. These two large brick houses are also referred to as the Ellicott houses. The early Victorian style house on the left was built when the Ellicotts operated the furnace in the early nineteenth century. The house to the right may have been built in the eighteenth century, dating to the very early days of the Elkridge furnace operation of Caleb Dorsey, the ironmaster. These houses have the Patapsco River located very close to the rear of the property and have experienced many floods rising around them. Enoch Pratt Free Library collection, reproduced by permission

Belmont, in Elkridge, is one of the oldest surviving homes in the county that can be documented by surviving records. The original center portion was built by Caleb and Priscilla Dorsey in the 1730s. Later descendents added the hyphens and wings. Edward Dorsey inherited the property from Caleb and Priscilla and passed it to his daughter Priscilla who married Alexander Contee Hanson. In later years the property stayed in the Hanson family until it was sold to Howard Bruce. The Bruces enlarged the center portion adding the chimneys to the rear. For many years the Smithsonian operated Belmont as a conference center. Today it is owned by the American Chemical Society, which retains it for use as a conference center. Belmont is in Elkridge. The Peale Museum, Baltimore, Maryland

John H. B. Latrobe was a resident of Lawyer's Hill in Elkridge and was one of the early attorneys to settle in that area. The publication The American Farmer carried this picture of the cottage built by Latrobe, in August 1845 and stated that the residence has been there for two years. The original Fairy Knowe burned and was rebuilt immediately by Latrobe. There appear to be two styles to the cottage with an ornamental style to the rear. Other pictures of the house show an extremely elaborate eclectic and unusual style architecture, which may have been added to this earlier house as it was rebuilt. The ground plan marks an area 'D' but in the legend there is no explanation for 'D'. The second Fairy Knowe also has disappeared and only the stables remain on the Latrobe property. Maryland Historical Society

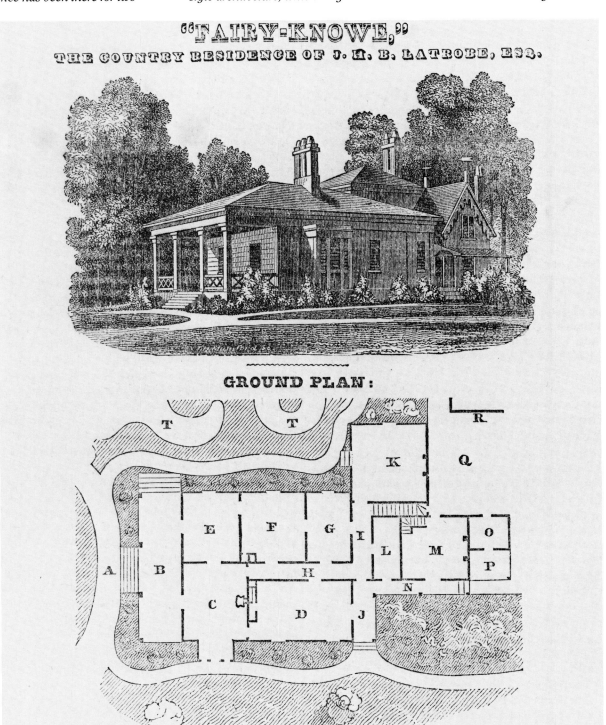

"FAIRY-KNOWE,"
THE COUNTRY RESIDENCE OF J. H. B. LATROBE, ESQ.

GROUND PLAN:

DESCRIPTION—A. Carriage Road. B. Piazza, 10 by 34 feet. C. Parlour, 22 by 15. E. Chamber, 13 by 15. F. Chamber, 14 by 15. G. Chamber, 10 by 15. H. Passage, 3ft.6. I. Passage, 4ft.4. J. Gateway, 6 ft. K. Chamber, 17 by 17. Pantry, 15 by 6.6. M. Kitchen, 15 by 15. N. Gallery, 4 ft. O. Store-room, 8 by 10. P. Shed, 7 by 10. Q. Kitchen-yard. R. Ice House. S. Shrubbery. T. Flower Garden.

George Washington Dobbin bought property in Elkridge for a summer home for the family. He built a small bungalow to which he made many additions through the years. It became his year-around home, which he called the Lawn. Dobbin was one of the Judges of the Supreme Bench of Baltimore City and remained active in Baltimore affairs. He was a founder of the Maryland Historical Society, a regent of the University of Maryland, a trustee of the Peabody Institute and of Johns Hopkins University. Dr. George Dobbin Brown, a grandson of the judge, kept the family home very much like it was when the older generations lived there. This interior view shows the faded walls covered with large paintings. The dark woodwork and the unusual carved fireplace mantels are eye-catching. Carved animal heads and a pink marble front were distinctive features of the fireplace, according to Mrs. Joe Cobb, who, along with her husband, bought the Lawn in 1951 from Dr. Brown. The house has many rooms that reflected the judge's hobbies, including metal working, astronomy, glass blowing, and photography. Maryland Historical Society

An 1870 view of the Patapsco at Elkridge shows the dam and falls west of the Thomas Viaduct. The Hockley Mill stood on the Howard County side (left) and was a gristmill in Colonial days. Each mill operation along the river built a dam and a millrace to produce water power. Although the Patapsco was navigable in its early days, the falls at Elk Ridge kept ships from sailing into the Patapsco Valley. Courtesy of the Baltimore Sun

An early sketch of the Great Stone Viaduct at the Washington Junction, the Thomas Viaduct, portrays the small engines that the viaduct was originally designed to carry. Skeptics doubted that it would withstand the weight of those early trains. More than 150 years have passed since the 1835 structure was completed and modern day trains continue to use the viaduct regularly. The B & O railroad is no longer an operating corporation, thus the viaduct is now a part of the company known as CSX. The great falls on the Patapsco can be seen through the viaduct. At this early date, in the 1850s, the Hockley Mill was in operation near the viaduct, grinding grain. The viaduct was named for Philip Thomas, the first President of the B & O. Enoch Pratt Free Library collection, reproduced by permission

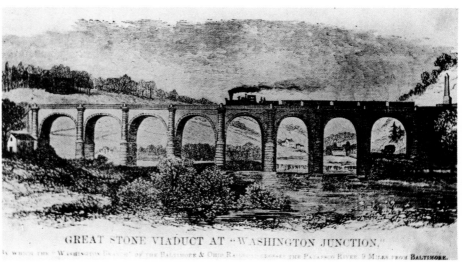

GREAT STONE VIADUCT AT "WASHINGTON JUNCTION,"

IN WHICH THE "WASHINGTON BRANCH" OF THE BALTIMORE & OHIO RAILROAD CROSSES THE PATAPSCO RIVER, 9 MILES FROM BALTIMORE.

The Civil War found the Union forces camped at the Thomas viaduct to protect it from sabotage attempts by the Confederates. Gen. Benjamin Butler identified the Viaduct as the most important target in central Maryland and stationed the Bouquet Battery here in 1861. These men are situated on a hillside of Howard County. Other forces protected the Baltimore County end of the viaduct as well as the B & O mainline into Ellicott's Mills. Courtesy of Howard County Historical Society

Viaduct House, situated on the Baltimore County end of the Thomas Viaduct, was built in 1872 as a station-hotel on the B & O Railroad. It could serve both the Old Main line into Ellicott City and the Washington branch into the District of Columbia. These hotels provided the evening meal and overnight accommodations for railroad travelers. With the advent of sleeping and dining cars in the 1880s, the railroad put their own hotels out of business. The Viaduct House at Relay remained popular into the early twentieth century as a vacation spot. It was dismantled in the 1950s and not one of these handsome old station-hotels survives in Maryland. Enoch Pratt Free Library collection, reproduced by permission

Viaduct Manufacturing Company listed itself in 1886 as manufacturer's of telephone, telegraph and electric light supplies with A. G. Davis as president. Although their business offices were on the northwest corner of Charles and German streets in Baltimore, their plant was in Howard County, near the Thomas Viaduct. One of the special items manufactured was the Hess improved 'guest call.' It was a form of an intercom system that could also be used as a fire alarm. Enoch Pratt Free Library collection, reproduced by permission

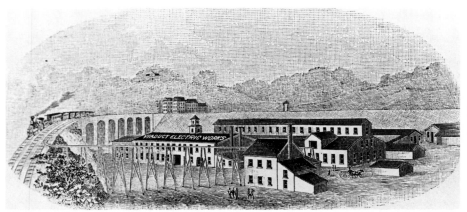

Davis and Hemphill is an old company now located near Furnace Avenue. The business started in the late nineteenth century near the Thomas Viaduct. This picture shows workers outside the building. They are from the left, Marion B. Davis, Ethelyn M. Mitchell, Arthur B. Davis, William T. Clifford, Ida Flood, Laura Hudson, Mabel Horsey, Harriett Dowling, J. Edward Hook, Walter Perkins, C. J. Eberhart, J. J. Crook, William G. Clifford, Harry F. Carter, Lerdy Vane, Walter Carter, John M. Fritz, John E. Horsey, Carl Jerns, H. F. Owens, R. C. Owens, Howard Bennett, J. F. Ege, T. A. Lyon, and J. M. Hemphill. Elkridge Heritage Society

John Brinker purchased a lot in 1847 and leased it to Martis Lupke for ten dollars a year. A condition of the lease was that Lupke would build a framehouse sixteen by twenty-one feet and one-and-a-half stories high. The following year, in 1848, Brinker paid Lupke ninety-five dollars to terminate the lease. In 1860 Brinker owned a number of lots near St. Augustine Catholic Church. This picture is one of those properties, which in 1860, served as a hotel. In 1900, when the church was being enlarged, the structure was torn down. Part of this building may be the house built by Lupke in 1847. From the author's collection

Few photos or drawings of Elkridge have survived to show us the early town. This old photograph shows a muddy road where Main Street, or the Washington Turnpike, was located. At one time this was a part of U.S. 1 with many busy shops lining the road. On the far right was the Earp home, where the post office was located for many years. Some of the buildings on the left were torn down but the old home of the Elkridge Country Club still stands. A wooden water pump can be seen near the front of it. Maryland State Archives, Robert G. Merrick Archive of Maryland Historical Photographs, Md. HR-G 6583

In 1920, this property was purchased by the Elkridge Country Club. The club was formed a year earlier for the initial purpose of forming a strong baseball team, according to the club's history. The purpose as stated in the Certificate of Incorporation was for literary, social and athletic purposes, for the mutual pleasure and benefit of its members. The presidents from 1919 to 1948 were Gabriel Retalliata, Dr. George B. Sybert, Harris E. Rodgers, John F. O'Malley (for twenty years), Richard T. Newman, Gordon A. Rodgers, C. Andrew Shaab, Robert J. Shanks, J. Elmer Dowling, and John J. Cook. Other than Mr. O'Malley, the terms were for one year. Although baseball was the predominant interest, there was a basketball team and some tennis players. The club's annual picnic was called "Elkridge Days" and helped to raise revenues for the club. The building to the

left is gone from Main Street but the country club stands at the corner of Levering Avenue. Elkridge Heritage Society

Tilghman's Store on Main Street in Elkridge was a large handsome building, which also provided a home for the family. The building stands on the east side of the roadway across from a building later operated as a store by the same family. In the mid-nineteenth century, the Pocock family owned this property. Today the building stands unoccupied, after having been converted to apartments. The awning, shutters and fine trim are gone. Until it is renovated, it is posted as condemned by local authorities. But it once served as a busy store during the days when Main Street offered many choices of shops and merchants to the citizens of Elkridge. Courtesy of Howard County Historical Society

Two old brick buildings in Elkridge stand near the northeast corner of Main Street and Furnace Avenue. Pictured here in the 1930s, they probably date to the early 1800s when the new turnpike road was built through the village. According to Cleora Thompson, former archivist in the Office of Planning and Zoning, Howard County, the structure to the right was built as a carriage house, with the groom's quarters on the second floor. In the middle 1800s the Pocock family operated a store at this corner. Main Street later became U.S. 1 until the route was relocated to the west where it runs today. Other merchants on Main Street one hundred years ago included the Earp, Kyne, McCauley, Stimpner, and Laffy families. Enoch Pratt Free Library collection, reproduced by permission

Elkridge was proud of its championship baseball teams, sponsored by the Elkridge County Club. Directors of the club joined players for a 1923 photo. Front row, from left, are: Dick Merson, left field; Henry Kessler, catcher; Johnny Gill, son of the local magistrate; Hiram Soper, second base; and Nally Bell, shortstop. Second row: John Bullock, third base; Jack Kilner, pitcher; Gaston Davis, right field; Morton Bond, manager; Gordon Rodgers, center field; Murray O'Malley, pitcher; and Charlie Peddicord, first base. Third row: R. Christopher, utility; "Pap" Hubbard, treasurer; Carlyle Earp, secretary; John O'Malley, president; Roger Laynor, corresponding secretary; John Cooney, and William "Bud" Clifford, right field. These men played teams from other towns and communities, providing recreation for themselves and their crowds of fans. The Hoplites in Ellicott City were a regular opponent. This information was provided by Jack Merson, son of Dick Merson. Jack's talents earned him a spot with the Pittsburg Pirates after World War II and he continued a professional baseball career until he chose to return to Elkridge to raise his family. Maryland Historical Society

These ladies in Elkridge started to sew during World War II and stayed together for more than thirty years. Mrs. Brumbaugh served as the first chairman of the group and later Mrs. Hastings. The Red Cross workers, from the left, are Mrs. Wilford, Mrs. Sybert, Mrs. Dudrow, Mrs. Borcherding, Martha Hastings, Mrs. Smith, Bertha Iglehart, Mrs. Ebberts, Ida Hartke, and Mrs. Brumbaugh. Elkridge Heritage Society

In 1931, the Sunoco Station occupied a busy corner at U.S. 1 and Levering Avenue, Elkridge. Not only did they offer fuel for the automobile, but sandwiches and drinks for the hungry traveler. Although the buildings to the rear are still standing along the old Main Street, the gasoline station did not survive the widening of the various roads. Maryland State Archives, Robert G. Merrick Archive of Maryland Historical Photographs, Md. HR-G 6586

Dead man's curve, one-mile south of Elkridge, was removed by the State Roads Commission in 1919 along U.S. 1, which was the first road rebuilt by the state in 1906. Before this each county paid for road improvements. There was much opposition to this reconstruction of the thirty miles between Baltimore and the District of Columbia line. It was built of fourteen-foot wide macadam, gravel, and some concrete. A new concrete bridge replaced an iron structure over the river at Elkridge. It was completed in 1915 and had cost over twenty thousand dollars a mile, a shocking expenditure to the citizens. This started the popular travel between Baltimore and Washington on this fine new roadway. With the travel came the "little shacks" to provide for the needs of the drivers. Soon the heavy army vehicles in World War I tore up the new road. It then was rebuilt after the war, bringing the cost to over thirty-two thousand dollars a mile. In 1925 Maryland 1 became a part of U.S. 1. About six thousand cars and trucks a day used the old road, by then twenty feet wide, causing many serious accidents. From 1928 to 1930 the roadway was doubled to forty feet and resurfaced.

During the thirties, traffic continued to increase but no further expansion was possible since the road, then called the Boulevard, already ran close to the buildings. The road became dotted with souvenir stands, restaurants, and bars. It was described as a nightmare. Soon the plans for the Baltimore-Washington Parkway were developed and U.S. 1 would be "junked." The parkway was built and the use of the old road changed. U.S. 1 continues to be a busy highway serving a more local use and offering a third north-south alternative route to I-95. Enoch Pratt Free Library collection, reproduced by permission

Fishing for gudgeon in the shadow of the Thomas Viaduct was a popular Sunday afternoon pastime in the early years of this century. Obviously the gudgeon was a small fish looking at the size of the fishing poles. It appears that any Sunday activity called for wearing your "Sunday best"—even the sport of fishing. This A. Aubrey Bodine photograph is especially appropriate when discussing the history of Elkridge because Bodine was raised in Elkridge. He would catch the train and ride into Baltimore to his first job with the Sunpapers. Later he was to become an award-winning photographic artist. The Peale Museum, Baltimore, Maryland

41

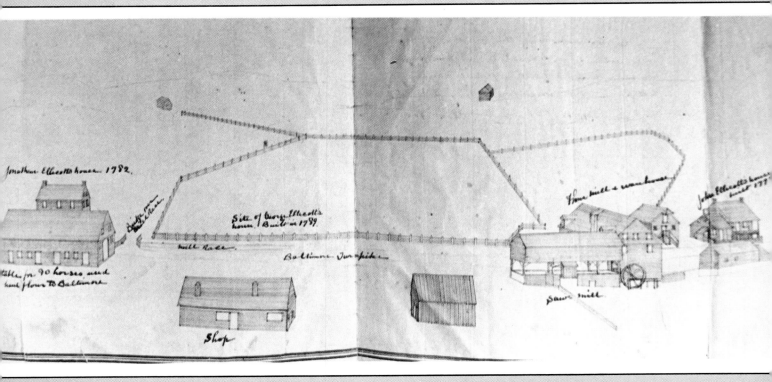

The earliest sketch of the settlement at Ellicott's Mills shows the very first buildings erected by the Quaker craftsmen and millers who came into the "Hollow" in 1771. John Ellicott's house and store to the far right were built in 1772. The flour mill and warehouse were adjacent to it along with the sawmill. The two homes best remembered in recent times stood on the left side of those in the photo. Jonathan Ellicott's home, which was destroyed in 1972, is labeled. The site of his brother George's home is labeled. George's stone house was recently moved across Frederick Road, out of the flood plain, to be restored. It is the last remaining structure from the early settlement. The Ellicotts cultivated the soils around their buildings to grow the wheat for their flour mill in the earliest days. About 1806, the first mill burned. After that time the mills were rebuilt, later enlarged and changed many times through the centuries. Today there is still a milling operation near the original site, across the river from Ellicott City, Howard County, in Baltimore County. It is operated by the Wilkens-Rogers Company.

Part of the fascination of this early sketch, drawn by George Ellicott in 1782, and later labeled by his granddaughter, is the detail of the buildings and the fencing. They are a series of very fine lines drawn in pen and ink showing another skill of George Ellicott, the mathematician, surveyor, and miller. Courtesy of Mrs. Henry Fitzhugh III

Chapter 3

Arrival of the Ellicotts and Other Millers

Although families were settling throughout the County during the 1700s, the arrival of the Ellicotts played an important role in the development of the county.

A family of Quaker brothers who combined their ingenuity and mechanical abilities with hard work, the Ellicotts can be credited with the founding of the county seat, Ellicott City. An incidental fact is that the original settlement was in Baltimore County, on the opposite shore from the location of today's town.

The immigrant founder of this family, Andrew Ellicott, came to Bucks County, Pennsylvania, from England for a visit in 1730 with his son, Andrew, following a financial setback as a woolen manufacturer. Intending to stay only a brief time, the elder Andrew left his wife and family in England. While visiting at Buckingham in Bucks County, the younger Andrew fell in love with and married Ann Bye and neither Ellicott ever returned to England. This young couple, Andrew and Ann Bye Ellicott, both about twenty-three years old when they married, were the parents of the founders of Ellicott City. Their five young sons, Joseph, Andrew, Nathaniel, Thomas, and John, were left fatherless in 1741. The three older boys were placed in apprenticeships by their guardian, Samuel Armitage and learned the trades of milling, carpentry, and blacksmithing. By 1750, the eldest of the brothers, Joseph, who displayed an ability with mechanics, directed the construction of a gristmill with the aid of his four brothers. The mill was for the use of Samuel Armitage.

First Maryland Settlement

Although there were five Ellicott brothers, Thomas did not join with Joseph, Andrew, Nathaniel, and John in the adventures in Maryland. He remained in Pennsylvania and Nathaniel also soon withdrew from the partnership and returned to Bucks County. The remaining three, Andrew, Joseph, and John are generally regarded as the founders of Ellicott City.

Mills

Having constructed a successful gristmill in Bucks County, the Ellicotts searched throughout Maryland for land and water for the location to construct a mill for their own use. This search led them into the Patapsco Valley in 1771 and to the construction of a flour mill in "this wild place, the Hollow," as Martha Ellicott Tyson recounts in her *Settlement of Ellicott's Mills*. They found the water power necessary to operate the mill and the fertile land to grow the wheat for such an operation. By 1774 the Ellicotts were ready to manufacture the finest wheat flour. Sylvio Bedini in *The Life of Benjamin Banneker* describes the first gristmill as follows:

> It was an impressive structure, with its gable end toward the river and stretched 100 feet long and stood 36 feet wide, one and a half stories high, and built entirely of stone. The five pairs of millstones were five feet in diameter. A wide arch under the center of the mill allowed the horses and wagons to unload their grains, which were then hoisted up to the top of the mill, where it was processed, cleaned and brought to the millstones below. The Ellicotts later added an elevator, conveying screw and hopper box. At first the ground flour was carried up manually to the bolting cloths, passed to the flour chest, and packed in sacks and barrels, after which it was lowered through another opening to the mill boys and placed in the waiting carts and wagons.

John McGrain in his *Grist Mills in Baltimore County, Maryland* tells the story of Oliver Evans, a fellow Quaker and an engineering genius. He explained that Evans had invented a steam engine and five devices to improve mills. The Maryland General Assembly granted him a patent on two devices: the "elevator" and the "hopper-boy." The elevator was a series of small scoops of belting that carried the ground grains from bins on the lower stories and dumped it where needed. The hopper-boy replaced a real person who spread the freshly ground flour on the top floor of a mill for it to cool and then swept it down a chute. Evans toured Maryland trying to sell licenses for the use of his inventions and the Ellicotts signed up. The Ellicotts, already operating the most productive mill in the country, could now, with Evans's devices, drive every element in the plant by the power of the main water wheel. This raised flour output and decreased labor costs significantly.

The first dwelling for the residents at Ellicott's Mills was a large, rude log structure. It contained apartments and accommodated the mechanics and laborers and their families who had come with the Ellicotts. Other early buildings included the saw mill to prepare the lumber for the other structures, a stable for the horses, a shop, John Ellicott's house and the store. Ellicott and Company, as the family business was called, carried a fine quality of merchandise at the store. Coming from New York and Philadelphia, these goods included linens of fine and coarse qualities, silks, satins, brocades, dinner and tea sets, mirrors and other glassware, mathematical instruments, iron-mongery,

and groceries. After the revolutionary war, Ellicott and Company imported merchandise themselves and sometimes sent directly to London for goods. According to Martha Ellicott Tyson, the store was a resort for all the influential men from miles around who came to sell their grain, to make purchases, to receive their letters and papers from the post office opened in one of its rooms, or to discuss political, legal or scientific questions.

John Ellicott, the youngest son, married in 1771 and brought his bride to Maryland. Andrew, the second son, lost his first wife to smallpox in 1766 and was left with five children. He married the first cousin of his first wife a year and a half later and in time had six more children. Esther, Andrew's second wife, refused to accompany Andrew to Maryland to raise the children in such a wilderness. So Andrew traveled often between Bucks County and Maryland. Jonathan and George, Andrew's sons from the first marriage, joined their father in the mill operation and built large stone houses along the Patapsco River near the mills. By 1797, Andrew and Esther finally moved to Maryland.

The Ellicotts attended the Quaker Meeting in Elkridge for many years. By 1799, a new meeting house was constructed at the Ellicott's Mills location and served as the location for the Preparatory meeting. In time the younger generations of Ellicotts and other Quakers moved to Baltimore and the meeting house was closed.

For the Ellicotts to obtain wheat for the original milling operation, it was necessary for them to clear the fields they owned and to grow their own grain. They were also able to convince Charles Carroll at Doughoregan Manor to grow wheat in some of his fields. To enable them to bring this wheat to their mill, the Ellicotts laid out and built the road to Carroll's property, now called Frederick Road. In the 1790s Jonathan Ellicott led in the construction of the Frederick Turnpike, extending it from the road to Doughoregan Manor westward to the town of Frederick. For transportation to Baltimore, the Ellicotts built a road into the town—at their own expense—to property they purchased in 1783. Here they built their first wharf, partly with stone and partly with sediment removed from the bottom of the dock. This dredging was also an attempt to deepen the water in the harbor. Elias Ellicott, one of Andrew's sons, moved to Baltimore, built his home and managed the export part of the business. Interestingly enough, there is an Ellicott dredging company in Baltimore, which was started in the later 1800s by descendants of this original Ellicott family.

By the time the Ellicotts moved into Maryland in 1771, many of the first families were seeking more fertile soils in the Piedmont region of the colony. Tobacco had exhausted the soils and made them unproductive. The Ellicotts learned that the use of plaster would fertilize the soil and experimented with it. They imported blocks of plaster of paris from Nova Scotia, ground it into dust and sold it for the farmer's use. It improved the soil and enabled wheat to be grown in these once-depleted lands.

Upper Mills

The Ellicott's Upper Mills, which became the homestead of the Joseph Ellicott family, were located three miles up the river from the Lower Mills, where the James Hood Mill once stood.

While living in Pennsylvania, Joseph received word from England informing him that he was heir to a large legacy. In December 1766, he traveled to England in the ship *Hibernia* to receive his great-grandfather's estate in Collumpton, Devonshire. By June 1767 he had completed the sale of the inherited real estate and realized 1,500 pounds sterling, a large sum of money. Tradition recounts that he spent time with a relative, John Ellicott, who was a clock maker in London, and he improved his skills in his trade. On his return voyage, he spent fifty-two days coming from London to Philadelphia.

From 1768 to 1769, Joseph was the high sheriff of Bucks County and a member of the Provincial Assembly. He gained prominence in the arts and sciences and particularly in the pursuit of clockmaking. In 1769 he constructed his musical clock, assisted by his fifteen-year-old son Andrew. The four-sided mahogany clock case stood about eight feet high. Made to be observed from all sides, it had four faces. One face represented the sun, moon, earth, and the planets, all moving in different orbits. Another face marked the seconds, minutes, hours, days, months, and years, all having their different hands pointing to the true time. On the third face were the names of twenty-four musical tunes, which were favorites before the American Revolution. A pointer in the center of this face could select the tune to be played. From the fourth face the mechanism of the clock could be seen.

Joseph built a new mill on the Upper Mills site following the 1774 purchase of property. In addition to a modern mill with all the latest inventions and improvements, he added a storehouse for merchandise, stables, houses for laborers, and a fine mansion for his family.

Joseph and Judith Ellicott, along with their nine children and six orphaned children of their friend and former neighbor, William Evans, moved to the Upper Mills in 1775. A normal consequence transpired when four of the Ellicott children married four of the Evans children. Their home was described as very pleasant and beautiful, with tasteful furniture and fine possessions, many of which Joseph brought back from England. He built a special hall in the home for his large, four-sided clock. His residence was a picturesque sight including the falls, the milldam and race, the fountain supplying the fish pond, and the gardens. In 1780 Joseph died of pleurisy at forty-eight, just five years after moving to Maryland. After this the Upper Mills did not fare well. Joseph's sons followed occupations that took them away from Maryland and there was no one to operate the mills.

Joseph, a son of the founder Joseph, became the first land agent for the Holland Land Company. It was his duty to direct land surveys and to sell parcels of land to settlers for farms and homes in western New York. The Holland Land Company owned three-and-a-half million acres of land. Joseph directed the surveys for the city of Buffalo. His brother Benjamin worked with him. Brother Andrew, a surveyor, traveled while locating the boundaries of many states. He was commissioned to survey the boundaries for the country's capital and reached great prominence in these duties. The majority of the descendants of Joseph and Judith Ellicott settled in New York state when they inherited lands from the two Ellicott brothers who were a part of the Holland Land Company, since neither of these men, Joseph and Benjamin, ever married.

Benjamin Banneker

To learn of the Ellicotts and not to include Benjamin Banneker leaves a story half told. Sylvio Bedini in his *The Life of Benjamin Banneker*, wrote the definitive biography of the first black man of science. Just as the founding Ellicotts did not live on the Howard County side of the Patapsco River, neither did Banneker. But the story of his life crosses county boundaries as well as those of states and countries. Born about 1731, Banneker was a man in his forties when the Ellicotts moved to his neighborhood. Banneker farmed with his parents on 125 acres of land northeast of the original Ellicott's Mills, off present-day Oella Avenue between Westchester Avenue and Old Frederick Road. The grandson of an African slave and an English woman, Banneker inherited intellect and curiosity as well as other fine traits. Banneker had shown a talent for mechanics and mathematics, with the construction of a striking clock, which stood in his cabin. Nothing provided Benjamin with new horizons like the arrival of the Ellicotts and their activities not far from his place.

Young George Ellicott, living at the new family mills, developed an interest in astronomy. He acquired books and instruments that enabled him to learn his subject and to share his knowledge with others through informal evening lectures. Over the years a close association developed between him and Banneker as Ellicott recognized Banneker's natural genius for mathematics. With the loan of some of George's texts and a few of his instruments, Benjamin taught himself how to make calculations necessary for the mathematical projects that he desired. In time he was able to prepare an ephemeris and looked forward to publishing an almanac, often the only book in a family's home in those early days.

Circumstances and his relationship with the Ellicotts led Benjamin Banneker to the greatest adventure of his life. Major Andrew Ellicott, eldest son of Joseph, the founder of the Upper Mills, had received the commission to survey the boundaries of the new federal city, the capital of the country, in 1791. Major Ellicott was usually accompanied by his brothers, Benjamin and Joseph. However, they were completing a survey in New York and Andrew turned to his cousin George for assistance. When George replied that he was not available due to the pressure of the family's business, it's possible that he recommended Banneker, knowing his skills and competence. Banneker agreed to the task and welcomed the opportunity to work with Ellicott's sophisticated instruments. He learned much in the late winter and early spring, months that were damp and cold, and not too pleasant for a man sixty years old. However, he was eager to work with the renowned Andrew Ellicott and to assist in the task. His main responsibility was the maintenance of the astronomical clock, which was a complicated instrument. When the younger brothers were able to rejoin Andrew, Banneker returned to his farm.

Banneker proceeded with work on his own almanac and with the assistance of the Ellicotts in finding a publisher, his almanacs were published for five years, starting in 1792.

Early Howard County Industrialization

Even today there is silent evidence of the extensive milling that was a part of Howard County's economy long before it became an independent county. To look through the index of street names, particularly in the western part of the county, one finds, Rover Mill Road, Triadelphia Mill Road, Roxbury Mill Road, Dorsey Mill Road, and Carroll's Mill Road. These names did not come from the creative pen of a developer. They indicate that along the roadway one would find a milling operation where the county farmer could have his grains ground or sold for market.

John McGrain, an authority of Maryland mills, states that the mill was a farmer's nearest point of contact with the market of a money economy and the farmer could do as well selling a wheat or corn crop to his nearest miller as by hauling it to Baltimore. Gristmills were the sign of a highly developed rural economy.

The Dennis Griffith map of Maryland of 1795 shows sufficient detail to identify many mills along the borders of Anne Arundel County, as Howard was then known. On the Patuxent River the following names are associated with the symbol for a mill: Pigman, Gaither, Howard, Ridgely, Crow, and Snowden. The Patapsco River harbors such names as Hood, Lawrence, Asquith, Ellicott, Mendenhall, Cornthwait, Dorsey, and Hockley. Within the interior of upper Ann Arundel County appeared the names of Roxbury, Carroll, Owings, and White.

This scene is identified as the store and home of John Ellicott. The store was probably the large structure to the left. It was a popular gathering place in the community and was well furnished with fine items from the earliest days of settlement. John was one of the mill's founders and moved to Maryland early with his wife and four young children. None of these buildings survive. They may have been torn down when the mills expanded or when the road changes were made. Courtesy of the Commercial and Farmers Bank

Three eighteenth-century Ellicott homes stood on the bank of the millrace, with the road into Baltimore passing in front of them. This view shows George Ellicott's house to the right, Jonathan's in the center, and John's to the left. George and Jonathan were the sons of the founder Andrew; John was their cousin, son of the founder John. John's home was lost earlier in this century when modern changes were being made in the area. Jonathan's home survived until the hurricane of 1972. It was so badly damaged that it was bulldozed. George's home was damaged in the 1975 hurricane, but has been stabilized and relocated across Frederick Road out of the floodplain, where it can be preserved as the sole surviving structure from the original Ellicott's Mills settlement. Courtesy of the Commercial and Farmers Bank

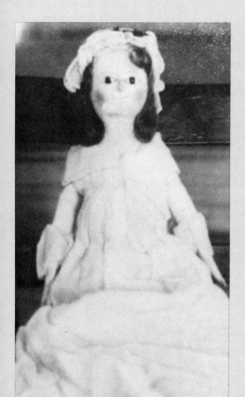

Martha Ellicott Tyson was the daughter of George and Elizabeth Brooke Ellicott. She was born September 1795 and married Nathan Tyson in 1815. Martha wrote interesting historical accounts of the family and their early settlement in Maryland. These were printed by the Maryland Historical Society. She and Nathan raised twelve children. She is considered a founder of Swarthmore College, as plans for the institution were discussed in her living room. American Family History, *Mrs. Lee Hoffman*

Martha Ellicott's doll from the 1790s was called a "Martha Washington" doll. Her face resembled the country's first "First Lady." The hair on the doll appears to be real hair. The eyes are of a glass-like material. Courtesy of Mrs. Henry Fitzhugh III

The Ellicott's Upper Mills were at their finest in 1781 as shown in this lithograph. Joseph Ellicott built a store and an improved mill on this site as well as the large family home, known as Fountainvale. On the property was a fish pond and a fountain near the home. The millrace ran beneath the mill. Joseph brought to his home the large four-sided clock that he and his son had built in Bucks County. He built a special place for it in the home. All four sons left this property sometime after their father's death in 1780, which occurred five years after moving to Maryland. Andrew was the renowned surveyor. Benjamin and Joseph attained great wealth as land agents for the Holland Land Company in New York. David disappeared after losing his wife and four young children through sudden illnesses. This location is now marked with an historical sign, along the

Old Frederick Road near the bridge that crossed into Baltimore County. No buildings survive. The cemetery stones, as shown on the hill, were relocated into the

Ellicott family cemetery in Ellicott City after acts of vandalism. American Family History, *Mrs. Lee Hoffman*

Major Andrew Ellicott was the eldest son of Joseph and Judith Ellicott. His title comes from an appointment to the Elkridge Battalion in the militia in 1778. He was a surveyor and extensively involved in the marking of the boundaries of many states. He was appointed the principal surveyor to locate the boundaries of the District of Columbia. In 1813 he was appointed professor of mathematics at West Point. He lived at the Ellicott's Upper Mills but left due to the unhealthy climate after his son George died. He visited Philadelphia and met with Dr. Benjamin Franklin and other members of the Philosophical Society. American Family History, *Mrs. Lee Hoffman*

The Elkridge Preparatory Meetinghouse was completed in 1799 across the Patapsco River from Ellicott's Mills. A simple rectangular structure, it had many uses after the Quaker meetings were terminated. It was used as a school and a residence, which is the present use of the building. However the structure has been altered. To the right of the picture is the Ellicott family cemetery, which is enclosed in a stone wall. In the iron gate across the top are the letters that spell Ellicott. Adjacent to the Ellicott cemetery is the former Quaker burying ground, which has not received continuous care, although some stone markers are still located there. Courtesy of the Commercial and Farmers Bank

By the 1850s Ellicott's Mills had grown into a sizable community. With the development of the mills in the valley and the coming of the railroad, growth was rapid in the 1830s and 1840s. Church and private schools arrived. By this period, the Ellicott flour mills had passed to the Gambrill family and there was talk of changing the name of the community to Patapsco. In the foreground, in Baltimore County, stands a rear view of the Ellicott homes. Between them and the river was the main road and the operating mills as well as a row of homes. According to an early newspaper article, these homes were built after the arrival of the railroad. Mrs. Elizabeth Ellicott warned about the construction of them so near the river

remembering the many floods and "freshets." These homes were destroyed and many lives were lost in the 1868

flood. Courtesy of the Commercial and Farmers Bank

The Granite Manufactory had a brief existence, directly across the river from Ellicott City, north of the bridge. It was built in the 1840s and destroyed in the flood of 1868. It was chartered in 1846 and was a four-story granite building with steam heat and gas light. In 1850 the machinery was described as the best in this part of the country. In 1850 it manufactured six thousand yards of muslin per day, operating 132 looms with four thousand spindles and employing 150 hands. Granite houses near the original site are called Granite Hill today, the only reminder of the short lived mill. Courtesy of the Commercial and Farmers Bank

Daniels Mill was located north of Ellicott City about five miles above the original Ellicott's Lower Mills. The name in the earliest days was Elysville, when the property was owned by Joseph Ely in the 1830s and 1840s. Once the O'Kisco flour mill operated there. By the 1850s James S. Gary purchased the property and operated the Alberton Mills at Elysville. Gary was a skillful manager and developed a cotton mill. His son, James Albert Gary, was associated in the family business. In 1940, the entire town was sold to the C. R. Daniels Company for $65,000, including the mill, churches and 118 houses. During the 1960s all of the mill housing was torn down and the families moved to nearby communities. When Hurricane Agnes hit in 1972, the mill property was so badly damaged that the company never returned to this original site. C. R. Daniels Company is now located on Ridge Road in Ellicott City. From the author's collection

This beautiful young girl died of a fever at age six. She was the daughter of cotton manufacturer James A. Gary. At the time, Gary operated a mill in Guilford, Howard County. In 1871 land was deeded to a congregation and the church was named in memory of Alberta Gary. The church bears her name and is located on Guilford Road near I-95, not far from Oakland Mills Road. Those mills burned and Mr. Gary moved his workers to his other mill in the county, at Alberton. They built new frame homes and called the homes Guilford, remembering their other village. Courtesy of the Gary family

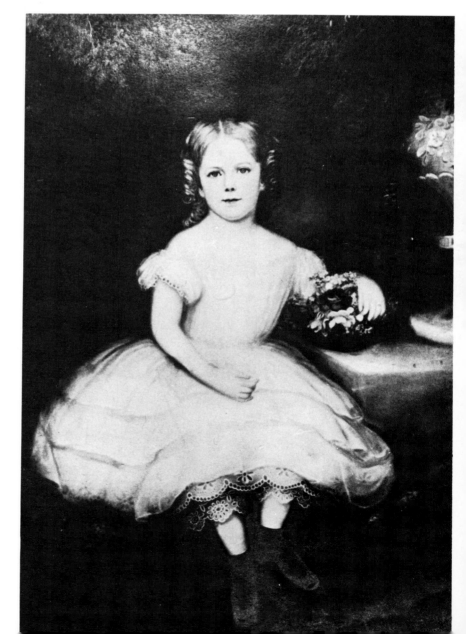

Following the 1868 flood, the bridges at Alberton (later Daniels) were replaced by 1870 with new Bollman bridges. This was the third bridge at this location on the B & O Mainline. The tools of workmen can be seen in the foreground. A man with a wooden leg is shown resting near one of the handsome portals. It was not unusual to lose a limb from a railroad accident. In the mill town of Alberton, to the rear, stood two houses that were torn down when the route of the railroad was changed many years later. These granite bridge footings are still visible in the Patapsco River at Daniels, the name given to the mill community in the 1940s. Courtesy of the Smithsonian Institution, National Museum of American History

In 1940, the mill town of Alberton was sold to the C. R. Daniels Company for $65,000. The original mill building with a white cupola stood in the center of a peninsula created by the Patapsco River. In the lower left were the homes called Guilford. Brick homes stood to the right and across the river in Baltimore County.

In the 1960s all of these homes were demolished after the town's residents relocated to other communities. They returned to the mill to work. Hurricane Agnes closed the milling operation in 1972 and swept away many buildings and bridges. A fire later destroyed some of the remaining buildings. Today some

commercial uses are made at this location. The Gary Memorial Methodist Church remains active and the community brass band continues to play on. C. R. Daniels Company has relocated their business to Ridge Road in Ellicott City. Courtesy of the Baltimore Sun

Elmer Rohrbach of Sykesville worked in the cutting room of the Daniels Mill. Three generations of the family have been employed by the company. Dandux is the tradename of the canvas products from the C. R. Daniels Company. However, the company has diversified and is making plastic products, also. Still located in Howard County after the 1972 flood put them out of business at the original location, they are located on Ellicott Center Drive near U.S. 40. Courtesy of the News American

An advertisement which was used by the Alberton Mills shows the variety of materials manufactured at Elysville. The owners of the mill were the Gary family with the business office located in Baltimore. German Street is called Redwood Street today. These were the typical products of a cotton mill and were being manufactured at the various cotton mills along the Patapsco. Courtesy of the Smithsonian Institution, National Museum of American History

178   THE MONUMENTAL CITY,

ALBERTON COTTON MILLS,
MARYLAND.

James S. Gary & Son,
MANUFACTURERS OF THE WELL KNOWN

Alberton Standard
SHEETINGS and DRILLS.

Alberton and Kentucky 7-8 and 4-4
OSNABURGS.

Alberton and Sagouan 28, 36 and 40 inch
TWILLS.

Western Star 29 and 40 inch
DUCK,
For Tents and Wagon Covers.

Baltimore 28½ inch
DUCK.

Alberton 40 inch Striped
BAGGING.

Alberton Blue and Brown
DENIMS.

Alberton Blue, Green and Fancy Colors.
AWNING STRIPES.

Cotton Warps, Carpet Chains, &c.

OFFICE, 24 GERMAN STREET,
BALTIMORE.

In the mid 1800s Ilchester presented the appearance of a bustling community. The stone house in the center of the scene was built by George Ellicott, Jr., after the railroad came into the valley. He visualized operating a busy inn along the railroad, which passed close by. He also modernized the old Dismal Mill, which stood to the right and operated the grist mill. The Patterson Viaduct carried the train while a wooden bridge served the horses, wagons, and pedestrians. A post office was established at Ilchester Mills in 1842 with Ellicott as postmaster. By 1877 the Mills was dropped from its name. The inn business never prospered and Ellicott sold his property to the Redemptorists in the 1860s. Courtesy of the Commercial and Farmers Bank

In 1809, Ellicott and Company sold land to the founders of the Union Manufacturing Company, the first manufacturing company to obtain a corporate charter from the Maryland General Assembly. In an attempt to found a cotton enterprise in Maryland, stock shares in Union Company were offered in an 1808 Baltimore American at the cost of $50 each. The first textile mill was completed in October 1809 and contained eight hundred spindles. In 1811 the company had the 865 acres resurveyed and patented under the name of Oella in commemoration of the first woman who applied herself to the spinning of cotton on the continent of America. To this day, any further identification of Oella has escaped discovery. A second mill was completed in 1813 and

two years later the first was destroyed by fire. Once the textile industry got into full swing, overproduction became a problem and in 1834 layoffs were necessary. In 1850 Union Mills was described as the largest cotton mill in the area. At that time they employed between three and four hundred persons and the mill consumed three thousand bales of cotton per year. Various circumstances strained the company's resources and Union Company was put on the market in 1887. William J. Dickey bid $125,000 for the mill and bought it. Dickey renamed it Dickey Mills and the community Oella. He produced wool kerseys, plaid linsey, cotton duck, brown sheetings, and cassimere. It was one of the finest manufacturing concerns in the area. In 1918 the

three main mill buildings were destroyed by fire. A new building was constructed and business continued. As manufacturers of woolen fabrics, W. J. Dickey and Son made fabrics for the Allied forces during World War II, as well as for civilian uses.

Life in Oella was typical of the mill company towns. The town had a brass band and a baseball team. The policeman patrolled the town on foot and even controlled the street lights. Doctors paid by the company kept a clinic at the community hall. Gradually, the economics of milling changed and Dickey Mills was closed in March 1972. Courtesy of the Commercial and Farmers Bank

Thomas Mendenhall of Philadelphia bought land from the Ellicotts in 1794 and developed a paper mill directly below Ellicott's Mills. This paper mill was advertised for sale in the American and Commercial Daily Advertiser on January 6, 1813. The improvements consisted of a stone paper mill about one hundred feet long and thirty-five feet wide with a shed at the east end for a sizing house and the accommodation of journeymen and apprentices. A convenient two-story frame dwelling house with a kitchen, a large stone barn and stables, a stone smoke and spring house, six small houses for the workmen, a sawmill and other improvements were advertised. It went on to state that it will be observed that immediately in the neighborhood of the property is the most flourishing settlement perhaps in the state of Maryland where a number of the best mechanics in various branches have settled. About this time Mr. Edward Gray became the manager of the mill, known as the Patapsco Manufacturing Company. In 1820 the mill experienced a fire and was once again advertised for sale. At this time the mill dam was described as nearly new with the race in good order and water wheel one-and-a-half years old and uninjured by the fire. The buildings were sound enough to rebuild. It could be used for anything other than grinding grain, which was a stipulation the Ellicotts included when they sold property along the river, thereby protecting their own milling interests. Gray appears to have purchased the property. After the tariff of 1823, business prospered through Gray's tireless efforts. By 1850, the newspaper reported that Gray employed 180 hands and manufactured osanburghs and heavy twills. Hugh Bone was the mill manager.

Edward Gray's daughter Elizabeth married John Pendleton Kennedy in 1829. Kennedy was a prominent Baltimore attorney who enjoyed politics more than the practice of law. Through Kennedy's interest in writing, Kennedy became acquainted with Washington Irving, who would visit the Kennedys and Mr. Gray at the Patapsco Mill. Irving, in one letter to Mrs. Kennedy wrote, "I should like nothing better than to have plenty of money to squander on stone and mortar and to build chateaus along the beautiful Patapsco with the stone that abounds there; but I would first blow up the cotton-mills (your father's among the number) and make picturesque ruins of them; and I would utterly destroy the railroad and all the cotton lords should live in baronial castles on the cliff; and the cotton spinners should be virtuous peasantry of both sexes, in silk shirts and small-cloth and straw hats with long ribbons, and should do nothing but sing songs and choruses and dance on the margin of the river." Courtesy of the Commercial and Farmers Bank

Thistle Mills was a cotton mill on the Baltimore County side of the river across from Ilchester. According to the newspaper in 1850, it was so named from having been built under many difficulties by two "indomitable and persevering sons of Scotia's Isle." The original stone mill was built in 1837 by George and William Morris from Philadelphia. The oldest mill is in the foreground with a gabled roof. At one time the mills are said to have spun silk thread, helping to keep the mills going during times of depression. In 1929 Bargis Brothers converted the operation from steam power to electric power. Three-and-a-half million gallons of water were consumed every twenty-four hours to convert waste paper to cardboard. Later New Haven Pulp and Board Company owned it. Simpkins operates a paper business at this location today. However in 1972 the flood did extensive damage that took months to repair. This 1940 photo shows many of the original stone houses and buildings no longer standing due to the floods and fires. Courtesy of the Smithsonian Institution, National Museum of American History

Another large flour mill was developed in the Patapsco Valley in the mid eighteenth century and was named the Orange Grove Flour Mill. Built on land owned by George Worthington and George Bailey in 1856, the property was sold to C. A. Gambrill in 1860. Orange Grove was one of three Gambrill mills. In 1873 a Corliss engine and boilers were added as auxiliary to the water power and in 1883 the mill was remodeled to the new roller system. In 1886 a substantial storage warehouse was built adjoining the mill. The Orange Grove Mill was located on the Baltimore County side of the river with the mill homes on the opposite shore in Howard County. There were various grades of flour manufactured with the Patapsco Flour as the top grade. At the turn of the century it was said to be the biggest flour mill east of Minneapolis, producing twelve hundred to fifteen hundred barrels of flour a day. A fire in 1905 destroyed the flour mill. Enoch Pratt Free Library collection, reproduced by permission

This swinging bridge was located at the site of the Orange Grove Flour Mill on the Patapsco River. This 1920 scene was long after the fire of 1905, which destroyed the mill. Thus the bridge was no longer used by the mill workers. The remains from the fire are visible on the Baltimore County side of the river. The workers lived on the Howard County side and depended on the bridge to get to the mill. At times the bridge was out of operation due to floods and ice floes which would damage it. Even then, large companies were concerned about liability. The sign above the bridge reads, "All persons using this private foot bridge do so at their own risk." A tragedy was recorded in 1925 when the bridge collapsed, killing a school boy. Youngsters from nearby Thistle Mills had visited the area on an outing and about eighteen children were on the bridge when it collapsed. Before the 1972 flood, the Orange Grove area of the Patapsco Park was one of the most popular in the system. The flood destroyed the road and picnic area on the Howard County side. The area can be reached on foot today. Enoch Pratt Free Library collection, reproduced by permission

An excellent illustration of the mill operations in the Patapsco Valley was Avalon Mills, which stood in Baltimore County near Elkridge and Relay. This 1850s Sachse print shows the extensive development the mill had reached. In the distance is the Thomas Viaduct. The railroad runs behind the mill and the artist has supplied three steam trains, including the one on the viaduct. John McGrain records that in 1850 John McCrone and Company owned the works and that 140 workers produced forty thousand kegs of nails annually. Later a renovated plant used steam to power seven puddling furnaces, three trains of rolls and forty-four nail machines. Very little remains at this site, following the series of floods that damaged these mills. At one time a Baltimore County water and electric company occupied the rebuilt building until 1926. Today the site is part of of the state park property. The Hambleton Collection; The Peale Museum, Baltimore, Maryland

Amos Adams Williams was one of the operators of the Savage Manufacturing Company. He and his brothers, several associates and John Savage of Philadelphia chartered the company in 1821-22 for the purpose of manufacturing and vending cotton goods. The three brothers, the youngest of a large family, were George, Amos and Cumberland. They had previously been developing a cotton mill at the falls of the Little Patuxent. Savage bought land in the vicinity called White's Contrivance. Although the Williams brothers held two-thirds of the stock, Savage loaned money for the enterprise and held a mortgage on the properties of the milling company. Courtesy of Vera and William Filby

The last surviving Bollman truss bridge stands across the Middle Patuxent River at Savage. This 1923 photo shows the bridge with a warning from the railroad. The old cotton mill is to the left rear. Wendel Bollman was a self-taught Baltimore civil engineer. He was the first to develop the construction of bridges from iron, not stone or wood. The Savage Bridge was built in 1869 and moved to its present location about 1887. It has been recognized by the American Society of Civil Engineers as a national landmark. In September 1966 the Howard County commissioners accepted the bridge from the B & O Railroad for permanent preservation. It has been restored by the county and is open for pedestrian use. The automobile bridge to the right has been replaced after floods removed it and later structures. Courtesy of the Smithsonian Institution, National Museum of American History

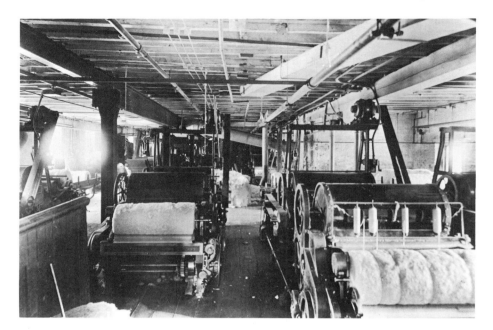

Savage was one of the important cotton milling operations in Howard County. This 1919 photo shows the picker room where the raw cotton was cleared of dirt and debris by machines that loosened the massed fibers and sifted out impurities. The cotton was run through a blower, which produced a long, smooth sheet or lap of cotton batting. The end fibers remained tangled and unaligned prior to carding. Carding was preparatory to spinning because it aligned the fibers by passing the lap between opposite layers of wire teeth. The carded cotton became loosely connected ropes called "slivers." The slivers were carried in cans to the drawing frame. *Maryland Historical Society*

Sometimes the slivers were doubled during the drawing process. Slivers from two or more cans were combined into one filament, drawn out and lightly twisted into a roving by machines called "speeders." The roving was removed from the can and wound on a bobbin. Quantities of bobbins were carried to spinning machines called throstles or mules. Throstles performed continuous spinning and mules intermittant spinning. After the speeder room came the spinning room. This process consisted of three motions, drawing, twisting and winding onto a bobbin or spindle. A mill's production was often described by the number of spindles. In 1825 the Savage mill had one thousand spindles; in 1941 it had twelve thousand ring spindles and three thousand twister spindles. Twisting was done to produce a strong warp yarn to weave cotton duck. *Courtesy of Mr. and Mrs. John A. Hartner and the Smithsonian Institution, National Museum of American History*

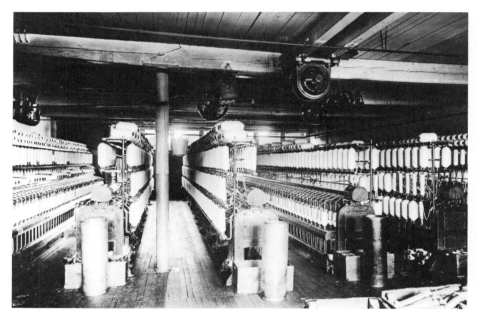

Railroad bridge pioneer Wendel Bollman received this hot water pitcher from the B & O Railroad as part of a nine-piece silver service in 1858. At this time he left the railroad after having served as master of roads. The custom-designed silver service carried a railroading and bridge motif, as shown in the detail on this piece. Each is encircled with scaled railroad tracks. The handles are model surveyor's telescopes. After 1868, Bollman entered business in the Canton section of Baltimore, constructing iron bridges. The Thomas Viaduct is engraved on the lower portion of this hot water pitcher. *Photo by Sidney Sussman, courtesy of the B & O and the Smithsonian Institution*

Warp yarns were wound by machine in preparation for weaving with the appropriate number of threads required for a particular kind of cloth. After being assembled and wound, the warp was usually packaged for transport to the weaver or the weave room. Many changes were made to looms in the nineteenth century, but the basic weaving process remained the same. There was one set of parallel elements, the warp interlaced at right angles with a second set of parallel elements with the weft or filling carried back and forth by a shuttle. The plain weave was the simplest. Duck is strong but light-weight plain weave cloth. The pictured new weave room was built in 1916 in preparation for increased production anticipated by World War I. It housed the automated looms for producing cloth in various lengths and widths. Duck looms were heavier than for less substantial cloth. This machine, called Big Bertha, could weave cloth 208 inches wide. Each machine weighed twenty tons and took six-and-a-half hours each to be moved

six hundred feet into place. Note the pipes on the ceiling for heating, the sprinkler system, electric lights, and leather belts connecting the looms to the drive shaft. Duck was used for sails, hoses, tents, tarps, laundry bags, brake lining for Model Ts, and backdrops for films, just to name a few uses. Courtesy of Mr. and Mrs. A. Hartner and the Smithsonian Institution, National Museum of American History

Wendell Bollman had left the employ of the B & O Railroad in the 1850s and opened his own business in Baltimore. His bridges were placed at many locations in Howard County, with his sole-surviving truss bridge located at Savage Mill today. Enoch Pratt Free Library collection, reproduced by permission

This portrait of Charles Carroll of Carroll-ton was made to hang in the State House in Annapolis, along with the other three Maryland signers of the Declaration of Independence. The Thomas Sully portrait was commissioned by the state of Maryland after the signer's death. Sully began the painting October 22, 1833, and completed it January 27, 1834. He based it on earlier studies and sketches that he had made for a portrait for the Marquess Wellesley. Enoch Pratt Free Library collection, reproduced by permission

Chapter 4

People of the Nineteenth Century

Although the eighteenth century brought settlers into the upper reaches of Anne Arundel County, it was in the nineteenth century that it grew and developed. Families reached prominence. As the new county emerged, slavery continued to flourish. Socialization began, which eventually led to the development of communities. The population grew and with it the churches and schools. The 1800s were important times for Howard County and its people.

Many prominent families called this county home throughout the centuries. Fortunately, a number of their large historic homes survive. These families have helped to preserve their own history through the pictures, diaries, silver, and other memorabilia that has passed down through the generations. A sketch of the Carrolls, one of these families, is appropriate to Howard County history. One outstanding Carroll estate, Doughoregan Manor, is in the county and remains in the family.

The Carroll Family

"Anywhere So Long As There Be Freedom," the motto on the Carroll family crest, was appropriate for a family so involved in the cause of freedom for the young American colonies.

Charles Carroll of Carrollton, illustrious Marylander and once a resident of what is now called Howard County, was one of the four men from the state to sign the Declaration of Independence and was, at the time of his death, the sole surviving signer.

The third generation of an Irish family who came to Maryland in 1688, Carroll inherited Doughoregan Manor, a large land grant in this county, along with thousands of acres of other lands. A portion of these lands and the historic buildings remain in the possession of direct descendants of Charles Carroll of Carrollton.

Carroll was born in 1737 and at age ten left for France to begin long years of education abroad, both at Jesuit schools in France and later to study the English law in London.

As the only heir in a wealthy family, Carroll felt a strong responsibility to marry. After two unsuccessful courtships, he married Mary (Molly) Darnell in 1768, a woman with the same name as his grandmother. Because of the interrelationships between certain family lines, Charles and Mary Carroll were first cousins once removed through the maternal line and second cousins once removed through the paternal line. Molly bore seven babies, three of whom grew to adulthood, Mary, Charles and Catherine.

Upon his return from abroad, Charles learned the management of the family estate and served as a willing apprentice to his father. According to Ronald Hoffman in the publication from the Baltimore Museum of Art, *Anywhere As Long As There Be Freedom*, Carroll did not play an active part in opposing British taxation policies during the 1760s, but he clearly sympathized with the Colonial protest. In 1773, through a celebrated newspaper controversy and exchange of letters, he became a prominent political figure. The argument concerned the validity of an action by Maryland's last proprietary governor, Robert Eden. Without the consent of the legislature, he increased the rate of fees charged for government services.

Daniel Dulany defended the governor's actions in the *Maryland Gazette*. Carroll opposed the governor.

As the newspaper debate continued, Carroll drew support and those men who sided with Carroll's opposition to the governor's action were destined to be the leaders in Maryland's role in the American Revolution.

Carroll attended the First Continental Congress, though not as a delegate. In 1776, he made a trip to Canada with his cousin Father John Carroll, Samuel Chase, and Dr. Benjamin Franklin in the effort to get Canada's support in the colonies' revolutionary cause. Later he took a seat in the Second Continental Congress and was appointed to the Board of War. When he signed the Declaration of Independence, he was placing his fortune on the line, a fortune that was possibly the greatest of any family in the colonies.

Carroll remained involved in the politics of the war but did not serve in the military. He was away from home frequently. During periods when he was at home, he and Molly entertained at their Annapolis home. In April 1781 they hosted a dinner party for the Marquis de LaFayette, General Smallwood, and other officers.

Tragedy struck the family in 1782 when Carroll's father died from a fall from the porch of their Annapolis home. So grief stricken from his death, the young daughter-in-law died within two weeks, leaving Carroll a widower with four young children. Mary, the oldest, was just twelve and the youngest child died soon after her mother's death.

His daughter Mary (Pol) married Richard Caton; son Charles of Homewood married Harriet Chew of Philadelphia, a sister of John Eager Howard's wife, Peggy; and Catherine (Kitty) married Robert Goodloe Harper.

After 1821, Carroll spent his winters at the Caton's town house in Baltimore and the summers at Doughoregan Manor, which he greatly enjoyed. He died at the Baltimore town house in 1832 at the age of ninety-five. After his death, mass was said at the Baltimore Cathedral, now the Basilica of the Assumption. His body was then taken by train to Ellicott Mills and by carriage to his beloved manor, where he was buried inside the chapel.

Average Families

During the early years of the nineteenth century, life was simple compared to the complexities of the late twentieth century. Leading a simple life, however, did not mean that life was easy. It was necessary to concentrate on necessities: food, housing and clothing. People provided for their own needs and that meant hard work.

The average family found little time for relaxation. Socializing usually happened through church and family relationships. Lectures and concerts were popular at the churches, which provided the early meeting places. Summer brought the church camp meetings, where people often attended for days at a time. Three camp meeting grounds in the county were Wesley Grove between Waterloo and Elkridge on the Washington Turnpike, Penny's Grove near the Guilford factory, and Rattlesnake Springs near Dayton. All denominations attended, often pitching tents for the week. It appears that these events were racially integrated, for in 1850 there were eighty converts at the Rattlesnake Springs camp meeting, sixty whites and twenty blacks.

The temperance societies were popular and groups formed throughout the county as a part of a national movement to encourage abstinence from alcohol. Originally male groups, the Daughters of Temperance were also formed. Politics provided an outlet for some residents, particularly in election years. Lectures and debates were held in the small communities. The Long Corner Literary Association debated "Does man have more influence in this world than woman?" in 1889. They concluded that he does not. At another time the same group debated "Are the works of art more pleasing to the eye than the works of nature?"

Unfortunately the history of many of these average and poorer families has not been as well documented and preserved as that of wealthy families such as the Carrolls. However, there are hundreds of homes, particularly from the Victorian era, that survive and have been carefully restored. Often these homes were composites of many additions. An older stone kitchen may have been enlarged with a frame addition, with new kitchens, baths, porches coming later. Many of these large homes have a front roofline with one or two gables and a cupola on the roof. Homes were changed as styles changed. Chimneys were removed when central heat became available. Later the Victorian styles were altered to appear more modern.

Nineteenth Century Life

Although county newspaper records are sparse between 1840 and 1870, some important events have come to light, including the commissioners meeting records.

The county commissioners kept busy maintaining the county roads which were identified by the families that lived along them. There was concern for paupers and the insane and some money was allotted for their care. The courthouse and jail were the primary county facilities under the direction of the commissioners. Government and county services were minimal.

One of the interesting stories from the 1850s, in the *Howard Gazette*, recounts the efforts of the people of Ellicott's Mills to have the state legislature pass a certain law. Herds of cattle were commonly brought on the hoof from the west through the main street of Ellicott's Mills enroute to the Baltimore stockyards. To get to the Monday morning market, the cattlemen would drive the stock through town on Sunday morning, like a stampede. It was dangerous and unpleasant for the residents to encounter these animals, especially on Sunday morning on the way to church. Meeting the cattle at the covered bridge that crossed the Patapsco River was a particularly harrowing experience. The state legislature would not respond to the citizens' appeal to ban cattle drives through Ellicott's Mills on Sundays.

Another interesting event from 1850 related to the visit of Henry Clay to the county. He was a very popular politician and when the citizens heard he was coming to the area they were eager to greet him. When his friend and local attorney, Robert Hare, picked him up at the Elkridge train station, they went immediately to the Carroll estate. This angered the local residents who verbally attacked Mr. Hare for not stopping in Ellicott City. Mr. Clay publicly reprimanded the citizens for accusing his friend Mr. Hare of any wrong-doing. Clay stated that he was exhausted from his travels and requested to be taken directly to his friend's home at Doughoregan Manor to allow him to rest. He did stop and make an appearance briefly in the town before leaving the area.

Slaves

Anne Arundel County was considered a Southern county and had a large slave population. Because Howard County was a part of Anne Arundel its statistics are difficult to separate from the entire county's figures. However, records indicate in the 1790s that the upper part of the county (later called Howard) had a slave population of about one thousand. Because the earliest settlers into the upper part of the county came from the Annapolis area, many were farmers and slaveholders. About seventy-five families held the one thousand slaves before 1800.

Runaway slaves proved to be a problem for the white community. In 1841 Charles Carroll, grandson of the signer of the Declaration of Independence, posted a notice that read as follows:

> I will give $5 for any one of my servants who may be taken at or beyond Ellicotts' Mills, night or day, and delivered to me or my manager on Doughoregan Manor, unless they have a pass, or are sent with a wagon, cart, or horse, on my business.

Michael Morgan recounts how the escape movement of slaves to the North accelerated about the time of the growth of the railroad in the 1830s. Slaves were said to be using the "underground railroad" in their passage North. Morgan writes that one of the major lines passed along the U.S. 1 corridor area, leading into Baltimore.

The account of two fugitive slaves from the 1850s is available. Bill Cole was a forty-seven-year-old slave of a judge of the Orphan's Court, a wealthy farmer in the vicinity of Savage. Cole said that his master sold slaves occasionally. Slave-trading had a stigma attached to it that was not attached to the actual owning of slaves. The master's family was known to have the slaves whipped. Cole decided to try to escape and persuaded Hansen, a slave owned by a relative of Cole's master, to accompany him. Hansen is quoted as saying:

> My master was a red-faced farmer, severe temper, would curse, and swear, and drink, and sell his slaves whenever he felt like it. My mistress was pretty cross, curious kind of a woman too, though she was a member of the Protestant Church. They were rich, and had big farms and a good many slaves. They didn't allow me any provisions hardly; I had a good wife, but they did not allow me to see her, only once in a great while.

The advertisement for their return carried the promise of a $500 reward. They were not captured.

In 1860 Howard County's population was about 13,300, including 2,862 slaves and 1,395 free blacks. Between 1843 and 1863, local records show that 132 slaves were manumitted (freed), many through wills of their masters. This form of freedom was usually reserved for those in their twenties to forties. The very young and the old were generally belived to be in need of someone to care for them and were not freed. Thomas Worthington of John (his father's name was John) freed sixteen slaves in 1829. Henry Welling freed eleven slaves in 1843. Rezin Hammond freed Nacky and Mary Green, ages fifty and thirty; Phoebe, age twenty, daughter of Nacky and Darky, Marcus, Catherine, and William Joice in his will of 1808.

When the slave statistics were recorded in 1868 by Claudius Stewart, commissioner of slave statistics, there were 259 owners of two thousand slaves. Although the inventory was made four years after freedom came to the slaves, it related the holdings as of November 1864. According to Phebe R. Jacobsen of the Maryland Archives, most of the former slaves still lived with or near their former masters. She has also observed that it is a myth that the freed slaves took their owners' names. Some names reflected occupations such as millers, coopers, sawyers. Many names came from prominent families in the community, or from neighboring whites, black religious leaders, or admired journalists.

This is borne out in the Howard County inventory. The most common name appearing for former slaves was Dorsey, although in only two instances did they belong to Dorseys. There were thirty-nine Dorseys who owned 406 slaves. The heirs of Charles Carroll (the signer's grandson) owned 131 slaves. The most prominent names found in the Carroll inventory were thirty-one Addisons, twenty-two Joices, and twenty Connors. Twenty-three Warfields owned 174 slaves. But half of all the owners had fewer than 5. Forty-four owners recorded just a single slave.

Other prominent slave names were Anderson, Brown, Blackstone, Clark, Cure, Green, Gaither, Howard, Johnson, Mathews, Snowden, Tyler, and Warfield. There were at least ninety surnames used by former slaves in the statistics. But Caleb Dorsey did not list last names for his forty-three slaves, nor did Reuben Meriweather Dorsey for his eighty-eight.

The inventory listed the name of the slave, age, sex, physical condition, term in years of slavery, and information about military service. The statistics were taken because owners were to be compensated when their slaves were freed. This did not happen.

In many instances, you could identify families of slaves. Helen Dorsey had eight slaves. Seven were named Holland, Caroline, age thirty-three, and six children, ages one to fourteen. Dennis Gaither had fourteen slaves; Elizabeth Todd was thirty-five and had seven children. Freeborn Hipsley had eleven slaves, Maranda Bell, age forty-three, with her nine children. Thomas Hood's seven slaves were Sarah Dorsey and her six children ages three to ten years. Joshua Anderson held eleven slaves, Sarah Nicholson, age thirty-five, and her ten children.

Isaac Anderson of Marriottsville was a large slave holder with thirty-nine. According to an interview with Ed Dorsey of Sykesville some years ago when he was in his 90s, Dorsey stated that Anderson was a slave trader. He remembered stories from his mother, whose mother belonged to Anderson. Anderson would buy "unruly" or "undesirable" slaves and sell them to the Southern states. Dorsey's grandmother worked in the Anderson home and observed the master's dealings. The slaves to be traded were imprisoned in a stone building.

First Map

In 1860, the first detailed map of this young county was made by Simon J. Martenet, a surveyor, and published by John Schofield at Ellicott's Mills. It was customary that when surveying business was slow, these men would prepare maps of the various jurisdictions. Schofield ran the Patapsco Enterprises at the new town hall in Ellicott City. In 1859 the commissioners granted $300 to Schofield to aid him in publishing his map. He was to provide one copy to each public office and to each primary school in Howard County. This map identifies the property owner on each parcel of land. There were five election districts and the county commissioners referred the map to five citizens to review and certify for its accuracy of information. These men were W. Baker Dorsey, W. W. Watkins, Thomas Burgess, Gustavus Warfield, and William Welling. Three communities were large enough to warrant enlargement of the area, Elkridge, Ellicott's Mills, and Lisbon. The detail shows each lot owner and in many cases the business of the shop owner. The map identifies churches, schools, mills, and other specific uses such as hotels, blacksmith shops, wheelwright shops. Unfortunately few black families are identified on the map since they were not property owners. A very few are with the designation (cold.) meaning colored, after the name. About twenty years later the *Hopkins/Atlas* of 1878 was published, which gave similar information. By this time there were six election districts and new communities that had developed since 1860 were included. It was also after the Civil War and some black families continued to be identified as (cold.) but many were excluded since they were tenants and not property owners.

Crimes

The county experienced many unpleasant events that the newspapers found proper to report. Toward the end of the nineteenth century the county had matured enough to find "city" crimes occurring. A highly respected physician in one of the mill towns was found guilty of performing an abortion and was sentenced to prison for the offense. A second event concerned a murder in Ellicott City. A young black man was found guilty of slaying an Ellicott City merchant. Before he could be hanged, as sentenced, he was lynched by a quiet mob in the middle of the night. The newspaper recorded it as the county's second lynching. A third crime involved the county's school board before 1900. A grand jury investigated the activities of all three board members. One problem was an expenditure of $150 for the board members to attend an NEA meeting at Richmond. A second charge was against the doctor who served on the board. He was reimbursed from school funds for vaccinating the school children and collected forty cents per child as well. A third irregularity involved a reimbursement to the board president of seventy-four dollars for traveling expenses throughout the year to inspect the school buildings.

WATERLOO INN.
the first Stage from Baltimore to Washington.

Spurrier's Tavern was a popular stage-coach and travelers' stopping point between Philadelphia and Georgetown. In Colonial days, one diarist recorded that he left Baltimore at 6:00 a.m. and reached Spurrier's for breakfast. It was also stated that George Washington traveled this route and remarked that the roads were so muddy that his horse died from exhaustion when trying to make his way along that road. By the early nineteenth century the stopover became the Waterloo Inn. The community along U.S. 1 near Maryland 175 was known as Waterloo for many years. There is no evidence of this old structure. By 1878 the inn no longer served this purpose. *The Hambleton Collection, The Peale Museum, Baltimore, Maryland*

Iris Hill stands east of U.S. 29, at one time remotely removed and difficult to locate, when this photo was made in 1940. It was then the home of Hans Kindler, the first conductor of the National Symphony. Today a road in the vicinity is named for him. An early Worthington family home, it now stands surrounded by trees, but closer to neighbors in the new town of Columbia. An old Worthington cemetery and the tomb of Mr. Kindler, are located on the property. Other names for the house were Whitehall and Worthington's Addition. *Courtesy of the* Baltimore Sun

Miss Liza Jane Crowner was the daughter of Elijah Crowner of Elkridge. Her sister, Bessie Crowner Snell, was a teacher at the school on Meadowridge Road and at the Odd Fellows Hall at Gaines church. Mrs. Laura Simms recalls that she was related to the Crowners and that they referred to one another as "cousin." Courtesy of Laura Simms and the Howard County Chapter of the NAACP

Troy was a Dorsey land grant patented in the late 1600s. Col. Thomas Dorsey lived in a frame dwelling on this patent until his death in 1790. His widow sold the 652 acres in 1808 to Vincent Bailey for $6,520. Bailey appears to have built this large stone house in the 1820s. In the mid 1800s, it was called Troy Hill Farm. The Pfeiffers owned the property at that time and occupied it until 1905. The front addition with tall white pillars had collapsed by the time the state declared Troy excess property and deeded it to Howard County. Once a showplace, it is boarded up and unused. It can be seen at the interchange of I-95 and Maryland 100, sitting on a high hill overlooking the modern highways. Courtesy of the News American

Carroll Mansion in 1853.

Charles Carroll of Carrollton spent his years as an active, patriotic citizen at the family's mansion house in Annapolis. Located on Carroll (Spa) Creek, the home was started by his father about 1735. It, too, was a property that grew through the years. By 1853, it was this large stately home. Today, the smaller section is gone. The property is a part of St. Mary's seminary. A connection has been made from newer buildings to what was the front entrance; therefore, it does not present this same appearance. Courtesy of M. E. Warren

These two large brick buildings are still standing at Doughoregan Manor. Both are used today as dwellings. The one to the rear served as a barn. The building to the right has four large brick chimneys and has been called the laundry by some sources. It may have served that use for the entire facility at one time. It has also been conjectured that the building was a part of the wool milling operation at the manor. Enoch Pratt Free Library collection, reproduced by permission

The old stone building on Doughoregan Manor sits behind the overseer's house on the east side of Manor Lane. Although it has been called the slave jail because of the bars on the windows, that use has been questioned by recent historians. A more probable use of the building was the storage of food, which was rationed to the slaves and tenants on a regular basis. Rather than keeping prisoners inside, the bars were used to keep people from raiding the food supply. Maryland Historical Society

7 "Doughoregan": Old catalpa in the garden under which President Washington and Mrs. Carroll sat and conversed. 17 April 1926

Knarled old catalpa trees line Manor
Lane leading into Carroll's Manor from
Maryland 144. In 1926 three gentlemen
were photographed standing under one
of these old trees. Family legend records
that it was under this tree that Mrs.
Carroll sat and talked with George Washington. *Maryland Historical Society*

The "necessaries" at Doughoregan
Manor served the residents until
Governor Carroll made indoor improvements. The interesting structure is used
for storage today. Privies or outdoor
toilets were found at every home and
today many homes have kept them in
addition to modern plumbing which has
become available. However, these unusual double privies were far grander
than those that were used generally in
this county. *Enoch Pratt Free Library
collection, reproduced by permission*

71

St. Charles college, a preparatory seminary, stood on 253 acres donated by Charles Carroll of Carrollton, a part of his land at Doughoregan Manor. A charter was obtained in 1831 for the college with the purpose of educating pious young men of the Catholic persuasion for the ministry of the gospel. After some delay, the college opened in 1848. It is shown here with later additions as the enrollment grew. By 1898, the golden anniversary, nine hundred students had been ordained. Cardinal Gibbons was one of the illustrious alumnus. Fire destroyed the buildings in March 1911. Few possessions were saved, but no lives were lost. A few ruins remain. The school was rebuilt in Catonsville. The property later was Brendel's Park and had other uses including a Gospel Park. Today the property holds a private residence. Courtesy of Howard County Historical Society

An interesting old house, which poses more questions than it answers, is located where Folly Quarter Road, east of Glenelg makes a right angle turn. Called the Folly Farm and once owned by Charles Carroll of Carrollton, this property was given by Carroll to his granddaughter, Emily Caton McTavish. An old plat of the property indicated that there was a dairy and bathhouse at this location, not far from the site of the large home built for Emily and her family. This 1920 photo shows a large white portico added to the stucco-covered building made of field stone. At one time a road passed directly in front of this structure to the family home on the hill to the west. Today the house sits with its rear to the roadways. Enoch Pratt Free Library collection, reproduced by permission

Generations of school youngsters have learned the story of the 1830 race between the Tom Thumb steam engine and the horse on the newly laid railroad tracks between Baltimore and Ellicott Mills. Recent research by John Hankey concludes that such a race probably never happened and even more shattering, the fact that the engine was probably never called the Tom Thumb. While working as a historian with the B & O, Hankey did extensive research on this subject, as reported in the Baltimore Sun in 1980 by Frederick Rasmussen. There is no evidence of the legendary race between an engine and a horse-drawn rail car. An imaginative publicist somewhere created a captivating story. Hankey has traced the first reference to the early engine to a speech by John H. B. Latrobe in 1868 when he referred to "that Tom Thumb of an engine," meaning Peter Cooper's early steam invention. At that

time the use of the phrase "Tom Thumb" was popular because of the circus midget touring with P. T. Barnum. From the author's collection

Waveland, as photographed by the Jones sisters, is a brick house painted white, not far from Oakland Mills Road. Larkin Dorsey built the home in the early 1800s. Later it was the home of Reuben M. Dorsey and his descendants. Family stories recall that Mrs. Dorsey's brother worked with the Confederates during the Civil War and often came to Waveland in disguise. The Union soldiers knew of the activity and made surprise visits hoping to catch him there. He was never discovered but used ingenious means, such as hiding among his sister's gowns in the large wardrobe, to keep from being captured. The Dorseys sold the property to the Sewells who operated a farm and orchards for many years, including an operation for picking one's own produce. Today Sewells Orchards is a housing development. The Jones sisters were prominent recorders of history through their hobby of traveling about Maryland and photographing their favorite spots. Miss Elsie made the photographs, Miss Ida did the artwork, and Miss Frances wrote the brief histories. Courtesy of Howard County Historical Society

Arcadia was the farm of the Dorsey family who lived north of Frederick Avenue and west of St. John's Lane. This home stood north of U.S. 40 near the Valley Mede development. An overgrown cemetery nearby holds the remains of dozens of members of this prominent and prosperous family. Caleb Dorsey of Thomas (1747-1837) and his wife Elizabeth Worthington Dorsey (1758-1840) settled here to raise their family of thirteen children. This couple provided the land for St. John's Episcopal Church. Their son, Reuben Merriweather Dorsey, (1796-1880) kept a diary, which is reviewed in the Maryland Historical Magazine. Whenever he mentioned his only son Caleb, it was in capital letters. The youngster was named for his uncle who owned Dorsey Hall. At Christmas they dined on oysters, raisins and almonds brought from Baltimore, turkeys, puddings, hams, and "corn beef." The house disappeared about thirty years ago. From the author's collection

Judge Thomas Beale Dorsey resided on his farm, Mount Hebron, in northern Howard County, bordering the Patapsco River. His two thousand acres of land reached from near Daniels Road west to McKenzie Road. Although a farmer, he is remembered for his professional contributions. Born October 17, 1780, he was admitted to the practice of law in 1803. He was a state delegate in 1807 and a senator in 1808. In 1820 he served as the attorney general. On the court of appeals he was chief judge until 1851. His home is owned by the Mount Hebron Presbyterian Church. He married Milcah Goodwin and moved to Howard County about 1815, when he built his large stone house. Construction appears to have been of various periods. During interior renovations, the walls of the double parlor were found to have been stenciled. The pattern resembled wood paneling. Often traveling artists of the early 1800s performed this art work prior to the use of wallpaper. Both of the Dorseys died in the 1850s. Enoch Pratt Free Library collection, reproduced by permission

William Henry Goodwin Dorsey was a son of Judge Thomas Beale and Milcah Goodwin Dorsey. He inherited property at his father's death and built the home called Wilton. He was an attorney and married twice. Each of his wives had the maiden name of Dorsey. This was a not uncommon practice that families followed. The Dorsey family was so large that there were many, many cousins. *Courtesy of Mrs. G. Arthur Brownley*

Wilton was one of the Italian villa style homes in Howard County designed by architect Nathan Starkwether. It was built in the 1850s by William H. G. Dorsey. In the 1880s and 1890s it was the home of states attorney Richard McGuire. When the property was unoccupied in 1939 it burned. The last owner bought the property to develop orchards on the farm and was not interested in the granite house. Two adjacent developments, The Orchards and Wilton Acres, take their names from this farm property. If it were standing today it would be near the interchange of I-70 and U.S. 29. Local legend reports that the stones were used to build the parish hall at St. John's Episcopal Church. *Maryland Historical Society*

WILTON

Res of Wᵐ H.G. Dorsey, Esq.

Woodlawn, which stands near U.S. 29 and Frederick Avenue, was the home of John T. W. Dorsey, a son of Judge Thomas Beale Dorsey. Woodlawn was a popular name for a home and there were others called by it. The structure was considerably altered when the rear addition was removed and the peak on the front of the house was removed. In recent years, this house was popular as the fine French restaurant, the Papillion with a small pub operating in the rear with summer entertainment. Currently there is no use being made of the property. Courtesy of Mrs. G. Arthur Brownley

Dr. Arthur Pue, Jr., was the builder of the house Temora, which stands on Columbia Road, west of U.S. 29. He was about fifty years old in 1857, when he constructed the Italian villa style home designed by architect Nathan G. Stark-weather. His earlier home stood along St. John's Lane where the home Woodley is located today. Mechanics liens were filed against the property at the time of construction. They provide the following information about the construction of Temora. Jacob Timanus was the stone-mason and his fees were $535.97 for the materials, including the stone, sand, and lime for the cellar of the house. Bevan and Sons supplied the marble mantles at a cost of $260.00 for ten mantles. It cost $16.50 for six day's work of setting the mantles. John Cavana of Baltimore was the painting contractor and was owed $543.00 for his work and materials. He painted for 182 days at $2.00 a day. Colors used were yellow ochre, Spanish Brown, black, green, and blue. Roofing and spouting cost $484.94. Windows and shutters ran $369.08. The question of the liens was answered in an interview with an elderly grandson of Dr. Pue. He recalled that his grandfather had to pay for the construction of the house twice since he gave the money to the contractor who ran off and did not pay the bills. Therefore the liens were filed and Dr. Pue satisfied the debts of the subcontractors. Dr. Pue married Sally Dorsey, daughter of Thomas Beale Dorsey, Jr., of Gray Rock. His father and grandfather were also physicians. He was the father of eight sons, three of whom moved to Texas and one who was killed in the Confederate Army during the Civil War. Maryland Historical Society

Dr. Charles Alexander Warfield married Elizabeth Dorsey in 1771 and settled on thirteen hundred acres called Bushy Park. He purchased half of the property and the other half was his wife's marriage dower. Near Glenwood, west of Maryland 97, the original home does not survive. As a member of the Whig Club and a recent graduate of the University of Pennsylvania, he participated in the burning of the Peggy Stewart in 1774 in the Annapolis harbor. Anthony Stewart had brought into port his vessel, loaded with tea, against the colonists' wishes. When confronted with the choice between "firing his own vessel or hanging by the halter before his door" Stewart set fire to the ship. Enoch Pratt Free Library collection, reproduced by permission

A portion of a lovely sampler done in 1829 shows that Mary Thomas Warfield made this work of art for her mother, also Mary Warfield, at the age of eleven. The entire sampler is preserved in perfect condition by a member of the family. The remainder of the sampler produces the alphabet completely four times in various sizes and includes the name of the family home, Longwood. Courtesy of Jean Warfield Keenan

Longwood, west of Maryland 97 near Glenwood, was built by Dr. Gustavus Warfield, son of Charles Alexander Warfield, about 1820. Dr. Warfield practiced medicine in the small building to the right. He and his wife Mary Thomas raised eight daughters and one son at Longwood. A family cemetery remains near the home. Their only son, Evan William, carried on the medical profession of his father and grandfather. From the author's collection

Red House Tavern provided a stopping place along the Old Frederick Road for those making the journey from Frederick to Baltimore. As early as 1795 the tavern was located in the western part of the county on the Griffith map. Today the old tavern sits near I-70 and Maryland 97. From the author's collection

The invention of the self-raking reaper occurred in the 1850s. It was a popular new farm machine because it dispensed with the labor of one man. In 1855, Owen Dorsey began to sell reapers. According to his patent, he lived at Triadelphia, but the 1878 Directory listed him at Glenwood. The reaper appeared to be a fine piece of equipment because Jess Higgins and Bros., Montgomery County agents for C. H. McCormick in Chicago, wrote on August 15, 1855 about the concern that Higgins had for the competition from the Dorsey Reaper. "It has taken the attention of the people like wild fire and the interest taken in his machine is truly astounding." Higgins was located at Poolesville in Montgomery County.

In 1855 Dorsey made five machines and took orders for 40 or more for the next harvest. Higgins felt that about half of those orders were potential customers of his. Dorsey's price was $135, apparently cheaper than McCormick's. Furthermore, Dorsey was expected "to make a great parade with his self-raker" at the Montgomery County fair. In November of the same year, Higgins wrote again about competition from the Dorsey reaper. Higgins' clients reported that it had performed well at the Frederick County fair and had impressed many people. In December Higgins urged McCormick to get someone to judge the Dorsey machine to see if it used any of

McCormick's principles and violated the patent.

This Adriance Platt and Co. self raker was very similar to Dorsey's. In 1856 Dorsey was granted patent No. 15,174 for an improved harvester rake. His reaper consisted of raking arms mounted on a vertical shaft geared to the drive-wheel. A universal drive mechanism coupled to the rake arms caused them to vertically enter the crop, one at a time, gently bring the crop back to the cutter-bar, sweep the cut material across the platform quadrant and then deposit the gavel on the ground, before withdrawing to repeat the cycle, according to "The Grain Harvester" by Graeme R. Quick and Wesley F. Buchele. They related that on the first Dorsey machines, the sweep of the raking arms left no room for the driver, forcing him to ride the drafthorse. Later an operator's seat was provided in Whitenack's 1861 design and others. This style was known as "pidgeon-wing" reapers which were popular on the farm for nearly 50 years. Courtesy of the American Society of Agricultural Engineers

William Winchester Welling (1813-1882) lived at the stone house Clifton, which was built in 1818 by his father. William married Mary Crawford in 1835. They raised thirteen children at the family home, which stands where the new village of Columbia will be built. He farmed extensively along both sides of what is today Maryland 32, Guilford Road. William also served as a tax assessor. Many of their descendants live in the county today. Courtesy of William B. Welling, Jr.

The Lawyer's Club in Baltimore was photographed in the mid-nineteenth century, now faded and stained. At least three of these attorneys lived in Howard County and are joined by prominent Baltimoreans. Standing from the left is Benjamin Presstman, judge of the superior court in 1866; George W. Brown; Charles Pitt; Thomas Donaldson, resident of Lawyers Hill, Elkridge; and Frederick W. Brune. Brune died at age sixty-five in 1878 from overexertion and intense heat while arguing a case concerning the Annapolis and Elk Ridge Railroad before Judges Hammond and Hayden in Anne Arundel Circuit Court. Seated from the left, are Henry Winter Davis; Severn Teackle Wallis; Frank Frick; George W. Dobbin, the builder of the Lawn and resident of Elkridge; William A. Talbott; William H. Norris; and William H. G. Dorsey, son of Judge Thomas Beale Dorsey and builder of Wilton. Note the assorted poses, the formal clothing, and the draped table with cane and hat. Courtesy of Howard County Historical Society

The gold rush beckoned to young Howard County residents, and by 1850 many had found their way West to seek their fortune. David Feelmeyer received a letter from his son-in-law, George Anderson, and the letter was printed in the local newspaper. From Camp Baltimore in California, George mentioned that as he was writing he could hear the wolves howling. In March it was raining three to four days a week. He reported that T. Pue, William Canby, and William F. Mercer were well. A letter from Charles Partridge was also published and reported that they would average twelve dollars per day at the mines. There was much sickness and many deaths. By his choice, he would rather work in Maryland for fifty cents a day. In August, Anderson wrote from the Calaberas River. Others in his party were Canby, George W. Feelmeyer, D. Taylor, and A. J. Barney. They were averaging eight to ten dollars per day working from 4:00 a.m. to 7:00 p.m., digging harder than the railroaders. Many miners were not making their board. Thousands were doing nothing. Dinner was hard crackers, fat pork and a little tea. Library of Congress, Prints and Photographs Division

This scene, circa 1860, at the Patapsco Female Institute in Ellicott City must have been made on a Sunday afternoon. Many people, both women and men, appear on the front steps and sloping lawn of the school. The long flowing skirts and the style of the men's clothing help to date the photograph. It could be an early warm spring day before the leaves appeared. Courtesy of Howard County Historical Society

Stockwood was the home of Dr. Thomas Galen Stockett before 1860. In 1871 Arthur Burns, M.D., owned this property and advertised in the Times *that he had removed to the farm of Geo. L. Stockett but would continue his practice in Ellicott City and at the factories. "During the day, one should leave a message at Mrs. N. B. Brook's book shop and at night at Cap't. McCrea's Livery and coal office on Court House Lane." By 1911 the property passed to Charles D. Gaither. His widow sold 115 acres to the county in 1950 and this is the location today of Howard High School. Courtesy of Jane Trollinger*

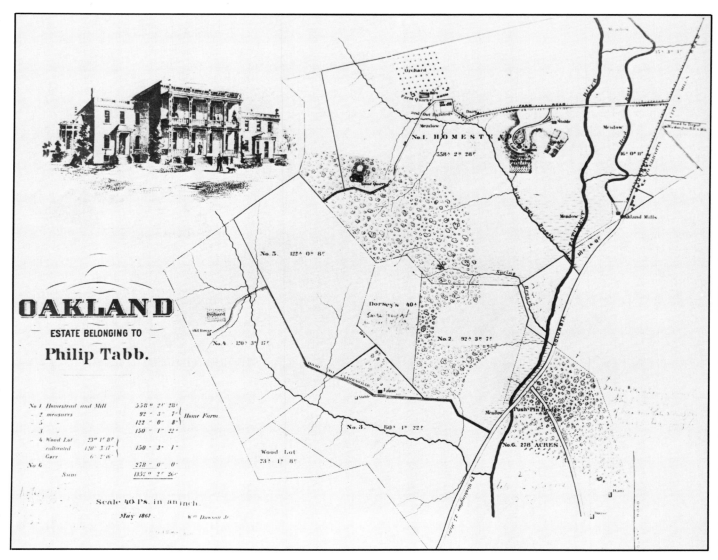

An 1867 survey of Oakland was done by William Dawson, Jr., and included 1,352 acres of land. The mansion house is sketched on the upper left corner. Although it is shown with a wrought iron porch, no photos exist which show other than a wooden portico. This house sat within the circular area at the top of the plat. A stable, garden, a dwarf fruit orchard were close by. A larger orchard was to the west where the farm quarters included a stone barn, dairy and out buildings. The Oakland Mills sat on the Columbia Turnpike, fed by a head race. A stone quarry was in the forested area. The mansion house is standing near Town Center in Columbia, along with a large renovated barn. The barn and other stone buildings are also still standing near Wilde Lake. Courtesy of Mr. R. L. Lee

Wheatfields was the home of James Clark after he purchased the property in the 1850s. The eighty-year-old family patriarch celebrated his birthday in 1889 at the home, as shown here. The newspapers reported that all thirty-four of his descendants were on hand for the celebration. Clark married Jemina Ward but she was not living in 1889. They had ten children. Wheatfields is located on Montgomery Road between Maryland 104 and U.S. 29. James Clark was the great-grandfather of Senator Clark. Courtesy of Howard County Historical Society

Fairfields was the home of Thaddeus Clark in the mid 1800s. His first cousin James lived at Wheatfields. Later John L. Clark, who married Mary Corinne Talbott, lived at Fairfields. Thaddeus and James were second generation Clarks in Howard County. John L. and Mary Corinne Clark developed beautiful gardens around their home and farmed in the vicinity of Running Brook in Wilde Lake Village. This home stood on the south side of Maryland 108 between U.S. 29 and Centennial Lane. It has not survived. Courtesy of Howard County Historical Society

An unusual piece of family memorabilia is this hairbarium, given to the Howard County Historical Society by Shepherd Snowden Dorsey. The collection was made for Mr. Dorsey's grandmother, Elizabeth Warfield Snowden by her aunt, Martha Ann Knowles and given to her the summer of 1867. The locks of hair, usually from a child's first hair cut, are encircled and tied neatly with a ribbon. Dozens of members of the family are represented, with the earliest date being 1752. Most of the family names are Warfield, however others are Bowie, Gray, Horner, Knight, Knowles, Shepherd, Snowden, Stinson, and Thomas. Included is Dr. Charles Alexander Warfield of Bushy Park. Courtesy of Howard County Historical Society

Four children of Sarah "Sally" Gorsuch and William Davis of Ivy Hill, Marriottsville, were photographed in 1873 at the Gallery of Artistic Photograph in Baltimore. They are from the left, John, William F., Gussie, and S. Louise. Louise married Francis Brown and they had three children. Her two daughters, Frances and Ruth Brown, taught school for many years in the county. The Times reported in 1872 that William and Samuel E. Davis purchased the village of Marriottsville and opened one of the largest and best-stocked county stores, which handled dry goods, groceries, and liquors. The year before, a fund raiser for an organ for St. James Methodist Church was held at Samuel Davis Hall in Marriottsville. A comedy, Handy Andy, was presented. Courtesy of Ruth Brown

Samuel and Ruth Davis Brown were photographed about 1907 when baby sister Frances Louise was too young to be included. The Browns are descendents of Ranger Thomas Brown who was assigned in the 1690s to patrol upper Anne Arundel County to protect the early settlers. Eventually he settled in the Woodstock area. Today the Brown's farm is called Mt. Pleasant. Samuel received his education at Johns Hopkins and worked as a civil engineer for Baltimore. Ruth and Frances were trained as teachers at Towson Normal School and received degrees from the University of Maryland. Ruth started her teaching career in September 1924 at the Alpha school not far from her home. In 1925 she was assigned to the first consolidated school in the county, West Friendship. Both sisters had long teaching careers. Neither they nor their brother married. Courtesy of Ruth Brown

A typical country Victorian style farm house stands between Dayton and Clarksville off Maryland 32. Patented as Gaither's Chance in the 1730s, it was occupied by the Gaither family for more than one hundred years. The original two-story log cabin was enclosed within this structure when the house was enlarged in the later nineteenth century, probably by Dawson Lawson. In the 1930s the Marshalls moved to Maryland from Chicago and purchased this farm so they could commute to jobs in Washington, D.C. Their son, Henry C. Marshall completed the restoration on this property in the 1970s and calls it Great Expectations, a name selected by his mother. Marshall has added a large pond. During the restoration the siding from the old barn, which was in disrepair, was used for the walls in the new bathrooms. George Ricketts, a local carpenter in his eighties, was responsible for the fine craftsmanship that restored the old home. Courtesy of Henry C. Marshall

Georgia Gaither Talbott (1842-1922) was the youngest of eight daughters and two sons of Greenbury and Catherine Gaither who lived at Gaither's Chance until 1852. The home at Dayton is now called Great Expectations. She was forty years old when she married George Edward Talbott. Most of her sisters did not marry and stayed on a farm with their parents. Her brother Samuel was past sixty years old when he married and moved to Baltimore. Her father, Greenbury, served as a school trustee for the public school on the Main Road to the Friendship Meetinghouse. She had one son, William Edward. *Courtesy of Howard County Historical Society*

Young people enjoyed a Sunday picnic in the 1890s at the farm called Rockland on Ellicott Road near the Cabin Branch in the western part of the county. Seated from the left in the front row are Miss Floid Fenny and Martha (Pattie) Ellicott (Hoffman); in back are Eddie Ellicott, Selma Cone, Willie Carr, and Beulah E. Haines (Hunt). The Times recorded in 1889 that William Carr opened a new roller mill for grinding the finest flour. Carrs Mill Road is northwest of this farm. *Courtesy of Ann Lekebusch*

Rockland Farm on the Cabin Branch was "grandmother's house" to Lee Hoffman, visiting as a youngster and arriving from Baltimore by train at the Woodbine station. His uncle, Eddie Ellicott, would meet them with the sleigh when there was snow and they would drive the seven miles in less than an hour. George Ellicott, the son of founder Andrew Ellicott, was Mr. Hoffman's great-great-grandfather. Mr. Hoffman's grandfather, also George Ellicott, married Catherine Duval in 1867. She lived in the western part of the county and they settled on Duval property, Rockland. The Duvals operated a mill nearby on the Patuxent River. In this 1895 photo, Ellicott family members at Rockland were from left, Franklin, cousin Beulah Haines (Hunt), Mrs. George Ellicott, a cousin Martha Lea (in her 70s), Mary Augusta and Martha (Pattie) who was Mr. Hoffman's mother. Mrs. Ellicott was widowed young and raised her family at Rockland. Courtesy of Mrs. Lee Hoffman

Saplin Range was the homestead of Levin I. G. Owings on Triadelphia Road in the fifth election district. Seated in the center are Levin Owings and his second wife Ella Mae Linthicum. The young people standing were the children of Levin and his first wife Maria Dorsey; from the left are Ruth, Gillis, Minnie, and Samuel. The youngsters from the second marriage, Lloyd, Katherine, and Susannah, are seated in the front. The baby, Mary, born in 1895 is held by the black woman who worked for the family along with her husband, standing beside the lawn mower. Seated to the left is uncle Nick Dorsey, who came for a weekend visit and stayed the rest of his life. The original section of the house in the rear is log. The stylish Victorian addition was built about the time of Mr. Owings' first marriage in 1865. The house stands in use today. Courtesy of Bettie Owings Summers

Farm work was shared by all the men in the family as the Owings on Saplin Range pitch in to help in the fields. This early 1900s photo shows the family and hired hands. The young boy was Lloyd Owings who spent his life working this same farm on Triadelphia Road. He recalled that the use of teams of horses continued most of his life. In the 1970s he retired from the farm and lived with his sister at the Asbury Methodist Home in Gaithersburg. Courtesy of Bettie Owings Summers

A year before he was elected governor, Edwin Warfield invited many of the former slaves at Oakdale back to the estate for a reunion. Warfield sits on the porch of the tenant house in August 1902. The "old folks at home," as the picture is captioned, are from left, Asbury Snowden, Hanson Dorsey, Warner Cooke, Remus Cooke, Laura (daughter of Henny Bond), "Aunt" Betty Bowie; "Aunt" Henny Bond, Claggett Bowie, Susan Garner, George Garner, and Charles Harriday. NAACP collection

THE OLD FOLKS AT HOME AGAIN
AT OAKDALE
Reunion--August 16th, 1902.
Governor Warfield seated on porch of old Servants' Quarter.
(1) Asbury Snowden, (2) Hanson Dorsey, (3) Warner Cooke,
(4) Remus Cooke, (5) Laura, daughter of Henny Bond, (6) "Aunt"
Betty Bowie, (7) "Aunt" Henny Bond, (8) Clagett Bowie, (9) Susan Garner, (10) George Garner, and (11) Charles Asa Harriday.

Oakdale became a grand residence when Edwin Warfield enlarged it in the late 1800s. He had met with considerable success as a state senator, surveyor of the port of Baltimore, director of the Patapsco National Bank, owner of the Daily Record and founder of Fidelity and Deposit Company of Maryland before becoming governor. The elegant pillars, ceilings, fireplaces, arches and other fine details attest to the stylish home that Warfield created at Oakdale. These handsome features survive and although no longer in the Warfield family, it remains a gracious home today. Maryland Historical Society

Teasing Uncle Albert was great fun for these cousins back in the early 1880s on the lawn of Oakdale. The children are John Warfield, Mildred Gill, and Marian Hoopes. The girls were the daughters of Albert's sisters. Available information indicates that Albert G. Warfield, Jr., is reading in the hammock. He was one of six sons and two daughters of Albert G. Warfield, Sr., the builder of Oakdale. The younger Albert served in the Confederate Army, became a civil engineer, and went to Japan in 1873 as a member of the American Scientific Commission. Maryland Historical Society

A Wehland home in the vicinity of Pfeiffer's corner off Waterloo Road shows the family of Herman Wehland about 1880. He is the bearded gentleman to the right. Three of his sons are pictured. Seated third from the left is Frederick. Standing in the rear left are Harman Hammond and George Henry. Although not identified, the others are the wives and children in the family. The attractive frame house was later enlarged but does not survive today. Courtesy of Granville Wehland

John Joseph and Hanna Driver Fleming lived on a large farm near Poplar Springs. Of Swedish ancestry, they were born in the 1850s. Hanna's father was a local preacher at the Watersville Church. John Joseph and his brother helped with the construction of that first church. Mr. Fleming operated a canning business before he went into the dairy business. They shipped their milk in five-gallon cans, meeting the seven o'clock train at Watersville. They stayed on the farm their entire lives. Farming was a family business with the children and grandchildren helping each other at threshing time. Courtesy of Mr. and Mrs. Aubrey Fleming

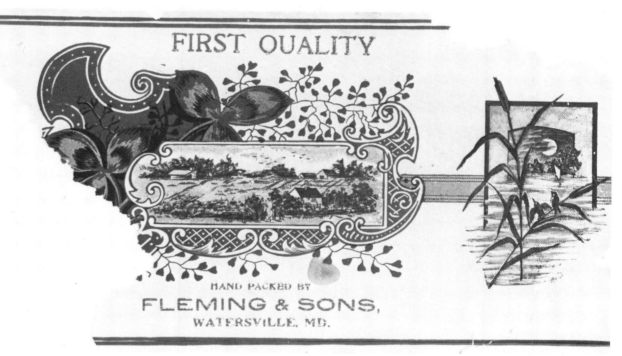

Canning tomatoes and corn were the business of Fleming and Sons from 1890 to 1905. Although the label reads Watersville, the cannery was located at Poplar Springs, across the Patapsco River from Watersville. This colorful yellow, green, and red label was used on the cans of vegetables sold to the stores. It was a Fleming family business, assisted by foster children raised by the family. Such canning operations were common throughout the county in the early twentieth century. Courtesy of Mr. and Mrs. Aubrey Fleming

Oliver Amoss moved from Harford County after the Civil War, following the death of his first wife. He married Emma Mar and raised a second family of seven children. Originally the family lived in a log cabin until Amoss added the front addition, a two-story house similar to hundreds of farm homes in that era. Note the arched window in the peaked roof-line, the shuttered windows, the windows above the front door. A young black boy stands beside the house. A dairy farmer, Amoss would send his milk in cans to Sykesville to be picked up by the train. The two older sons had that twice-daily task. Later he owned property on Maryland 144, near West Friendship and his son operated the toll gate on the Frederick Turnpike, as it was then called. Two of his sons served as postmasters. Courtesy of Russell Shipley

Toll gates were common along many roadways. This gate halted traffic on Frederick Avenue on the road from Elli-cott City into Baltimore. At one time the path of the road weaved uphill, making a gradual slope enabling the horses and wagons to climb the grade. These homes were built along the winding path. Today the road has been straightened, leaving the houses off the beaten path. Fees were paid to the gatekeeper depending on the size of the vehicle, the number of horses and the number of people. Enoch Pratt Free Library collection, reproduced by permission

Votta's Band, or orchestra, was a popular attraction around Baltimore for over a quarter of a century. In 1895 the orchestra played in Marriottsville for a dance at Aker's Park. In 1917 Guilford Day was the occasion for the band from Little Italy to journey to Howard County. Frank Votta's son John recalls that often the band continued playing past the hour of the last streetcar's trip into Baltimore. The men would bed down for the night at Gaither's Livery stable on Main Street. Howard County was one community the band toured for weddings, picnics, fairs, and other occasions. Joseph Pente re-called crab feasts and oyster roasts near Dundalk, Middle River, and on Eastern Avenue. The waltz and two-step were popular, but the schottisch, quadrilles, square dance and other forms were often played. Frank Votta would call the figures and played the fiddle over his head, delighting the dancers. The musicians earned two to three dollars each per night's work—plus tips for special requests. The band once traveled west with an itinerant circus. Other times they boarded the Latrobe to entertain youngsters on summer bay excursions. For formal occasions the men wore dark blue uniforms with braid and caps. The man in the far back is unidentified. In the back row, from left, are N. Roberto, F. Petarra, Nick Barone, unknown, Gus the guitar player, and unknown. In the front row, from left, are Tony Scatti, harp; Benjamin de Rosa; young Louis Votta, son of the leader with his trap drum; Frank Votta, violin; unknown trombone player; Mr. Milano, snare drum; and Joseph Pente, trumpet. On the ground in front are Nicholas Pente with his tambourine, and Lawrence Votta with his trumpet. Courtesy of Mr. & Mrs. John Votta

One of the old barns on the property known as Chatham and later the Dunloggin Dairy, was an attractive stone barn, which displays a circular window at the gable roof. After the sale of the dairy, most of the barns were torn down. However, the builder used this barn, with an addition as his early sales office. Today it has been tastefully incorporated into a home that includes additions, making it one of the most attractive homes in the development. Courtesy of Howard County Historical Society

Joseph Ellicott's home at the Upper Mills was still standing close to the railroad tracks in 1911. Ellicott built the house in 1775 and operated a mill and store at this location until his death in 1780. Fifty years later the railroad tracks were laid close by the house making the appeal of the location far less desirable. Local men loaded these wagons with feldspar in 1911. Potash was also mined in the near vicinity of this area, known then as Hollifield's. Courtesy of the News American

What was more fun that to dress up silly and go out on a picnic? About 1910 Willie Carr and Beulah E. (Haines) Hunt decided that they would have such an outing. Beulah was the granddaughter of George Ellicott, Jr., Ellicott City's first mayor. She married Thomas Hunt, Jr., and was left a young widow with six children. She purchased Font Hill on Ilchester Road and supported her family on that farm. Courtesy of Ann Lekebusch

Font Hill was the name by which this property on Ilchester Road was known as early as 1875. When Beulah Hunt purchased these ninety-two acres from Samuel Fort in 1911, she paid $8,500. Dr. Samuel J. Fort operated Font Hill as an institution for feeble-minded children, according to the 1891 Times, with a neat frame cottage that had a dormitory annex. Two years before, in 1889, Arbor Day was celebrated at Font Hill when they set out five cedars and five chestnuts. It was called the first institution for the feeble-minded in the Southern states. Fort purchased the property in 1886 for $5,000. The structure pictured no longer stands. Courtesy of Ann Lekebusch

Pictured is the dining room of Font Hill, at the time of operation by Mrs. Beulah E. Hunt, the widow of Thomas Hunt, Jr. Mrs. Hunt advertised her establishment as a place where guests, threatened with a breakdown could rest and recuperate. The food was supplied from Mrs. Hunt's farm. A booklet in the family advertised the facilities of Font Hill. It could be reached over a state road by automobile, by B & O trains to Ilchester or by trolley to Ellicott City. Courtesy of Ann Lekebusch

This lovely stone house, the Lindens served as the home of the Sykes family for many years. Surrounded by other homes now in Chapelview, it has been enlarged. This turn of the century photo records the warm winter dress of the ladies. From the left, Louise T. Cleggett, Cora T. Isaacs, and Mayanna Tabler Sykes. Mayanna was the wife of Carlton Reid Sykes and they were married in 1886. Their only child was the young man in the foreground with his school books, Guy Carlton Sykes, born October 7, 1888. This branch of the Sykes family name will no longer be extended since Guy Carlton Sykes, Jr.'s family consists of two daughters and he was the only male Sykes to carry on the family name. Courtesy of Frances Gist Sykes Piekert

This late nineteenth century picture captures members of the Sykes family outside their home, the Lindens. From the left are Carlton R. Sykes, Annie Sykes Keyes, her husband Frank Keyes, Mayanna Sykes, Dr. Claude Sykes, and Dr. Mordecai Gist Sykes. Front row are Guy Carlton Sykes, son of Carlton and Mayanna, and Edith Keyes, daughter of Annie and Frank. The siblings were Carlton, Annie, Claude, and Mordecai. Their parents were Sylvanus and Rachel Gist Sykes who moved to Ellicott Mills about 1844. Sylvanus had studied dentistry in London and practiced in Ellicott Mills until his death in 1872. All of their children were well-educated. Their three daughters attended the Patapsco Female Institute. William, the oldest son, was an Ellicott City lawyer. Mordecai and Claude followed their father's profession, dentistry. Claude practiced in Elkton for thirty years before becoming a banker. Mordecai practiced in Ellicott City and also served as the town's mayor. Carlton attended Rock Hill College, farmed and was a banker with the old Washington Trust Company in Ellicott City. Courtesy of Frances Sykes Piekert

The Hugg mansion stood on 276 acres of land owned by the Hugg family from 1877 until 1917, when the property became a part of the Maggie V. Hugg Memorial Fund, as a condition of her will. The house stood until 1933 when it burned. Originally this land was owned by members of the Sykes family, founders of the town of Sykesville. The mansion may have included a portion of an older Sykes home, but it was enlarged in 1884, according to an article in the Howard Gazette. The News American reported in 1967 that the Huggs were wealthy merchants in Baltimore who outfitted ships, importing especially from the Orient. They had a large home on Eutaw Place. Capt. Jacob Hugg had four sons and two daughters, with only two children surviving to adulthood. The daughter, Margaret V. Hugg, never married and left the family fortune to the family lawyer, William S. Thomas. There were legal entanglements and the transfer of the 276 acres to the state was not finalized until 1949, thirty-two years after Margaret's death. The transfer of the land

to the state formed the Hugg-Thomas Wildlife Park in Howard and Carroll counties, near Sykesville. It is an area of preservation, managed by the state, in the vicinity of St. Barnabas Episcopal Church. *Courtesy of Fred Church, former publisher of* Sykesville Herald

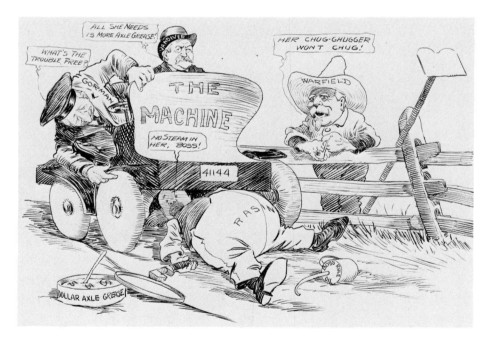

Two Howard Countians, both Democrats are portrayed in this 1890s cartoon. Arthur Pue Gorman, Sr., controlled Maryland politics from 1875 to his death in 1906 according to James B. Crooks in Maryland, A History 1632-1974. He became aligned with Isaac Freeman Rasin in 1870 and they became recognized as a powerful political machine. However they were not geared to solving the problems of urbanization and industrialization and that lead to opposition from reformers. By the 1890s the newspapers, churchmen, college students, and Republicans pushed for election reforms and better government. In the mid-1890s the Machine had run out of steam, as observed by Warfield, who was later the governor. *Maryland Historical Society*

In May 1907 Mark Twain (Samuel Clemens) visited Annapolis as the guest of Gov. Edwin Warfield. The two men had become friends and the governor invited the famous author to Annapolis. He enjoyed the famed Warfield hospitality at a special dinner in his honor. As a kindness to Mrs. Warfield, Twain presented a "Mark Twain Evening" to benefit her church. The event was given in the new Hall of the House of Delegates. Courtesy of M. E. Warren

Four generations of Moxleys represent a family that had been in Maryland before the time of the revolutionary war. Charles Moxley, left, farmed on Maryland 108 near Harper's Farm Road. His son, Ezekiel, right, moved to the area of U.S. 40 in 1891, when he purchased a farm, Mt. Aetna. In time he had purchased four farms in the vicinity of Rogers Avenue, Church Lane, and the Oaks farm. He married twice and raised two families. His son, Mark, center, is holding still his own son, Ezekiel, to catch the photo. Russell Moxley, also a son of Ezekiel, served as a policeman in Ellicott City when the police force numbered just one. Another son, Norman, was in the construction business. The Normandy Shopping Center, located on the family farm, was named for his company. Courtesy of Norman Moxley

An illustration in W. C. Bryant's "Pic-turesque" shows the Patapsco River at Ilchester in 1874. The B & O Railroad crossed from Baltimore County into Howard County at this location. The original stone Patterson Viaduct was built on the Main Line in 1830. This iron truss bridge replaced the original, which was damaged in the 1868 flood. A single arch from the first bridge remains visible from Ilchester Road at Bonnie Branch Road, however the train no longer crosses here and the iron bridge is also gone. The Ilchester Tunnel was built in the early 1900s, which changed the route slightly. Courtesy of the Smithsonian Institution, National Museum of American History

Chapter

Communities

Feeling a sense of community is increasingly important to people who are transient in the twentieth century. Communities in Howard County developed slowly and took form after the Civil War.

In the earliest days Maryland was settled by individuals who lived scattered about the countryside. Some people lived in towns but they were in the minority. This situation held true in Howard County. Although Elkridge developed into a landing, with merchants and tradesmen who worked the iron industry and the shipping, there were few other early communities. The Dennis Griffith map of Maryland in 1795 shows upper Anne Arundel County with enough detail to discern this information.

Howard County's two border rivers were settled by 1795 with a series of mills. Other mills were scattered through the 251 square miles of Howard County. In time, some of the mill sites developed into villages or small towns; others disappeared. In the late eighteenth century, the town of Hilton (now extinct) clearly stood on the road leading from Ellicott's Mills south at the crossroad to Elkridge Landing. Poplar Springs was on the Frederick Turnpike in the western end of the county, where it remains today.

Fifty years later, there were a total of thirteen villages in Howard County, described in the 1852 *Gazeteer of the State of Maryland.* These were Elkridge, Ellicott Mills, Ilchester, Hilton, Elysville, Marriottsville, Cooksville, Lisbon, Mathews Store, Poplar Springs, Clarksville, and Savage.

Most were described as principal villages. Elkridge Landing was said to have considerable manufactory and to have a population of 1,128, including 246 free colored. Ellicott Mills offered productive industry and was one of the greatest centers of flour milling in the Union. The population was 1,059 with 196 free colored. Its newspaper was the *Howard Gazette.* Elysville contained one cotton factory, one oakum factory, one store, one church, one school and 106 inhabitants. The houses were generally built of stone or brick and the vicinity was thickly settled in a highly flourishing condition, both in industrial and agricultural interests. The lands were described as fertile and afforded considerable quantities of produce. Hilton was a village, Ilchester had a post office, and Lisbon was thirteen miles from Ellicott Mills and twenty-three miles from Baltimore.

Marriottsville was located on the south side of the Patapsco River and on the B & O Railroad. Mathews Store was on the post road three miles southwest of Cooksville, a principal village on the headwaters of the Cat Tail Branch. Owingsville, Clarksville, and Poplar Springs were all principal villages while Savage had extensive iron works in its vicinity.

Twenty-six years later, in the 1878 directory, there were changes. Elysville became Alberton, Ellicott Mills was Ellicott City, Mathews Store became Glenwood, and the new towns of Jonestown, Woodstock, Long Corner, Florence, Simpsonville, Oakland Mills, Pine Orchard, West Friendship, Annapolis Junction, Dayton, and Glenelg appeared.

The Washington Branch of the B & O Railroad produced communities that straddled the border between Howard and Anne Arundel counties. One was Hanover with the Anderson post office. Pierceland's post office was at Hooversville, an area which would become Jessup. Dorsey was called Dorsey's Switch station.

The Patapsco River and the Main Line of the B & O presented the same situation with communities developing on both sides of the river. Those northwest of Ellicott City were Alberton, Woodstock, Marriottsville, Sykesville, Gaithers Siding, Hoods Mills, Morgan's Switch, Woodbine, and Watersville.

The post office was often located in the country store. This location would change after an election if the political party in power changed and new post masters were appointed. Therefore, it could move across the river or down the road, changing counties as it did so. The homes, churches, and other village components of these early settlements were in both Howard County and shared by Anne Arundel, Carroll, Baltimore, and Montgomery, as the case may be.

The 1878 *Maryland Directory* presented a flattering description of Howard County:

This county is very undulating and the soil mostly good...with considerable fine limestone land...a large amount of excellent water powers, which are mostly improved by factories, mills, furnaces, etc. Inexhaustible quarries of granite exist in the county. Howard has 31 miles of the B & O Railroad on one side and 12 miles of the Washington Branch on the southeast...This accessibility with the eminent natural advantages of pure air and water...are promoting improvements and the vicinity of the railroads is being built up with fine country seats.

By 1878 Alberton was described as fast becoming the most flourishing village in the county.

The business...is extensive cotton mills...flourishing temperance societies and building associations. The mills and several other buildings are lighted with gas and a large reservoir on the adjacent heights furnishes an abundant supply of pure water...The factory grounds are regularly laid off with gravel walks and adorned with trees and shrubbery. The population is 800.

The 1878 directory placed the population of Elkridge at 150 and spoke of the past with the great tobacco market. "Where now there is a meadow and a marsh, vessels came for their cargoes of tobacco." The land was valued at fifty to five hundred dollars per acre and produced fifteen to thirty bushels of wheat, twenty-five to fifty bushels of corn and two tons of hay. Land at Clarksville was worth forty dollars per acre and yielded ten bushels of wheat, forty bushels of oats, twenty-five of potatoes and thirty of corn. The population was twenty. Cooksville was two-and-a-half times as large with fifty residents. That land was valued at ten to thirty dollars per acre, producing ten bushels of wheat and fifteen to sixty bushels of corn and two tons of hay.

Ellicott City was splendidly described in 1878 as an incorporated city, "noted for its beauty and picturesqueness. The country around is healthful and the soil is fertile." Farm lands sold for sixty to one hundred dollars. Truck farms were numerous. The city was entirely recovered from the disastrous flood of 1868 and flourishing. Its population was twenty-nine hundred.

Florence, four and a half miles from Woodbine, had land with a clay subsoil and was valued at sixteen to fifty dollars per acre, yielding ten to twenty-five bushels of wheat, ten to fifty bushels of corn, eight hundred pounds of tobacco and one ton of hay. Glenelg was thickly settled with a healthy location and a population of seventy-five. Land values were the same as Cooksville and the farmer grew wheat, corn, tobacco and hay. Glenwood farmers grew wheat and corn on land valued at twenty-five to one hundred dollars per acre. The celebrated Dorsey reaper was manufactured there. Glenwood and vicinity was reputed to be the garden spot of Howard County with a population of forty.

Lisbon was very similar to the neighboring villages, with a population of fifty. However, it could boast of the Lisbon Female Academy as well as a public school. The Reverend J. T. Hall manufactured cigars at Lisbon. Long Corner's population was forty, including the blacksmith, carpenter, mason, and two millers.

Oakland Mills, just five miles from Ellicott City, had a population of 135, including S. F. Whipps, the postmaster. There were also seven carpenters, two millers, and three shoemakers. Pine Orchard was described as the location of nearby St. Charles College. The population was fifty. Poplar Springs had forty residents with Allen Dorsey running the hotel.

Roxbury Mills had just twenty-five residents, including two blacksmiths. Waters Store had a population of twenty-five and was six miles from Laurel. West Friendship had fifty residents and two public schools. Woodstock's population was twenty and the location of the noted Woodstock College, a Jesuit institution across the river in Baltimore County.

In addition to an inventory of the villages, the 1878 directory listed the farmers with their post office address. Cooksville had eight Hobbs families, Long Corner had sixteen Mullinix families, two spelled *Mullineux*, and throughout the county there were eleven Warfield families.

Although the directories are interesting and useful there were omissions. Neither Guilford nor Savage were included in 1878 when both communities had been in existence for some time. The Martenet map of 1860 clearly shows developed communities at both locations. The error was corrected in the 1887 directory when both appeared. Other new names in the 1887 directory were Alpha, near Henryton, population thirty; Columbia, three miles from Ellicott City, population eight. Again Columbia, had been missed in the earlier publication but it was shown in the 1878 *Hopkins Atlas*.

In 1887 Daisy, five-and-a-half miles from Woodbine, had a population of 18; Dayton had a population of 150 and a Temperance Society. Doughoregan had a population of 10. In 1887 Fulton appeared at the location of Waters store. Mention was made that mica abounded but there was too much water for the mines to be worked in the vicinity of

Fulton. The population was purported to be 400. Guilford had a population of 300 and the directory mentioned granite quarries and a large cotton factory. Hanoverville was on the Washington Branch of the B & O and had a population of 200. The well-known Baltimore Kennel Club was in the vicinity; mining iron ore was important. Highland's population was 50 and ten years earlier had been Wall's Cross Roads. Ilchester was listed with a population of 450. The Thistle Cotton Manufacturing Company and the Ilchester College (St. Mary's) were located at Ilchester. Ivory, near Glenelg with a population of 20 had a temperance association. Savage, with a cotton factory, had a population of 500.

In the thirty-five years between 1852 and 1887, the number of communities had tripled. The population was growing and villages were too. The 1850 Census placed the Howard County population at 11,857. Twenty years later the county had grown to 14,510. Recognizing that the earliest settlements had developed due to the waterways needed for milling, then it follows that the railroad and the crossroads provided the impetus for continued community growth.

As the population of the county grows, the small communities that had begun to fade when better roads and transportation came along are feeling a new sense of being. People are identifying with the small post offices and stores that formed the center of the village. Modern shopping areas are the new version of the crossroads that held the blacksmith's shop, the county store, the miller, and even the innkeeper.

The Redemptorists order of the Roman Catholic church purchased 110 acres at Ilchester from George Ellicott, Jr., for $15,000 in 1866. The first mass was said in George's stone house that August. It is visible in the lower left corner as part of a frame structure. By September 8, 1868, a large three-story brick building was ready for the Studentate and the three fathers who formed the entire faculty. The total cost was $80,000. The chapel was built on the left end of the building in 1882 and the name was changed from Mt. St. Clement when the chapel was dedicated to our Mother of Perpetual Help and it became known as St. Mary's College. Sometime after 1900 a fifth floor was added to the building. The property was sold in the early 1970s when the Redemptorists no longer needed this large estate. A new rectory was built in 1978 near the Our Lady of Perpetual Help School on Ilchester Road. This aerial view shows beautifully groomed grounds. Courtesy of Our Lady of Perpetual Help, Albert Riesner, C.S.S.R.

Astral Heights were at Ilchester, behind the cemetery of the St. Mary's College. The priests in their long black cassocks were obviously interested in the study of the stars at this Redemptorist community. Although there were open fields then, trees now cover the landscape and present an entirely different appearance. Our Lady of Perpetual Help, Albert Riesner, C.S.S.R.

At St. Mary's, Ilchester, a wooden addition was added to George Ellicott's stone house in 1872. It was a preparatory school, the Juvenate, for the young men planning to become priests. In later years these buildings served as a parish church and school. In 1955 new property was acquired for this purpose and Our Lady of Perpetual Help was built on Ilchester Avenue. The furnace system, including the boilers, were housed in the "lower house," as this was called. There was a covered passage from the "upper house" to this building. Later it burned and there is no trace other than stone steps. Courtesy of Our Lady of Perpetual Help, Albert Riesner, C.S.S.R.

Ilchester, one of the smallest post offices in Maryland, was also one of the earliest in the county. George Ellicott was appointed to the post in 1842. At one time located in the train station, this eight- by sixteen-foot building was built in 1950 for the postmistress, Teresa Schaad, by her father. Once located nearer the Patapsco River, it was moved to the Schaad's property. Elizabeth Airey is emptying the outside box. The front addition was added to the original structure, increasing the working area at the facility. Their two largest clients were St. Mary's College and Trinity School. It is now closed. Courtesy of the News American

The Savage Mill executive office force and leaders of the departments gathered outside the mill for a picture in the 1920s. In the back row, from the left are Howard U. Gosnell; Mr. Glass; Walter Baldwin; Frank Specht; Frank Fraizer; John Warters; unknown; Jess Ward Hartner; George Ward, Mill manager; R. Baldwin, mill owner; unknown; William Shorts; Albert Redmiles; and Scott Daywalt. In the front row, from left, are Frank Wheeler, Albert Williams, Les Harrell, Sam Bussey, Lot Walters, Bob Bussey, Joe Hagger, Bernard Ward, and William Perkins. Maryland Historical Society

Even with reindeer in residence it was difficult to transform Savage into Santa Heim. But for two brief years Harry Heim tried. He renamed the town and manufactured Christmas ornaments. In 1948 and 1949 there was a festive holiday season for a few weeks in December when trains ran from Baltimore and Washington to the old mill town to bring out the curious. In 1950 the experiment folded and the excitement faded. The old Savage mill has new owners who are making a more positive transformation of the property. They are creating a year-round center for artists, craftspeople, and visitors by retaining the feel of the old mill but with a freshness that invites exploration. Courtesy of Mrs. Marian Mathews

Obviously a progressive little town, Savage was receiving sewer service as early as 1919. But there were no heavy machines to dig the trenches. It was hard dirty work, purely by pick and shovel. Traffic was light on the street and the shade might have helped provide some comfort. Could it be the superintendent in the suit and tie leaning against the fence making certain that the job was being done properly? Maryland Historical Society

The Savage company store was remodeled in 1919 and served the mill families. It was customary to get credit at the store until pay day. A new refrigerator, seen behind the counter, was a fine improvement. Not only did the store stock food items, but pottery, luggage, clocks, and full shelves of medicines.
Maryland Historical Society

Although the Savage mill was founded in the early nineteenth century by the three William brothers, it was named for their associate John Savage. Some years later, the Baldwin family bought the property and built for themselves a summer home across Washington Street from the old mill. It was complete with a fine cupola, and wide porch, and handsome shuttered windows. Today the building is apartments. Maryland Historical Society

One Spot identified a location along U.S. 1 near Savage. In 1935 there was a public swimming pool called the Solarium at this location offering the opportunity to swim somewhere other than in a river or stream. Enoch Pratt Free Library collection, reproduced by permission

It's easy to understand why almost everyone who saw this building never forgot it. The building where they manufactured the flea powder was built in the shape of a large dog. It became a landmark and One Spot became the location of a community along U.S. 1, about ten miles from Baltimore. The structure is no longer standing and the term One Spot is seldom heard today. Library of Congress, Prints and Photographs Division

Camp Kelsey was a Civil War camp near Annapolis Junction. The junction was where the Washington Branch of the B & O and the Annapolis and Elk Ridge Railroad met. Here the Tenth Maine Company F was enjoying Thanksgiving dinner on November 21, 1861. Dinner was provided by their friends at Lewiston according to the sketch. Capt. William Knowlton was in charge. Later Annapolis Junction would be called Fort Meade Junction. Enoch Pratt Free Library collection, reproduced by permission

Buildings sprang up along the railroad where the B & O met the Annapolis and Elk Ridge Railroad, forming Annapolis Junction. This scene appears to be at the time of the Civil War, as many military figures are visible. The railroad from Annapolis provided a valuable means of transporting the Union forces and avoiding the hostilities in Baltimore. The New England troops sailed across the Chesapeake Bay to Annapolis and boarded the trains to Washington. The movement was not popular and the railroad attempted to stop it by taking up the tracks and disabling the engine. The resourceful troops made the necessary repairs and the soldiers moved on their way. Today there are not many buildings left along the railroad. A popular eatery still occupies one of the old buildings. Maryland Historical Society

The location on Maryland 108 at Ten Oaks Road where Toyotas are sold was the center of Clarksville, with the store and post office. Records show that for the year 1857, Postmaster McKnew earned $44.36 based on receipts. In 1871 William Clark was the grocer. That year there were four blacksmiths and wheelwrights; five stores; three carpenters; and three doctors, William Hardy, Robert Pue, and Jeremiah Nichols. In the 1878 Hopkins Atlas, Dawson Lawrence claimed that "Clarksville is now the Paris of the Fifth Election District." From the author's collection

Highland junction at Maryland 108 and Maryland 216 had a blacksmith shop at the turn of the century, which served as the location for the toll gate. In 1878 this area was called Walls Cross Roads, with W. F. Wall and Joshua B. Disney located there. Wall was a merchant keeping the store and post office. Disney was a wheelwright, operating the blacksmith shop. Land records show that in April 1870 there was a lease made between Disney and Wall. The location then was given as Old Annapolis Road (Maryland 216) and the road to Ashton (Maryland 108). For a five-year lease, until 1875, Wall promised to erect a dwelling house twenty-six feet long and sixteen feet wide, with one-and-a-half stories. Wall would hold the property rent-free for those five years and for the next five years, Disney would rent the property to Wall for $140 per year. Courtesy of Howard County Historical Society

The railroad opened up the Patapsco Valley. Woodstock is one of the communities that developed after the train came through the valley. In 1911 T. C. Worthington, Jr., made this picture of an old house along the tracks across the river from his home town of Granite. Although considerably changed, this house is standing east of Woodstock Road. It could date back to those early days if it survived the floods in the valley. Other homes along Woodstock Road are Victorian, coming after the Civil War era and having a similar style. A cluster of these Victorian homes stand on the bluff above the river, safe from the rampages of the Patapsco. Maryland Historical Society

The Woodstock Swells was a troupe that formed a minstrel revue in 1903, performing music and drama. Mrs. Josephine Oliver Peach, known as "Aunt Brodie" played the organ and piano for the group and for St. Alphonsus Church. The Swells performed for more than twenty-five years, drawing enthusiastic crowds. Mr. Warner W. Peach, Sr., Interlocutor, appeared at every Minstrel show with the exception of two. Members of the group standing, from the left, are John Puls, Frank Peach, Tom Webb, Tom Dunnigan, Eugene Gosnell, Joe Merkle, Charles Peach, Robert Wheat, Frank Parlett, Fred Peach, and Emslie Cavey. Seated are Patrick Feeney, James Bortell, Warner Peach, Michael Feeney, and James Driscoll. Courtesy of Howard County Historical Society

This 1940s photo shows the old hotel as it stood at Pine Orchard, on the south side of present-day U.S. 40. In 1860, Mrs. A. Hopkins operated this prominent landmark located at the fourteen milestone on the Frederick Turnpike. By 1878 Jesse W. Rhine owned the property, which stood near the eastern edge of Doughoregan Manor. Also at Pine Orchard was a "colored" Methodist Church that has disappeared, although a cemetery from that church remains. On the right is the "Atlantic" sign for the gas pumps that were used in this era. Today the building has been enlarged and there are new businesses that operate at this location. Courtesy of Emma Lacey and Betty Gerwig

This artist's painting of the Simpsonville Mill dates to the 1920s. At this period the Igleharts owned the property. An accident occurred nearby when a driver was injured after careening into the river. He recuperated with the Iglehart family and left this painting with them. The mill was used for a variety of activities, a woolen factory, gristmill and sawmill. Before it was known as Simpsonville, the community was Owingsville. Another early family associated with the property were the Warfields. However, John Martin had the original patent in 1719. As early as 1789, a mill was referenced in the deeds. When the Simpsons bought the property in 1852, the name of the community changed. Today only a few stone ruins remain from a flourishing nineteenth century village, which included mills, stores, a blacksmith and a wheelwright.

Improvements to Cedar Lane will remove the last visible identification of this early community, although the river's flooding can also bear responsibility for the loss.

In recent years the Simpsonville post office was relocated to a shopping center on U.S. 29, changing the location completely. Courtesy of Walter Iglehart

The Thomas Garage was an early 1930s business in Cooksville. Pictured are Daniel Howard, Effie Thomas, Dorothy Hawkins, and Neal Smith. These buildings are still standing. Business was good on old U.S. 40. Courtesy of Mrs. Mildred Thomas

Hog-killing time brought together the men of the community who were proficient in this task for a long day's work. These Cooksville men included Albert Dorsey, second from the left. According to Carl Johnson, Dorsey's son-in-law, most families raised a hog or two. When the time in the fall came, the hogs were slaughtered and hung in the smokehouse for the winter, which provided the family's meat for the year. Every part of the animal was used, permitting no waste. NAACP Collection

Pindell's store housed the Glenwood post office for decades. Before the post office was called Glenwood it was the Mathews' post office, where that family operated a store in the general vicinity. A new brick post office stands close by, as this store was closed. Later the building moved across Maryland 97 to become a part of the nursery business that operates on the opposite side of the road. From the author's collection

James B. Mathews and his wife Kitty Griffith Mathews were the founders of the community known today as Glenwood. They married in 1818 and lived at Roxbury where Mr. Mathews operated the mill and the store. They moved to Glenwood in 1822 and operated a store and post office known as Mathews. Later their son Lycurgus, one of twelve of their children who grew to adulthood, named the area where the family lived Glenwood. He founded private schools, one being the Glenwood Institute. The Mathews family home is called Bloomsburg. James B. Mathews lived past his ninety-fifth year and was one of the founders of Union Chapel. From the author's collection

113

Roxbury Mill stands in near ruin off Maryland 97. It was one of the last county mills where a farmer could have his grain custom ground. In 1795, there was a Roxbury Mill located at this site. The old Westminister Road has been realigned leaving this mill nestled away from the main road. James and Kitty Mathews started their married years at Roxbury before opening their own store along the same road. From the author's collection

Isaiah and Dena Harriday were the first black couple in Daisy to own their own automobile. Harriday was the chauffer for Governor Warfield, so this may have been one of the governor's fine automobiles. Note the small tires and the clever bumper on this open touring car, a truly handsome vehicle. Members of the Harriday family are still active in the Daisy community. Courtesy of Alice "Becky" Thomas

A portable sawmill was set up in Daisy about 1900 and ready to go to work. If there was lumbering to be done or if a building was to be built, the sawmill operator would be engaged to bring his equipment for the duration of the project. Sawmills that operate in a portable fashion are still used, although the equipment is considerably more modern. Courtesy of Alice "Becky" Thomas

In 1893, the Cat-tail Quarry was in operation. The men responsible for the back-breaking labor in the quarry are shown with their tools. Small quarry operations extended throughout the county, providing a variety of products. The stone used on the roadways before the modern hard-surfaced roads were built came from such operations. Courtesy of Alice "Becky" Thomas

Community bands were important. They provided entertainment at many functions. They were generally made up of brass instruments and the members were male. The Glenwood Community Brass Band was no different. Dressed in their fancy uniforms it was easy to see why they were a favorite in the community and in great demand for dances, parades, picnics, and other activities. The third baritone player from the right was Channing Dorsey of Daisy. Courtesy of Alice "Becky" Thomas

Buried under fifty feet of water in the Triadelphia Reservoir stands the remains of the town Triadelphia. These buildings were once a part of the old village that stood in Montgomery County but shared a Howard County post office. It was founded by three brothers-in-law, Isaac Briggs, Caleb Bentley, and Thomas Moore in 1809. The men all married daughters of Roger Brooke, hence the name for the town, which means "the three brothers." A flour, grist, and saw-mill operated here. Floods in 1868 and 1889 destroyed the village. Carroll Dulaney in the News Post related the fact that Moore, one of Triadelphia's founders, had invented the icebox in 1803 and patented it. It was used to carry butter on horseback to Alexandria. Library of Congress, Prints and Photographs Division

School exhibitions were popular activities within a community. In 1867, one could attend the event at Poplar Spring for fifteen cents. The school stood on the west end of town along the Frederick Turnpike. By 1876 it cost twenty-five cents for an adult to attend the exhibition at the Long Corner School. There were recitations separated by musical selections. An abundance of Mullineaux family members participated in the program, as well as those from the Becraft, Penn, Burns, Reed, and Stackhouse families. Edwin Warfield, Esquire, gave the address. Later he would become governor. Courtesy of Tracey Stackhouse

SCHOOL EXHIBITION,

POPLAR SPRINGS,

Dec. 4th, 1867, 7 o'clock, P. M.

TICKETS 15 CENTS.

WOODS, PRINT. BALT.

SCHOOL EXHIBITION
AT
Long Corner School.

Friday, April 14, 1876, at 7 P. M.

PROGRAMME:

OPENING ADDRESS..........................S. E. BECRAFT.

Music

RECITATIONS AND DECLAMATIONS..........BY LITTLE BOYS AND GIRLS.
THE GIRL'S VISIT..........................SIX LITTLE GIRLS.

Music

THE FORSAKEN SCHOOLHOUSE..............DORSEY STACKHOUSE.

Music

SCHOOL..........................BOYS AND GIRLS.

Music

THE FARM..........................GEO. MULLINEAUX.
MARCO BOZZARIS..........................JOHN W. PENN.

Music

MRS. POTTS.......................... { IDA Z. MULLINEAUX,
LAURA V. MULLINEAUX.

Music

DOUGLAS AND MARMION..........................J. E. BURNS.

Music

THE RAINBOW..........................SEVEN GIRLS.

Music

SOUTH CAROLINA..........................E. MULLINEAUX.
MASSACHUSETTS..........................JASON MULLINEAUX.

Music

AUNT PEABODY'S VISIT....................... { S. R. BURDETTE,
SALLIE PENN,
LAURA V. MULLINEAUX.

Music

HENRY'S WAR SPEECH..........................CALVIN BECRAFT.

Music

CINDERELLA'S SLIPPER........................... { LAURA B. MULLINEAX,
MARY A. BURNS,
C. V. MULLINEAUX,
SUSAN H. MULLINEAUX,
J. E. BURNS,
JASON MULLINEAUX.

Music

THE VIRTUES.......MISSES PENN, BURDETTE, REED, BROWN, MULLINEAUX.

Music

BLUE BEARD.......................... { J. E. HILL,
ELDRIDGE MULLINEAUX,
CALVIN BECRAFT,
LOTHE H. REED,
SALLIE PENN,
GUARDS, &C., &c.

Music

ADDRESS..........................EDWIN WARFIELD, ESQ.

Admittance—[For paying expenses and procuring library for school], 25 cents;
Children under twelve, 10 cents.

117

Charles D. and Catherine Pickett relaxed on the front porch of their house at Poplar Springs. Mr. Pickett kept a store at Florence and a store at Poplar Springs. Their house is one of the oldest surviving buildings in the old town, which grew up on the Frederick Turnpike. Courtesy of Aubrey Fleming

One of the oldest surviving houses in Poplar Springs sits at the corner of Watersville Road and Maryland 144. Mr. and Mrs. Charles D. Pickett raised a large family in this home, which looks considerably different today. Mr. Pickett kept a store at Florence and at this location in Poplar Spring. Mr. Pickett's father, John Thomas Pickett, returned from the Civil War, married and built a log cabin for his family. He died at age twenty-five before his only child, Charles was born. Poplar Springs is an early community, in existence before 1795. At one time it had hotels to accommodate summer vacationers. All those hotels, have since burned. In the Civil War era, the community had hotels, stores, a blacksmith, churches, and a school. The old spring from which the name comes is still flowing fully but the poplars have long disappeared. Courtesy of Aubrey Fleming

Clara and Aubrey Fleming were mighty proud of that 1930 Ford, even in the mid-thirties when this picture was made. Two of their four children, Donald and Mildred, stood on the old running board before taking a family ride. Aubrey recalled that he paid seven hundred dollars for the vehicle and then the Depression came and the bank wanted the rest of the money. He still owed two hundred dollars on the car and was fortunate enough to have a crop of peas to sell that brought in the needed amount. The Flemings farmed for many years near Poplar Springs but moved into town to enjoy their retirement years. They live across the road from his Grandfather Pickett's old home and store and not far from the old faithful Poplar Spring. Courtesy of Aubrey Fleming

Canneries were a business supported by the agricultural nature of Howard County and its neighbors. Employment was offered and often immigrant workers came out from Baltimore to provide some of the seasonal labor. The canneries in Woodbine were located near the railroad. Mullinix, Leatherwood, and Weller operated one. The Corbin-Gosnell factory was the other. Farmers brought their loads of corn or tomatoes by wagon and lined up to wait their turn. The towns were crowded on these days. The favorite day for the factory workers was Saturday when the pay was handed out. Courtesy of Herbert Kessler

Engines along the B & O's Main Line were a familiar sight. Not often did they appear in the Patapsco River as did Engine 4449. A derailment sent this engine down the bank. However it flipped completely over and landed upright in the riverbed outside of Sykesville. Courtesy of Herbert Kessler

Lisbon was situated on the National Pike, as the road was called in the early 1900s. The large building on the left with a second-floor porch was once the hotel, owned in the 1870s by Fanny Webb. It served passengers from the railroad who were seeking overnight lodging. Visitors also came out to escape the city during the summers and vacation at these small towns convenient to the railroad. The road to Woodbine was also called Madison Street. Warfield's Folly is the early patent name, according to a booklet from the Lisbon PTA. Caleb Pancoast purchased land in 1802 and soon built his home here and laid out a town of one hundred lots, approximately a quarter acre each. Churches were established, services were provided to travelers and the town grew in size. Schools were established, and in 1899 a high school operated for about a year. Pancoast's home stood to the rear of the hotel until it was recently demolished. This roadway became U.S. 40 and today is Maryland 144. Many of the old houses remain and the PTA walking tour booklet provides an interesting guide to the town. *Maryland State Archives, Robert G. Merrick Archive of Maryland Historical Photographs, Md. HR-G 5881*

A SKETCH FROM ROCK HILL.

Lith. of Thomas Campbell, Baltimore   *Drawn by R. C. Long.*

VALUABLE REAL AND PERSONAL PROPERTY
BY
LOTTERY,

This 1834 sketch by Robert Carey Long is the earliest view of Ellicott City's Main Street. Andrew McLaughlin was authorized by the legislature to hold a lottery to distribute his estate. The first prize was the Patapsco Hotel, valued at $36,500 including two additional lots. Another prize was Angelo's Cottage, valued at $2,650. The hotel is in the foreground, right, adjacent to the railroad tracks. The cottage is the castle-like home behind and above the hotel. Lottery tickets were $10 each. Other prizes included lots valued from $200 to $800, furniture, bottles of wine, books, and silver. In the lower right corner is the railroad station in its earliest days with the doors on the end for bringing the small steam engines inside. Other buildings on the north side of Main Street include the four-story stone building with dormers and porches, which would later be modified to add a top floor and be called the New Town Hall. The wooden walkways were necessary to provide a safe travelway for townspeople separate from the muddy roads, horses and other livestock that used the main street. The home, Mt. Ida, is on the hill to the left and the Patapsco Female Institute is in the distance. Gazebos were popular and whether they existed or were added by the artist is unknown. The Hambleton Collection, Peale Museum, Baltimore, Maryland

Chapter  6

Growing into the County Seat, Ellicott City Matures

Ellicott City went into a gradual decline in the mid-1940s. The wars brought changes so that many town residents moved away from Main Street. New state roads soon led businesses away. After a period of dormancy, the old town began to take on a new look. Fortunately, Ellicott City is sturdy and tough. To survive all of the fires and floods, she's had to be. New people are helping to build and rebuild where necessary. Once a thriving shopping village, Ellicott City now has a sparkle and charm that attracts new shoppers and retains old friends. It's been designated a Historic District to help retain the nineteenth-century atmosphere that leads visitors to remark, "It reminds me of a European village."

It was early in the nineteenth century that Ellicott City developed into the commercial center for large milling operations throughout the lower Patapsco Valley.

The earliest description of the community, aside from the work of Martha Ellicott Tyson, comes from Joseph Scott's *Geographical Description of the States of Maryland and Delaware,* published in 1807. Ellicott's Lower Mills were situated nine-and-a-half miles southwest of Baltimore and forty-one miles from Washington City. The Patapsco at the falls was about the size of the Brandywine or Gunpowder rivers. The great Western Turnpike from Baltimore to Frederick Town passed through this place. Mills that Scott described included the largest and most elegant merchants mills in the United States, capable of manufacturing 150 barrels of flour in a day. The wheat was obtained from Loudon and Jefferson counties in Virginia. Another mill with one water wheel and a pair of burr stones manufactured plaster of Paris. Wagons from the western country loaded with plaster of Paris stopped to have it ground. The mill would pulverize a ton in forty minutes. Other mills were the sawmill and an oil mill. The proprietors (Ellicotts) had a mill for rolling and slitting iron. These mills belonged to and were occupied by Jonathan,

Elias, George, and John Ellicott who were also the owners of the greater part of the dwellings. Several of the elegant houses were built of hewn stone, dug from a valuable quarry of gray granite at the place. The Ellicotts also had a large store of groceries and dry goods. Several kinds of mechanical trades were carried on such as coopers, blacksmiths, tanners, shoemakers, and saddlers. There was a very handsome meetinghouse built of stone, belonging to the Quakers, and a good tavern for the accommodation of travelers. At this place was one of the largest paper mills in the country, the property of Mr. John Hagerty. The inhabitants were well supplied with water, which was conveyed in pipes from a remarkable cold spring at a distance of 420 yards.

The location of these mills was beautiful. The adjacent hills were lofty and fertile and the meadows were covered in the season with a rich verdure, which gave the whole a delightful and pleasing appearance according to Scott. The arched bridge and the extensive walls erected by the turnpike company added to the beauty of the place. A post office was established at the mills.

The next available description comes from the lottery poster of 1834, when Andrew McLaughlin advertised for sale four hundred prizes valued at nearly $60,000. The poster read,

. . . from all its meandering walks nothing can be more interesting to the eye than the ever varying landscapes formed by the bold and romantic scenery of this delightful village. Upon the summit of the hills, which appear like a succession of rolling billows rising in every direction, here and there is seen a splendid mansion, beautiful as a stately ship riding upon the mountain wave.

Continuing, the poster read,

In the valley below, the clink of the hammer is heard from every quarter, splitting the gray granite, which abounds in inexhaustible quantities; the dull noise of the forges and the rapid motion of saw mills, the hum of ten thousand spindles in the cotton factories, the whirl of the many mill stones and the white spray of the pure water which is constantly tumbling over the dam, mingling with the cheerful bustle of the industrious and enterprising villagers, give to the whole scene a most animating character and make it the happy resort of thousands of admiring visitors.

The poster also refers to the academy of Mr. Sams on the summit Rock Hill, immediately opposite the hotel and the Patapsco Female Academy, which was building in the rear "upon a magnificent scale, situated on a beautiful commanding eminence 224 feet above the level of the turnpike" several extensive stores, two churches, and a bank about to be erected also bore evidence of the prosperous condition of the village.

The advent of the B & O Railroad and the industrialization of the Patapsco Valley were rapidly changing the Ellicott's Mills community. The B & O Railroad built a stone station in 1830 which served as the terminus on the railroad when the first trains traveled the thirteen miles from Baltimore to Ellicott's Mills. It is the oldest railroad in America. The building has been designated a Registered National Historic Landmark and has been restored as a museum. It preserves the history of the B & O and of Ellicott City's role in the history of railroading. In 1833 Andrew Jackson was the first U.S. president to ride a railroad train. He made a trip from Ellicott's Mills to Baltimore on June 6.

From the biography of Amelia Hart Lincoln Phelps, by Bolzau, we learn that in the 1840s the village supplied its own needs and its own amusements. Such organizations as the Patapsco Patriots with their local band, five lyceums, and temperance societies furnished interesting occasions for the town.

In reporting national news on July 30, 1842, the *Howard District Press* spoke of the temperance progress in New York where 179,624 had enrolled, with 120,000 of them pledging total abstinence. Included in this number were 237 members of the clergy, 426 physicians, 4,976 Germans, 900 colored, 13,380 seamen and 23,300 Irish, both Protestant and Roman Catholic. The Baltimore newspaper reported on those signing the pledge in February 1844, in Ellicott's Mills. The "temperance fever" continued to prevail to an extraordinary extent. A Mr. Scott was instrumental in forming the local society and through his speaking on three occasions 110 signed the pledge. By the 1850s the *Howard Gazette* reported temperance societies in Elkridge, Ellicott City, Lisbon, and Union Chapel, with Daughters of Temperance also being formed.

Bolzau also reports that with the development of the county court in 1851, the village lost some of its provincialism. Lawyers and their clients from all parts of the county took up their abode in the village and the happenings in the courthouse were the chief concern of the moment.

The early county commissioners were busy men in the 1850s and 1860s, tending to the management of the county—in particular the care of the roads, the public buildings (courthouse and jail) and the schools. Or possibly as a rare occasion as on September 7, 1857, there was simply no business. If the old minutes are any indications, the meetings were brief and possibly quite dull. In June 1857 William Hollifield presented the plan for the bridge at the old Upper Mills, and it was approved. (Is that one reason why that area is called Hollofield?)

In September 1857 Mrs. Haines complained about the condition of the road past her place and she was told to inform B. F. Nichols, the supervisor, about the problem. On December 5, 1858, Thomas Welsh presented the county with a bill for ten dollars for burying a dead person that was found near Simpsonville. In March 1859, the commissioners ordered pantaloons and cotton shirts for the three men in prison. They approved the repair of the pump at the courthouse in 1860. In 1861 the sheriff was ordered to buy six comforters, six blankets, six husk mattresses, two pairs of andirons and three pairs of leg irons and to repair the stove at the jail. In June 1862 the jailer was paid fifty dollars to use for lights and soap through December.

An early undertaker in the community was William Fort, whose primary occupation was that of cabinetmaker. Fort's place of business was opposite Brown's Hotel (also called the Patapsco Hotel). He manufactured bedsteads, bureaus, tables, wardrobes, chairs, pictures, looking glasses and other items, according to an advertisement in an 1840 newspaper.

As an undertaker, he advertised that coffins of various kinds were made at short notice out of poplar, walnut, or mahogany, being lined when required with cambric, flannel, florence, or satin with breast-plates suitably and neatly engraved. He furnished his hearse and promised every exertion used to give entire satisfaction in this part of his business.

The ad also stated that he would take poplar, walnut, buttonwood, cherry, or maple sawn logs, plane or scantling in exchange for furniture, or a fair price paid for a good article in cash. Bernard Fort was also in business at the same location, as a painter and advertised that he could paint and glaze a house or letter a sign to please any critic or he could imitate any kind of wood or marble.

The Fort Undertaking business later became known as Eastons and operated in Ellicott City for many years. When "Barney" Fort died, Daniel Laumann and his son-in-law, W. Clinton Easton purchased the business and property, according to the Century Edition of the *Times*. Mr. Easton later bought out the business and in time it was Easton and Sons. At this early period, when a death occurred out in the county, a relative rode horseback to town bearing a notched stick indicating the height and width of the deceased, whereupon the cabinetmaker would manufacture the necessary size casket. An 1870s advertisement offered coffins at a price reduced by 20 percent due to a new style coffin, so there must have been some ready-mades available. A "hack" to the Quaker, Catholic, or Union burying ground would cost three dollars, while the trip out to Whipps cost four dollars.

In 1867 a charter was granted to change the village of Ellicott Mills to an incorporated town, Ellicott City. This was a natural development in the town's growth.

The town limits included the property of the neighboring mills on the east bank of the Patapsco, so it crossed county lines, including both Howard and Baltimore counties. George Ellicott, grandson of the founder Andrew, presided as mayor at the first Common Council meeting, April 15, 1867. Others present were Dr. Thomas B. Owings, E. H. Soper, A. Wallenhorst, T. H. Hunt, William B. Collier, and Dr. I. J. Martin. Mr. Collier was elected president of the council.

According to the minutes, the first acts of this council were to order a corporate seal "for the use of the Mayor and Council, two books for the registrar to record the proceedings of the Council and the Ordinances of the City," and the purchase of a lamp and oil.

In July 1869 the council approved the purchase of twenty lamps at a cost of $13.50 each and seventeen lamp posts, at $3.00 each. Soon, everybody in the town began demanding that a lamp be placed directly in front of his home or place of business.

According to research by Mark M. Moxley, Ellicott City had electric power and lights in 1891 through the efforts of Herman Shriver who sold stock to form the new company. The electric plant was located at the old gristmill on Tiber Alley. The power to operate the generators came from dams upstream. When necessary it was supplemented by steam power. Ezekial Moxley was the first operator. The first lights were on Main Street, Fells Avenue, Church Road, St. Paul's Street, and New Cut Road.

In 1914 the commission form was adopted by the town and the Patapsco River was made the boundary of the city. On June 1, 1935, the town's charter was revoked by the Maryland General Assembly at the request of local residents. The cost of government played a role in this change. Before Prohibition, due to a high license fee for saloons, the town charged a very small real estate tax. With Prohibition, the tax increase led to the many bitter protests that finally brought about the surrender of the town charter.

Ellicott City Flood of 1868

Destruction by fire and flood. Considering the disasters caused by these fearsome enemies, it is surprising that there remains today so many of the important historic and meaningful structures in the old town.

The Ellicotts experienced flooding very early upon their arrival into the valley. Undoubtedly this flooding influenced the location of the old school and the meeting-house in placing them high on the hills above the valley.

Newspapers often spoke of "freshets" that occurred at the mills. Defined as a "sudden rise in the level of a stream, or a flood, due to heavy rains or the rapid melting of snow and ice" a freshet aptly fits the activities of the Patapsco River.

When Hurricane Agnes assaulted little Ellicott City in 1972, it was termed a "hundred years flood" recalling the horrible events of a little more than a century earlier in 1868. The newspapers, particularly *The Common Sense*, on July 29, 1868, recorded the events that ended with a loss of at least thirty-nine lives and destruction for miles throughout the river valley.,

That descriptive account read in part:

A dreadful calamity befell the Valley of the Patapsco on Friday the 24th day of July. A flood of unprecedented dimensions and incalculable powers swept nearly the whole valley from Mount Airy down to the Ridge, carrying along with it destruction to annihilation and misery to a maddening extent. What handicraft and human genius had wrought, what nature herself had beautifully built up, what human industry and self-denial had accumulated, all went swept away as if it had never been, or leaving only the saddest of ruins, the most mournful reminiscences. . ."

Fourteen houses were swept away at the location of the original Ellicott's Mills and many of the residents lost their lives at this one place. Since the families had often experienced flooding they did not leave their homes, but merely retreated to the upper floors. However, the power of the flooding waters, joined with the floating debris and

finally the collapse of the Granite factory not far upstream, utterly destroyed these homes and the people within them. Dr. T. B. Owings' wife, Margaretha, thirty-six years of age and six of their children, ages ten and under were lost that day. William and Ellenore Patterson along with their five young children perished.

All of the mills and operations through the valley were damaged. The Granite Company was never rebuilt. The Union Factory stood highest and received the least damage. The Avalon nail factory near Elkridge was never rebuilt.

These homes at the Ellicott's Mills were some of the earliest dwellings. Homes were never built again on the banks of the river, as the flooding was never controlled and continues to wreak sporadic havoc through the valley.

- ROCK-HILL-COLLEGE -
- MARYLAND -

Rock Hill in Ellicott City was the location of a private boy's school from as early as 1820. This 1894 view is while the Christian Brothers operated the school. They purchased it in 1857 and operated it first as an academy, during the Civil War as an institute and after 1865 as a college. Brother Aphrates was the first director and added new buildings to an existing structure. The architecture changed as additions were made to the property. Brother Tobias of Jesus and Brother Azarias were also notable teachers at the facility. This sketch is by Osmun Latrobe, Jr. Library of Congress, Prints and Photographs Division

Angelo's cottage is an Ellicott City landmark that attracts attention with its distinctive architecture. This early twentieth-century photo shows what was probably the original plaster construction of the 1830s home. Many remember the "Castle" as it is often called, with a brown shingle exterior. Later white siding returned the home to better visibility, as it is perched above the river overlooking Main Street. Courtesy of John Kirkwood

Mt. Ida was built in the 1830s by William Ellicott who married Mary Elenora Norris. William was the sixth of Jonathan and Sarah Ellicott's twelve children, thus making him a grandson of Andrew the founder. Married at age forty, William died three years later. The couple had no children. The home next belonged to the Tyson family, who were related to the Ellicotts. Although Mt. Ida is still standing it has lost many of its attractive architectural features, as well as the chimneys. It has been used commercially. A yellow-stuccoed building, it sits near the courthouse parking lot. Courtesy of the Commercial and Farmers Bank

An interesting 1850s view of the area south of the railroad station in Ellicott City shows a number of buildings on the rolling hillside. Nearly in the center was St. Peter's Episcopal Church, which stood until it burned in 1939. To the right are the original Patapsco Bank building and the St. Paul Catholic Church. On the hill in the distance and to the right of St. Peter's is the Quaker meetinghouse. To the left of St. Peter's and in the distance is a structure that was the original building of the boys' academy, later known as Rock Hill College. In its earliest days it was Sam's Academy. Courtesy of the Commercial and Farmers Bank

A stereoptican scene of Ellicott's Mills affords a rare photographic view. It must have been the late 1850s or early 1860s since the buildings that were destroyed in the 1868 flood are still standing. Dense construction of buildings gives the appearance of businesses that may have been built across the river itself. A covered bridge with small windows angles into the main road, where horses and buggies can be seen. The stone house in the center foreground was probably the home of John Ellicott, a cousin of George and Jonathan whose historic homes are out of view on the left. The homes in which people were trapped and lost in the flood are clearly visible with their rears to the river. A stone wall separates the roadway from the millrace. Looking across the railroad tracks and up the hill, none of the frame houses on Church Road were constructed. The trees are small. Steps to Angelo's cottage are visible. *Maryland Historical Society*

Destruction along the Patapsco River was evident from this 1868 scene at Ellicott City. The ruins of the Granite Factory stand to the left and the ruins of the Patapsco Flour Mill are in the center. Men assisting in recovery of items or people lost in the flood are working from shore or in boats. Stories were later told of household goods recovered under mud and sand downstream from the town. Some of these pieces came to light years later. *The Peale Museum, Baltimore Maryland*

Ellicott descendents identify this gentleman as George Ellicott. There were four generations of George Ellicotts during the 1800s. It's likely that this George was the first mayor of Ellicott City, elected in 1867, when the town changed from Ellicott's Mills to Ellicott City. Known as George Ellicott, Jr., he built the stone house at Ilchester in the 1830s and operated a gristmill at that location. In the 1860s he sold the property to the Redemptorist Order. He was married to Mrs. Agnes Iglehart and they had three children. Courtesy of Ann Lekebusch

A sketch by Osmun Latrobe, Jr., in 1894, though not identified is clearly the large stone house, Lilburn, which stands today on College Avenue, Ellicott City. Henry R. Hazelhurst built the house in the 1850s for his second wife, Elizabeth McKim. His first wife died in childbirth while Hazelhurst was in Cumberland involved with the construction of the railroad. Later, he raised a famiy at Lilburn and ran his own business in Baltimore. After Hazelhurst's death in 1900, the property was owned briefly by the Oddfellows. However, they never put it to use. The first structure burned in the 1920s and was rebuilt by the Maginnis family. For a brief time in the 1930s it was operated as a facility for mentally retarded children. The tales of ghosts that linger with the house may relate to the two daughters of the Hazelhursts who died there and the death of their mother Elizabeth. In recent years private families have lived in the lovely old home with an unusual tower. Library of Congress, Prints and Photographs Division

In the 1850s Henry Hazelhurst was working in his own business as a civil and mechanical engineer. He advertised his skills and noted that they manufactured iron bridges along with spoke car wheels, boilers, etc., made of the best Baltimore Iron. It was during this time period that he built the home, Lilburn, on the hill in Ellicott City. Enoch Pratt Free Library collection, reproduced by permission

In 1892, the first pumper fire fighting equipment was purchased for Ellicott City and located in the new frame station on Ellicott Street, as it was then called, now Church Road. The equipment was drawn by horse or man to the location of a fire. It was then hand operated. A hose would run to the closest pond, stream or river to supply the water. Often the volunteers would build a dam on the stream to collect the water for the pumper.

On the side of this pumper, which is pictured inside its original home on Church Road is the identification, Ellicott City F.D. Courtesy of B. H. Shipley, Jr.

In 1888 Ellicott City acquired its first fire fighting equipment, a ladder truck drawn by horse or man. One year later this frame station was constructed to house the truck. In 1894 the first bell, donated by the B & O Railroad, was placed in the cupola. In 1896 a new bell was purchased from the McShane Bell Foundry and placed in use. The first bell was moved to the large white frame school that stood for the first quarter of the twentieth century on the hill not far from the courthouse. When the new granite school was built on College Avenue in 1925, the bell was loaned to and is still located in the St. Luke's A.M.E. Church on Main Street. After the fire station was moved in 1924, the bell was removed and the cupola lowered. It has served as various offices and today houses a branch of the county library. Courtesy of B. H. Shipley, Jr.

Tailor and merchant Henry Buetefisch operated his place of business across from the county's first firehouse on Church Road. He is shown with his son Victor. Buetefisch played an essential role in the early days since fires would be reported to him and he would dash across the road to ring the fire bell, thus alerting the volunteers. Courtesy of John Kirkwood

Artist Osmun Latrobe, Jr., made this picturesque sketch of Ellicott City's new jail in 1893. It was built in 1878 at a cost of $8,000. It held sixteen cells with a brick interior that was whitewashed. Masonry work was done by Robert Wilson, carpentry by James Rowles, ironwork by Truman and Derans of Laurel, plumbing by R. Kirkwood, and painting by O. Mercer. The 1851 jail was connected at the rear and used as warden facilities. Willow Grove, as it was called was used for over one hundred years as the county's principal jail facility. It is in use today by the sheriff's department. Far from the tranquil appearance it presents, the old granite jail saw turmoil. An 1894 lynching began here. In 1927, a dope raid was recorded. Hangings occurred near this area when a prisoner was sentenced to death. The appearance of the Emory Street Jail can be recognized but the grounds are changed. Library of Congress, Prints and Photographs Division

Dr. William Hodges built his Victorian frame home on Church Road (then Ellicott Street) about 1870 to get away from the river after experiencing the flood of 1868. His dining room exhibits his portrait. The large china closet had survived earlier floods and remains in the family. A Latrobe stove in the fireplace helped to warm the rooms. Dr. Thomas Herbert continues the practice of medicine at this home, as did his father. Courtesy of Mrs. Andrew Adams, Sr.

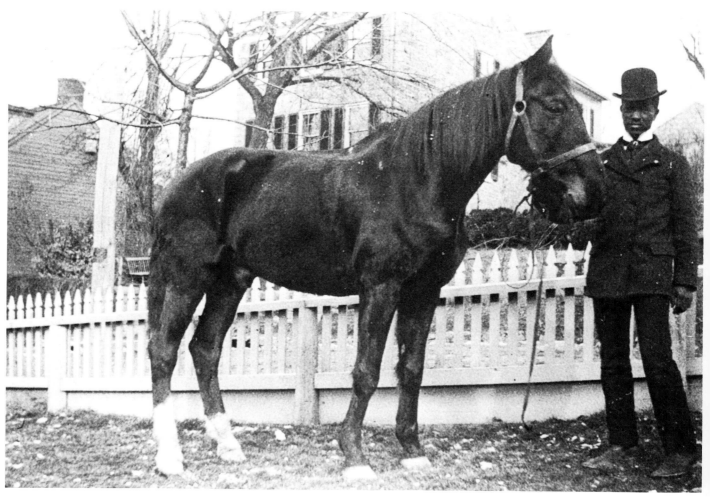

Standing with Dr. Hodges' horse is the young man who worked for the doctor. It appears that this may have been a Sunday call for the doctor judging from the young man's fine dress. In the rear of the picture is the parsonage of the Presbyterian Church, the "old manse" as it is called, which is located opposite Dr. Hodges' home of Church Road. Courtesy of Mrs. Andrew Adams, Sr.

Robert Yates once operated a florist shop on the west end of Main Street. At this time it was a grocery with dry goods and notions. Yates served as the mayor of Ellicott City. This building is still standing but no longer operates as a store. *Courtesy of Howard County Historical Society*

The harness shop was an important business when the horse and buggy was the popular means of transportation and horses were the farm power. This shop was located west of Columbia Road on Main Street, where the brick Church of God is located. On the left is Mr. W. F. Mayfield, to the right is Charles McCumsky and his grandson Cleb. *Courtesy of Howard County Historical Society*

A very early view of the Quaker meeting-house in Ellicott City shows it as it looked when it was abandoned as a meetinghouse before 1850. Built in 1799, this simple building later was altered for other uses. Porches were added to the front and rear as it was used as a public school, private school, and a private home. *Enoch Pratt Free Library collection, reproduced by permission*

A nineteenth-century view of Main Street, Ellicott City shows a wide, tree-lined dirt road with the Howard House Hotel on the left. On the right where Taylor's Store is located are older buildings which generally have not survived. A dark-suited officer appears to be talking with two men on the steps of the old hotel. Hitching posts and water pumps as well as lanterns are visible. By 1900 the building would be enlarged considerably. Trees are scarce along Main Street today. *Courtesy of Howard County Historical Society*

Weber's Quarry in Ellicott City, was an active operation in 1898, as shown in the Maryland Geological Survey. The Ellicotts used this available granite in the construction of their first homes. The quarries on either side of the river produced granite used in construction of the Baltimore Cathedral from 1806 to 1812 and 1815 to 1821, hauled in huge wagons by nine yoke of oxen. Now abandoned, these quarries are concealed from view along the railroad tracks, hidden among growing trees. Enoch Pratt Free Library collection, reproduced by permission

This post card scene of Ellicott City can be dated between 1894 and 1900. The new Presbyterian Church stands near the courthouse. Oak Lawn is visible above the church and adjacent to the church is a small house with three dormers. This was the old Quaker school built before 1790. It has been enlarged and is known as the Weir building. The Howard House had been enlarged to a full five stories but the addition to the west was not yet added. Earlier pictures of the Howard House showed it with three stories and a dormered fourth floor. Courtesy of John Kirkwood

The trolley was an important asset to the residents of Ellicott City and welcomed by them. However there were problem times. In this view the trolley was entangled with a telephone pole on the lower Main Street near the railroad overpass. A pole was knocked over, but the passengers seem undisturbed as they remain seated on the vehicle. Observers watch from the tracks above, in this early 1900 accident. Adjustments were made to the stone Oliver Viaduct to improve travel conditions and the two arches were removed to try to help prevent such situations. Courtesy of Howard County Historical Society

An early 1900s Main Street scene in Ellicott City shows the front of the City or Union Hotel, as it was known. The business was operated in the 1840s by Mrs. Deborah Disney. Scott Starr bought the property to the right and built his funeral home. All of these buildings are still standing. The Fabric House on the north side of Main Street across from the post office occupies half of the old hotel. With the wagon and team are ten-year-old Harvey Thompson and his father Theodore C. Thompson, farmers from near West Friendship. Courtesy of Howard County Historical Society

The Burgess Carriage and Wagon Works later became an automobile dealership. In 1917 Samuel W. Burgess sold Buicks at his garage. A red brick home high on the hill to the rear of the building was the Burgess family home. This building is still standing. Courtesy of Howard County Historical Society

At the rear of the Burgess Mill and Waterworks, an aqueduct carried water across the Tiber Creek to provide power for the operation of the mill. George Burgess operated it until 1867. His son continued until his death in 1906. These buildings remain near Ellicott Mills Drive but are unused. Courtesy of Howard County Historical Society

Hamilton Oldfield's pump business stood on the west end of Main Street. The Times *recorded in 1882 that the new steam sawmill and pump manufactory was moving rapidly and nearly complete in June. The stream flowed in front of the building and provided the water to soak the wooden pumps in preparation for use. Oldfield pumps were used on Main Street as well as on many farms and private homes. This building is painted white and in use by a modern business. The stream no longer is open between the road and the building. Note the bare hills to the rear. Oldfield served three terms as the Ellicott City postmaster, 1889, 1897, and 1910. The family once lived at the old post office before building a large home on the north side of Main Street. Their home was torn down for the new Ellicott Mills Drive. A granddaughter Wilhemenia Oldfield was with the county school system for many years. Courtesy of Howard County Historical Society*

In 1939, Oak Lawn in Ellicott City was nearly hidden behind large trees. For a time, this building with the wrought iron porches served as the offices of the board of education. It was constructed in the early 1840s by Edwin Parsons Hayden, the clerk to the circuit court. The name, Oak Lawn Seminary, was used when the Haydens operated a private school. This structure has been incorporated into the recently enlarged courthouse. Enoch Pratt Free Library collection, reproduced by permission

An American Lafrance triple combination pumper was a proud addition in 1924 to the Ellicott City fire department and was put into service on June 10. The $10,500 engine was purchased by the county commissioners. The garage to house this first gasoline fire engine in the county was converted at the expense of the Ellicott City council. The B. H. Shipley family lived above the station. The volunteers pictured from left, top row, are John Lyons, Albert Greenwood, and Sydney Hyatt; middle row, Preston Miller, Frank Collette, B. H. Shipley, Raymond Meldrom, Thomas Lilley, and Carl Thompson; bottom row, G. Ray Helm, Leonard McNabb, Horace Makinson, Stephen McNabb, and Charles Delosier. The shiny bell from this first engine hangs in Station No. 2 on Main Street.

This engine house is one door west of Talbott's Lumber Yard. The department moved here with the new engine from the small white building with the cupola on Church Road.

When the new brick firehouse was built in the 1930s one-and-a-half blocks west, the police department used this frame building for offices for many years. It once was a teenage recreational center. Altered in appearance, it is still standing and used for storage. Courtesy of B. H. Shipley, Jr.

Edyth Tittsworth's Grocery stood on the west end of Main Street near Rogers Avenue in the 1930s. Although the building remains, it would be difficult to identify because the porch is gone. It is painted white, is occupied by a welding business, and the road is widened. The youngsters from the old frame school that housed the black elementary grades would stop by the store to purchase their goodies. Later it was a hardware store. Maryland Historical Society

The Gambrill milling operation expanded and by the turn of the century, mills stood on either side of the road leading into Baltimore. A connecting overpass spanned the road. The millrace flowed past the former Ellicott houses. A fire changed this scene and new buildings were constructed that remain today. The millrace was filled in, as water power was no longer important to the operation. A modern milling operation of the Wilkens-Rogers Company stands at this location. They manufacture Washington Self-rising Flour products and relocated here in the early 1970s from Georgetown. *Courtesy of John Kirkwood*

Which produced the greater disaster in Ellicott City, fire or flood? Both would have to be the answer. About 1919 this fire erased the flour mill, which had grown into a modern facility throughout the nineteenth century. There was no modern fire fighting equipment in Ellicott City then and the water was pumped by hand from the river and the millrace. The mill was rebuilt and the next decade saw the emergence of the Donut Corporation of America, which provided employment for the community for the next fifty years. *Courtesy of the News American*

Tongue Row in Ellicott City contains a variety of interesting stores that lure the shoppers and businesses by its quaint appearance. It was built in the 1840s by a widow, Ann Tonge. She would construct one double stone house during the year for three years, until she had these properties that provided income for her and her descendants. It is a picturesque scene, which attracts photographers and artists who seek to capture the attractive arrangement on the bend of the Columbia Pike. Enoch Pratt Free Library collection, reproduced by permission

Scott Starr purchased a lot for fifteen hundred dollars in 1919 on Main Street, Ellicott City. There was a structure on the lot attached to the large building adjacent, which was once the Union Hotel. He later built a modern brick building for his undertaking business. All of these buildings survive and stand opposite the post office. This 1920s photo shows Mr. Starr as well as John Lyons, Steve Hillsinger and others. The business had a limousine, a hearse and two touring cars. Note that part of the business was the hiring of autos—in essence, a taxi service. Courtesy of Howard County Historical Society

In 1937, "Old Brick," Christ Episcopal Church, presented a somewhat different look along Oakland Mills Road than it does today. A congregation that recently celebrated its 275th anniversary, it continues to serve the community. Founded under the Church of England, it was served by the Rev. James Macgill as its first full-time minister. Land was given for this early chapel by Caleb Dorsey. Queen Caroline Parish was formed locally so worshipers would not have to travel to Annapolis to attend services. This brick structure was built in 1809, replacing the early log building. Enoch Pratt Free Library collection, reproduced by permission

Chapter 7

Flourishing of Churches and Schools

C hurches and schools provided activities that isolated farm families could not find in other ways. Worship was a part of the settlers lives from the beginning, making the day of rest something special—socializing with friends, listening to the learned preacher, a stimulating change from a hard and often monotonous daily life. Education depended on your economic means. It was the nineteenth century before schools developed and after the Civil War before the state took the business of public education seriously.

The earliest records indicate that the Quaker meeting may have been the first religious establishment in upper Anne Arundel County, or Baltimore County as the county was in the late 1600s and the early 1700s. Martha Ellicott Tyson, in her *Settlement of Ellicott's Mills* wrote, "It was in this year (1800) that the old Elkridge Meeting House which tradition informs us, had been occupied as a place of worship as early as 1670, was abandoned with regret, by those that loved its rural situation and quiet shade, the trees in its vicinity being unusually large; but the old building was small and uncomfortable, and except for a few families, could only be approached by crossing the Patapsco. . . ." At the Herring Creek quarterly meeting, it was reported in the sixth month of 1745 that a member who had visited the Elk Ridge meeting was apprehensive about the April 21, 1745 meeting when all seventeen persons prayed and preached at once, continuing all night and several days. Several unfounded and improper speeches were made. In the third month of 1746, friends from the Elkridge meeting attended and acknowledged their misconduct and desired to be taken under care. Quaker records in the Hall of Records indicate that in 1747 the Friends of the Elkridge weekly meeting applied to be added to the Gunpowder monthly meeting. Later Elkridge was a part of the Indian Spring meeting, located in the vicinity of present day Fort Meade. Decisions which were made at the monthly meetings were then passed to the quarterly meetings.

On July 23, 1747, Nicholas Gassaway, Jr., was accepted as a Friend and he and Margaret Pierpont showed their intention to marry. Richard Richardson and Samuel Hopkins were appointed to look into this. At the August meeting their intention was approved and they were married September 4, 1747, at the public meetinghouse in Elk Ridge. There were thirty-five witnesses, of which eighteen were members of the Pierpont family. Others included Nicholas and Mary Gassaway, Mary Richardson, Mary Ridgeway, Sarah Brown, Deborah Baker, Richard Rideway, Basel Dever, John Roberson, Rebecca Dorsey, Priscilla Dorsey, Richard and Betty Reynolds, and Elizabeth Talbott.

At the 1778 Indian Spring monthly meetings, representatives from the preparatory meetings attended and discussed that those who "deviate from the truth and support war and bloodshed, would be disowned by the Society of Friends." Another problem developed in March of 1784 concerning Jonah Deaver who had been actively dancing in public company and wholly neglected attendance at religious meetings.

John Thomas and Edward Walters were to meet with him. In May it was reported that the committee had met with Deaver but he showed no disposition to condemn his misconduct. Isaac and Ennion Williams were to draw testimony against him, acquaint him with it and produce it at the next monthly meeting. In June the testimony was presented, signed and he was to be informed of his right to appeal. If he didn't deny it, it would be read at the first day public meeting at Elkridge.

In April 1784 George and Nathaniel Ellicott presented certificates from Buckingham, Bucks County, to transfer their membership. In March 1791 Nathaniel and Elizabeth Ellicott were condemned for marrying since they were first cousins and they were disowned from the Society. Five years later, they asked to become members again and were accepted.

In March 1796, discussion began on the proposition to build a new meetinghouse on the hill opposite the schoolhouse on the southwest side of the falls near Ellicott's Mills as it was more convenient than the present meetinghouse. In July 1798, it was reported that work had begun on the new meetinghouse. In 1799 it was reported that the new meetinghouse was completed. Martha Tyson recorded that at the first meeting for worship in the new meetinghouse, Joseph Thornburg and Cassandra Ellicott were married. He was the senior partner of the house of Thornburg, Miller and Webster of Baltimore, a mercantile house of great respectability, and Cassandra Ellicott was the widow of John Ellicott. That first meeting was one of peculiar solemnity with a large company in attendance and the ceremony impressive.

By 1816 the meetinghouse was closed. Mrs. Tyson reported that many Quakers had moved to Ohio, Pennsylvania, Baltimore and elsewhere. Also their numbers had generally decreased until finally came the deaths of Samuel Smith and Ezra Fell, who for several years had been the only male representatives of Quakerism in the neighborhood. Elizabeth Brook Ellicott, who married George Ellicott, died in 1853 at Ellicott Mills and her obituary in the *Howard District Press* stated that "She was the last Ellicott in Ellicott Mills where she had lived sixty-three years. Elizabeth had helped preserve the 1799 Quaker Meetinghouse after it was closed by having it 'tinned over and painted to preserve it, all at her own expense.'"

In the Howard County Religious Heritage Celebration booklet from the October 2, 1976 event held at Atholton High School, there is a time line for churches of the county that includes 113 churches.

It is impossible to include all these congregations, since information is not available and space is limited. Some of the earliest are reviewed.

Earliest Churches

Two Methodist churches can look back to the late eighteenth century for their origins, one at Elkridge, the other toward the western part of the county. An itinerant minister who would become a bishop in the church, Francis Asbury, performed his first preachings at Elkridge in 1772. In Asbury's diaries, he wrote about the families who extended him their hospitality, John Worthington, Honor Elder Dorsey, and Colonel Thomas Dorsey, as well as Caleb Dorsey, the ironmaster at Elkridge. At one time he noted that he was particularly incensed at John Worthington's home in June 1783 when he saw a Negro so cruelly treated that he could no longer accept his old friend's hospitality. It was seventeen years before he stopped there again. This time two other pastors were with him and his old friend had died. Worthington's widow welcomed them and he recorded, "We were kindly entertained and had a comfortable night's rest." The first structure for this Elkridge congregation was built by 1795.

St. James Methodist Church at Alpha, West Friendship, Slack's Corner, or just plain Maryland 99 and Maryland 32, however you would call it, built their first structure in 1792 but had evidence of services conducted in homes as early as 1775. Asbury wrote also of his visits to this congregation in August 1800, "We had a most severe ride, nearly twenty miles, to Daniel Ellicott's. At St. James Chapel, God hath begun to pour out his Spirit . . . we had an attentive, solemn sitting, and powerful prayer closed the whole. We dined and road five miles to Henry Hobbs'. The people heard of us and ran together in the evening."

Members of the early Roman Catholic church, prior to the time of the American Revolution, worshipped at private chapels, since they were not permitted to gather in public to worship. The chapel at Doughoregan Manor provided the private chapel setting during that period of time and continues to offer mass as a part of the St. Louis Church at Clarksville. St. Paul's in Ellicott City became the next Catholic church to be built, constructed and dedicated in 1838. The archives of the church indicate that there were only three white Catholics in Ellicott Mills in 1822 and one black Catholic. This source noted that the blessing of the cornerstone of the church in 1837 by Archbishop Samuel Eccleston was attended by two archbishops, two bishops and many priests and Catholic laymen. These clergymen were attending the Third Provincial Council in Baltimore and came out via the new steam train on the B & O Railroad. St. Augustine's Church in Elkridge followed in 1844 and in the next decade St. Louis Church in Clarksville came on the scene.

Presbyterianism came to upper Anne Arundel County, as the county was then called, in the 1830s, both in Ellicott City and in the west at Lisbon. In the eastern part of the county, the congregation had its beginnings at Thistle Mills, founded by the Scottish. In 1837 a ministry began at the mills, and by 1839 they were located in their new building in Ellicott City. Harmony Church in Lisbon was in existence about 1836. However, records were destroyed early in this century.

A "Chapel of Ease" served members of a parish when they were living too distant from an existing church. The first such chapel formed from Christ Church on Oakland Mills Road was St. John's in 1821. The land was deeded by the Dorseys as Christ Church land had been. The first building was stone and measured thirty-eight by thirty-six feet. The building that stands today was built in 1860 at the same location as the original structure.

Trinity, another "Chapel of Ease" was built near Waterloo, on U.S. 1, in 1857 with additions made in 1867 and 1890. It became an independent church in 1866.

Another early Episcopal church was St. Peter's at Ellicott City, which started with meetings held in the Brown's Hotel, in 1842. Originally called Grace Church, the name was changed so it would not be confused with the church at Elkridge.

Grace Church in Elkridge came into existence in the early 1840s, and experienced three fires through its lifetime. The new stone structure was completed in 1911, following the disastrous series of fires.

Joshua Dorsey wrote to London merchant William Hunt in May 1747 to order silver for Queen Caroline Parish at the request of the church's vestry. The congregation was able to pay for the silver with money in hand and the produce of two hogs-
heads that would be shipped. The silver was placed in the care of the Reverend James Macgill when it arrived in August 1748. The flagon, chalice and paten of silver are engraved with "Queen Caroline parish in Anne Arundel County, Mary-
land 1748." Christ Church on Oakland Mills Road celebrates communion with this historic silver. From the author's collection; permission from Christ Church, James M. Shields, Rector

In the 1870s two Lutheran churches were formed in the county, St. Paul's at Fulton and First Evangelical Lutheran in Ellicott City. By then the population of Germans had increased enough to develop churches. Earlier Germans in Ellicott City traveled to Catonsville to attend services. The St. Paul's Church held services in German and English on alternate Sundays.

Early black church history has not been well researched but it appears that the 1870s may have brought the first organized congregations. St. Luke's in Ellicott City, Locust Methodist at Atholton, and Mt. Zion in Ellicott City were formed in that decade. St. Stephen's in Elkridge joins as an early congregation.

St. Luke's started on Missionary Lane, off Main Street and built their new structure at the foot of Ellicott Mills Drive in the 1890s. The local newspaper recorded that in 1877, the Heptasophs (or seven wise men), a black lodge from Catonsville visited in town and entertained with marching. In the afternoon an address was given in the Missionary Church telling about the order, with the objective of starting a chapter in Ellicott City.

Locust was one of three churches in the Atholton charge, including Locust, Asbury, and Hopkins United Methodist churches. Near Freetown Road, this was the location of a community of free Afro-Americans.

Hopkins Church at Highland was in existence by 1882. The first structure was built on land deeded by Gerald and Samuel Hopkins. Tragedy struck not long after in 1901 when the church building burned to the ground and the pastor, Reverend Samuel Brown, died in the same month.

Education

The first effort in Maryland for direct taxation for general education was made through an act in 1816, which applied to Anne Arundel, Kent, Talbot, Cecil, and Montgomery counties. (Howard was then Anne Arundel). Its purpose was to provide education for poor children through a moderate tax on the wealthy. The law stated "Whereas want of an efficient and well-digested system of county school calculated to diffuse the advantage of education throughout the state has been long felt and sincerely regretted by every friend to morality and good government, and whereas there is no practical mode to accomplish so desired an objective in the present situation of the finances of the State but by laying a moderate tax on the wealthy for the education of the poorer classes of society. . . ."

In 1825 a state law provided for a general system of public education throughout the state. A state superintendent appointed by the governor and council named commissioners of primary schools for each county and a number of inspectors for the primary schools.

Locally the commissioners divided the county into school districts. District meetings were held to appoint a clerk, collector, and three trustees. The trustees were to build and maintain the schoolhouses and furnish them with fuel, books, stationery, and other supplies. The district meeting voted a tax to use for the schools. The school commissioners received the state money and divided it among the districts. This system operated locally until 1865.

Local school records begin in 1847. Each school district received approximately $195 for each school in the district, the state contributing one-third and the district two-thirds. The system did not work very well. The quality of schools varied from district to district. The schools were far apart and attendance was not consistent. In 1856 Governor Ligon (a resident of Howard County) reported to the legislature that the school system was in "a state of most utter and hopeless prostration. Our plan of public instruction must be constructed anew, made uniform in its operation through the State, and supported more liberally by State and County resources, and above all, should be made subject to some controlling supervising power."

The state constitution of 1864 required the governor to appoint a state superintendent of public instruction who would report to the General Assembly in 1865 a plan for a uniform system of free public schools.

The Reverend Libertus Van Bokklen, founder of St. Timothy's School in Catonsville, was appointed the first state superintendent and submitted a plan that was approved in 1865 and provided for a highly centralized system. The state board of education and the county boards of school commissioners held the authority for the organization and operation of the schools. The county was divided into districts and the president of the school board acted as a county superintendent. Each member of the board became the examiner for his district.

The school board in Howard County, Samuel K. Dashiell, Dr. Joel Hopkins, and David Burdette, first met on October 1, 1865. They elected Mr. Dashiell president, who supervised the school in the first election district. Dr. Hopkins was responsible for the second and fifth districts and Mr. Burdette the third and fourth.

A change in the state law in 1867 brought a reorganization and a new board was appointed in 1868 consisting of Dr. Samuel H. Henry, Edward A. Talbott, Henry O. DeVries, David Burdette, Dr. William H. Hardy, and Joshua W. Dorsey. This law also provided for the establishment of high schools but it would be thirty years before this was accomplished in Howard County.

Early Primary Schools

The original primary schools were numbered as a part of the Anne Arundel County school, starting with numbers 22 through 42, with some numbers missing. The following is the listing of the trustees for each in 1847:

Schools 22:	Thomas J. Talbott	School 33:	Benj. Hood Sr.
	George H. Pocock		John Thompson Senr.
	George Hopper		Thomas Barnes
26:	Seth W. Warfield	34:	James H. Hobbs
	Jonathan Marriott		James T. Henderson
	Thomas D. Griffith		Asbury Peddicord

27: George Bradford	35: Basil Duvall
Henry Warfield	James A. Meridith
Charles R. Simpson	Philomon Warfield
28: Philip Cissel	36: Nathan Shipley
Rezin Gaither	D. E. Hopkins
Greenbury Johnson	William W. Warfield
29: Evan Scott	37: Nathaniel Clary
George Stinchcomb	Luther Welsh
Richard Davis	Adam DeLauder
30: Anthony Smith	39: James B. Mathews
Thomas G. Davis	Mortimer Dorsey
Nicholas I. Barrett	Samuel T. Owings
31: George Hamilton	40: George W. Warfield
Charles G. Haslup	Ephriam Hobbs
Theodore Tubman	John N. Selby
32: Lenox J. Martin	42: Wesley Linthicum
Wilson S. Hobbs	William W. Watkins
Beal Whalen	James Treakle

In 1853, the schools were renumbered, starting with 1 through 22.

Early primary school records are sketchy. Between 1847 and 1851 each school received the allotted $195. By 1852, this increased to $250 and to $300 until 1858, when it was increased to $400 and stayed there until 1861, after which records are not available until 1865.

School board minutes exist from 1865. In August 1865, A. D. Warfield and William Denny passed as qualified teachers. In September it was decided to pay teachers $100.00 per quarter until December, then in proportion to the number of pupils attending. Salaries for the first quarter, for the entire county, came to $2,165.41, for the twenty-four operating schools. When a salary scale was developed per pupil, it read as follows: fifteen pupils, $100.00 per quarter; twenty-five pupils, $115.00; thirty-five pupils, $125.00; forty-five pupils, $135.00; fifty-five pupils, $145.00; sixty pupils, $150.00. So if you had four times as many pupils as the minimum number, you received only 50 percent more in wages.

Examiners

Mr. Samuel K. Dashiell, in his role as an examiner wrote to the school board in 1865:

The condition of the public schools under the old local law, I have found to be not so good as I would like. The schoolhouses with their furniture, in many cases, were wholly unfit for the purpose for which they were used. They were dilapidated, and in many cases out of the way, and inconvenient to be reached. I found the teachers in too many cases unfit for their profession; yet I found many honorable exceptions, and I gave them praise. Such changes will be made as the interest of the schools require

In 1868, Mr. Dashiell again noted the poor condition of the schools due to indifference of parents by keeping children home from school and the small salaries paid to the teachers. By 1870 he was more optimistic, writing,

I have visited every school in the county each quarter, and have found the interest in the schools on the increase. The patrons and pupils are active. I find that the more frequently the patrons visit the schools, the more the teacher and pupils are encouraged, and the better the work progresses.

The 1870s proved productive in local education. There was an increase in pupils, teachers and buildings. To stimulate teachers' interest, the board instituted a salary dependent on the average attendance percentage of those enrolled. However, writing at that time, Mr. Dashiell noted that the district trustees were inefficient, manifested little or no interest...and he would be happy to see the trustees abolished.

In 1868, the schools were once again renumbered, this time by district, with a location given. First district, 1, was at mine bank; 2, at the church; 3, near election house; and 4, at Bonny Branch. Second District, 1, was at Ellicott City (male); 2, Ellicott City (female); 3, Mount Hebron; 4, Jonestown; 5, Elysville; and 6, with Miss Strawbridge (In 1866 Miss Strawbridge had been hired to operate an additional school at Ellicott Mills, to receive both male and female children, over the number of sixty from other schools now in operation in the village.) Third District, 1, was near Dennis; 2, near Jem's; 3, at Sykesville, 4; Hobb's Mill; and 5, at Marriottsville. Fourth District, 1, was the new school house; 2, at Long Corner; 3, Lisbon; 4, Cooksville; 5. A. G. Warfield's; and 6, at Roxbury. Fifth District, 1, was near Bason's; 2, near Dr. Hardy's; 3, Pindell's; 4, Simpsonville; and 5, at Folly Quarters. Sixth District, 1, was at Savage; 2, near Bern's; 3, near Oakland; and 4, near Dr. White's.

In 1868 a committee was appointed to look into building a high school. Salaries were set at $500 annually if you held a First Grade Certificate and $475, a Second Grade Certificate, $300, if you were an assistant. Quacker's, *A History of the United States* (without the war section) was substituted in place of Willard's. The board decided in November that the teachers would not be paid for cutting wood; furthermore, any teacher who failed to collect money from the students for books for the fall term would be dismissed by the board.

In 1869, the board looked into establishing a high school at Clarksville or Carroll's Manor.

The first mention of "colored" schools was made in June 1870 when the treasurer was directed to report to the board the amount of levy paid by the black population to the school fund. In February 1871, the school commissioners were to distribute the books of old series in their possession, if needed, to the black school in their district. Finally in November 19, 1872, Colored School No. 1, District 4, was mentioned with the name of the teacher, Isaiah W. Somers, and the salary of $41.49. On April 26, 1873, record of money paid to black schools lists teachers,

Josephine Carr, $37.40; Jesse Wilson, $42.74; John Hendersen, $22.23; and Isaiah Somers, $42.74.

In April 1876, the treasurer was instructed to pay ten dollars to the trustees of any school district that had raised the same amount toward establishing a public school library. William Crapster asked for renumeration for the occupancy of his academy building as a public school for the past two years. In October 1878 a petition came from the black population near Freetown for a school. They wanted to open one the end of the fall term to continue for two terms, until end of spring 1879. Again in 1882, there was a petition for a school near Freetown for two terms. By 1884 there was one black school in each district with two in the second, third and fifth districts.

In 1878, John G. Rogers, then county examiner, wrote of additional expenses due to increased school attendance and reduced state taxes. Total attendance that year was 2,589, including 555 black children, 20 percent of the enrollment. Even though the county commissioners increased the school aid from $9,000 to $10,000, they still found it necessary to reduce the salaries of the teachers. In 1880 a study of illiteracy in the county and the black population was made. Twenty-eight percent of the county's population was black and only 15 percent of the whole population was illiterate.

In September 1883, a committee of Germans approached the board asking for a school to benefit "that element" but were refused for insufficient reasons. Three committees asked for additional black facilities in the first, fourth and sixth districts. The board declined all requests. Finally in January 1885 Myra Hobbs was appointed the teacher for a school at the German Lutheran Church in Ellicott City.

Discussion in 1887 centered on a new school for Ellicott City. The architect advised that a four-room, two-story building could be built for $3,000.00. John G. Rogers agreed to loan the money and it was advertised. All bids ranged from $5,400.00 to $7,720.00 so plans were canceled. A year later the decision was reversed and the new building was completed by October. A janitor was hired for $7.50 per month.

The 1890s were difficult times financially for the county schools, since the county needed to replace the schoolhouses and furnishings, but received no additional state support. In seventeen years the county built twenty-three new buildings. In 1892, there were fourteen black schools in the county and forty-three white schools. The white teachers' salaries ranged from $95 to $110 a term and the black teachers about half of that. The white schools were allotted $28 each for fuel for the year and the black schools $7 to $12. In 1893, the board closed the schools early due to lack of funds. The black schools closed in mid-April and white schools mid-May. When the Marriottsville school got six new desks that year, the old desks were sent to the black school at Alpha. A new white school was

built at Oakland Mills for $600.

In 1900 Phillip T. Harmon, examiner, reported 3,019 pupils in sixty county schools, with seventy-one teachers. Black pupils numbered 824, with fourteen schools and fifteen teachers.

The first regular high school was established at Lisbon in 1899, probably offering no more than a two-year course. The Ellicott City High School opened in 1902, Clarksville in 1914, Savage in 1921, and Elkridge in 1922, the latter two being two-year schools. In 1936 the Savage school was consolidated with Elkridge. A four-year school was established at West Friendship in 1928, reduced to two years in 1931 and consolidated with Lisbon in 1932, which had become a four-year school about 1921. In 1902 there were reported to be 20 pupils in high school, in 1910, 50; 1915; 154; 1925, 335; 1935, 582; and in 1940, 788.

In 1900, the *Times* reported where the white schools were located in the county. In the First District they were at Mechanicsville, Elkridge, near Waterloo, Overland, Wesley Grove, and Orange Grove. Second District schools were at Ellicott City, Hunts, Jonestown, Alberton, Elioak and Hilton. Third District was Alpha, West Friendship, Marriottsville, Ridgelys, Selbys, Woodstock, Mayfield, Mottu's, and Melia's. Fourth District was Long Corner, Poplar Springs, Lisbon, Cooksville, Florence, Roxbury, Hobb's, Providence, and Daisy. Fifth District was Dayton, Hardeys, Fulton, Owings, Highland, and Clarksville. Sixth District was Savage, Gormans, Guilford, Oakland Mills, near Laurel, between Savage and Waterloo, and Browns. In 1900 the black schools were in Guilford, Ellicott City, Cooksville, Alpha, Pine Orchard, Colesville, Daisy, Highland, Atholton, Elkridge, Jonestown, Dayton, and Folly Quarters.

An interesting evaluation was done in the late 1940s of the black schools in the county. Each school was found to be inferior. The schools were overcrowded. The stoves did not keep them warm and were dangerous for the children. Often the water was not suitable for drinking and had to be hauled from a neighbor's for drinking. The locations of the schools were undesirable, often in the middle of a lot with no playground room available. The furniture was generally described as old and in poor condition. The rooms and building needed painting. At the Ellicott City school it was noted that the outside toilets sat so close to the door of the schol that the odor penetrated the classrooms on warm days.

There continued to be discrepancies into the twentieth century between the salaries of the white teachers and the black teachers. In 1917 elementary white teachers were paid in a range of $30-$60 per month, high school $45-$95, black teachers $25 to $30 (there were no "colored" high schools). Ten years later white elementary teachers made $75 to $115, high school teachers made $110 to $140, while black teachers were paid only $57 to $85.

Although county superintendent W. C. Phillips, who came into office in 1900, wrote of consolidation in 1908, it was a long time coming. At that time they were taking steps to consolidate the two schools at Elkridge.

In 1948, the school system was expanded from eleven years to a twelve-year system. In 1949, there were seventeen white schools in the county, but no separate high schools, for each included the elementary grades. There were eight black elementary schools and one black high school The first consolidated high school, Howard, opened in 1952, with Clarksville and Lisbon high schools continuing operation. In 1965, integration of the school system was totally achieved. Before the beginning of Columbia and following integration there were twelve elementary schools: Elkridge, Waterloo, Ellicott City, St. John's Lane, Rockland, West Friendship, Lisbon, Clarksville, Atholton, Scaggsville, Savage, and Guilford.

The growth of schools was slow with a 1 percent increase per year until 1880 when the population remained stable for fifty years. The years of the 1940s and 1950s are when the school system exhibited its first growth. There were 4,175 enrolled in 1950; 6,984 in 1960; 10,308 in 1965; and 15,895 in 1970; more than a 300 percent increase in twenty years.

In 1974 another historic event took place with the board of education members being elected for the first time. Previously, the members were appointed to their position.

Private Schools

Private schools existed throughout the early years of the county's growth. The Ellicott's Quaker school, which opened before 1790, appears to have been the earliest. Families of means had private tutors before the advent of formal education. Private schools developed when there was no public education available in Howard County above the primary level before the turn of the twentieth century.

The most prominent of these private schools were Rock Hill College and the Patapsco Female Institute. Warfield's Academy, Lisbon Academy, St. Clement's Hall, Maupin's University School, Glenwood Institute, Dundee, and Mrs. Rivers Boarding School for Young Ladies were others that operated during the nineteenth century.

Although the *Howard Gazette*, in 1850, told of the first semiannual examination of students at Rock Hill Academy and stated that the school had been in existence for six months, it was operating prior to that time. Land records in the 1820s refer to Sam's Academy and to Isaac Sams as proprietor. Records prior to the opening of the railroad reveal that Mr. Sams engaged in litigation with the B & O concerning the railroad operation's cutting off the access to his academy with the construction of the tracks. Mr. Sams received a new right-of-way to his property,

which is probably the Maryland Avenue, St. Paul Street, College Avenue route up the hill today.

The Christian Brothers purchased the property and operated under the name of Rock Hill Academy. Some years later it gained the status of a college and the road by the property took that name. The Reverend J. P. Carter was an early principal. The summer session at Rock Hill in 1850 began May 1 with tuition and boarding expenses costing seventy-five dollars. For day scholars the tuition ran from ten to twenty dollars, depending on the studies.

Also in 1850, the Warfield Academy advertised that their summer session commenced May 1 and winter session, the first Wednesday in November. They further stated that the course of instruction in each department of English, mathematical, and classical was "full and thorough." Elocution, vocal music, and lectures on philosophy and chemistry entered into the course as well. The healthfulness, morality, and intelligence of the neighborhood gave superior advantages to the institution according to literature of the time. Cost per session of twenty-two weeks was sixty dollars, including board, payable one-half in advance. The Reverends T. J. Shepherd and W. T. Crapster could supply additional information about the academy.

After the closing of Warfield's Academy, the Reverend William Crapster opened the Lisbon Academy where, in 1871 board and tuition for forty-four weeks was two hundred dollars. Their curriculum offered higher English and math, Latin, Greek, Hebrew, French, German, Italian, and other subjects. By 1883 Ellen Crapster, presumably the widow, advertised for sale a building that could be used for a boarding school, hotel, or summer boarders.

In 1850 Mrs. C. M. Rivers ran a board and day school for young ladies at Ellicott City. Her advertisement in the local newspaper read that she taught all the branches of a finished English education including the French language, drawing, and vocal and instrumental music. Her fees for boarding, washing, and tuition with instruction on piano were $7.50 per quarter. The exact location of her school is not known.

Dundee was a girls' school located in the stone house just outside Ellicott City, at Rogers Avenue and Frederick Road. Originally Mr. and Mrs. Weems ran the school until Mrs. E. E. Baird Chenoweth from Easton came to town and took over the school in 1900.

Private schools continue to have an important place in Howard County. There are a number of church-related facilities and independent institutions. Statistics prove that the average adult in Howard County is better educated than the average U.S. citizen. Howard County supports a high-quality education for its children and this is reflected in the quality of the present county system and the fine private facilities.

W.P.A. PROJECT #294

Works Progress Administration (WPA) workers put the finishing touches on the new Elkridge High School in the mid 1930s. The construction of the new school was a joint project with the county. It was built directly across the road from the first high school in Elkridge on the Washington Boulevard. Although it has been renovated, the school building is still in use for the elementary grades. Enoch Pratt Free Library, reproduced with permission

The Donaldson School was founded in Baltimore in 1906 as a boys' school associated with Mt. Calvary Church, Baltimore. In 1912 the school purchased "Grovement" at Ilchester for $27,000. In the next twenty years they constructed a number of buildings in the Elizabethan style including this vinecovered brick building. It was then called the School House and now, minus the ivy, is called the Trinity Middle School, St. Kidwine's Hall. After the Depression the school closed, having lost its endowment. In 1934 the Maryland Academy of Notre Dame, Inc. purchased 183 acres of land. The Sisters of Notre Dame de Namur opened a high school for girls, both boarders and day students. In 1942 Trinity Lower School opened. Additions were made to some of the earlier buildings. In 1972, the high school was closed and the building leased to the elementary school, and the schoolhouse later became the Middle School. Trinity Preparatory School became Trinity School and is at present co-educational. When it was still Donaldson School, young men attended from along the East Coast states, as well as Maryland. In 1930 about six of the 60 students were from Howard County. Howard County Historical Society

Locust Chapel stood on Ilchester Road at the corner of Landing Road. Long before 1860, this chapel served the old established community of Ilchester. Over 50 years ago it went into disuse before this building was torn down. Now a grove of trees covers the old church yard. News American

Members of the Gaines A.M.E. Church, Elkridge, stopped to chat after Sunday services one morning in the 1920s. According to Laura Simms, the gentleman in the center is her grandfather, Alexander McCrory Mars, a man of Irish, Indian heritage. He married Ella Johnson and they lived in Elkridge on Montgomery Road and raised six children. Courtesy of Laura Simms and the Black History Publication of the Howard County NAACP

The identifiable front door of the First Presbyterian Church helped to locate the scene of this turn-of-the-century photo. The Rev. Henry Branch, pastor in the late 1890s, can be recognized without a hat and with the gray beard. It appears that this may have been the Sunday

school along with the teachers since there are many children and young people. Another interesting feature is the doll dressed in white, which is being held up by a girl in the second row. This may have been taken shortly after the completion of the new building in 1894. The original of this old print was printed in reverse. We have printed it properly. Some of the blurs resulted from restless youngsters who found it difficult to stand still for the photographer. But the handsome Sunday apparel, capes on the jackets, large bowties, high boots and hats on nearly every head, are interesting even though the identification of the people has not been found. Courtesy of John Kirkwood

Emory Methodist Church was founded in 1837 as Emory Chapel of the Methodist Episcopal Church at Ellicott's Mills, and named for Bishop Emory. Most early churches were built along these simple rectangular lines and had two entrance doors. The men and boys used one entrance and the women and girls the other. The sexes sat separately. At the time of the golden anniversary of the church, it was remodeled to the present appearance. The church stands on Church Road in Ellicott City and remains an active congregation. Courtesy of the Commercial and Farmers Bank

St. Peters Episcopal Church was first called Grace Church at its founding in 1842. This brick structure was consecrated in 1854, five years after the name was changed to avoid confusion with the Elkridge church. The original building was located on the hill behind St. Paul's Catholic Church. Fire destroyed the eighty-five-year-old structure in 1939. It was rebuilt on Rogers Avenue in the west end of Ellicott City. Courtesy of John Kirkwood

EPISCOPAL CHURCH, ELLICOTT CITY, MD.

This early engraving focuses on the young men's school, Rock Hill Academy. The students can be seen on the grounds of the school. St. Paul's Church and the Patapsco Bank are easily identified. The perspective that the artist used is confusing since the train seems to cross at the same level as the wooden bridge, leaving the question of where the Oliver Viaduct was. Obviously, the focal point is the Rock Hill Academy. A rare letter in the possession of Patricia Walker was written from Rock Hill in 1843 by B. T. Johnson to his mother Mrs. E. M. Tyler, Brotherton in Anne Arundel County. He reported to his mother that he almost missed the train because Rezin (a servant?) didn't have the horses ready and dawdled in the kitchen. At the academy, upon his return from home, he found Basil Norris and Potts recovering from the measles. He discussed how much they enjoyed the jar of oysters and the chestnuts. He shared the oysters the next day with Mrs. Holmead and Mr. McNeil, possibly the housekeeper and a teacher. Writing in March, he asked that his father bring him a bundle of summer clothes if he made a trip to Baltimore. Maryland Historical Society

Smouldering ruins of a granite shell was all that remained after the fire destroyed Rock Hill College in 1923. A boys' school had operated at this location on College Avenue in Ellicott City for nearly one hundred years. Before the fire, through the preceding years, newspaper articles had reported the possible closing of the school due to financial restraints. A need for a new Ellicott City high school had been discussed for many years before the decision was made to use the site of the old college for the new school. In 1925 the new Ellicott City School opened for all ages, from first grade through the four years of high school. Courtesy of the News American

Ellicott City High School was completed in 1925, designed by Pietsch and Emory, architects. Granite from the Rock Hill College may have been used for the new structure, which stands at the site of the college that burned. The old frame high school stood on an opposite hill, near the courthouse, at the top of Strawberry Lane, as the road up the hill was called. It was demolished after the completion of the new school, which housed the elementary grades, one through seven, plus the four years of high school for a total of eleven years of public school. In the 1970s the elementary school was closed, for the high school had been moved in the late 1930s to Montgomery Road. The building is privately owned. Courtesy of Mr. and Mrs. G. Carlton Sykes

OLD MAIDS

O+O+O=O

SPRING IS HERE!

+ AND -

"ME"

CAPITAL and LABOR

THREE CAKE EATERS

From the Oracle, *the yearbook for the Ellicott City High School in 1930 come the fun pictures that portray the lighter side of school life. The sponsors were an important part of the publishing of the book and the bigger sponsors included Provident Savings Bank, Patapsco National Bank, Ellicott City Parent-Teacher Association, Easton Sons, Eaton and Burnett Business College in Baltimore, Lucy Crescent Candy Company in Baltimore, Ellicott City Lunch, Johnson's Service Station, and Miller Chevrolet Sales. A section of jokes was included to add interest to the publication. Courtesy of Mr. and Mrs. G. Carlton Sykes*

Some of the members of the 1933 basketball squad from the Ellicott City High School are pictured standing in front of the school. The players were Nathan Clark, Norman Brosenne, Albert Lauman, Charles Gearhart, Severn Tittsworth, George Everly, Robert Donovan, Clarence Cook, William Moore, Joe Donovan, Paul Mumford, Lewis Iglehart, Pete Olson, and John O'Neill. They won eight of their twelve games, defeating Catonsville, Kenwood, Sherwood, the Ellicott City All-Stars, Randallstown, and Clarksville. The highest score was against Clarksville, 29 to 23. Courtesy of Mr. and Mrs. G. Carlton Sykes

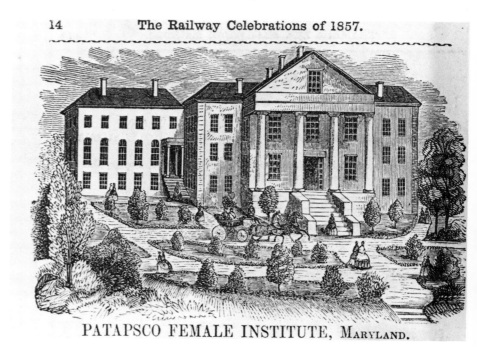

When Almira Hart Lincoln Phelps became the principal of the Patapsco Female Institute, its success soared. In 1841, she became the third principal and enrollment reached three hundred. Most of the young ladies attended from Maryland and the southern states, according to research by Doris E. Chickering. Homes included Virginia, North Carolina, South Carolina, Georgia, Tennessee, Alabama, Mississippi, Texas, and the District of Columbia. There were also students from the Midwest and the northern states. Mrs. Phelps, along with her sister, Emma Willard, were prominent educators in the early 1800s. They were raised in New England. Mrs. Phelps published her lectures on botany and books on chemistry, geology, and natural philosophy. Before directing the PFI, she served at the Troy Seminary in 1830, a new seminary in West Chester, Pennsylvania, and Rahway Female Institute, in New Jersey. Enoch Pratt Free Library collection, reproduced by permission

The PFI was enlarged and advertised in 1857 that the improvements were complete to increase the convenience and comfort of the pupils. The new chapel (to the left) was described as being a handsome and most appropriate structure for the exclusive use of the inmates of the institute. It was furnished with a new organ and had an excellent tone. The advertisement praised the excellent climate and the closeness to Baltimore to enjoy the benefits of a city without any of its evils. Mrs. Phelps had notified the trustees of her intention to resign and Robert H. Archer, Esq., had been selected as her successor. The trustees were Charles W. Dorsey, president; William Denny, M.D., secretary; T. Watkins Ligon; E. Hammond; and John P. Kennedy. Enoch Pratt Free Library collection, reproduced by permission

14   The Railway Celebrations of 1857.

PATAPSCO FEMALE INSTITUTE, MARYLAND.

St. Clement's Hall was the name of this property on Columbia Pike, now occupied as a doctor's office and residence. It was built after the Civil War by the Reverend J. Avery Shepherd as a school for boys. When Shepherd sold the property in 1875 the building was described as having three stories with basement, Mansard roofed, and frame. The property was in litigation in the late 1870s. During that time and into the 1880s, it appears to have been operated as Professor Maupin's University School for young men. By 1893, Edward A. Talbott bought the property. His son, Richard Talbott, in a 1964 interview, recalled living in the house. When his father bought it, the Kraft family was living in it while work was being done on their home across the road. Mr. Talbott was going to tear the house down because it was so large until it was suggested that he contact a Baltimore contractor who altered houses. Spick-

nall, the contractor, lowered the house, taking out the first floor entirely. The remaining house was moved onto a new foundation. Dr. Taylor has held the property since 1943. From the author's collection

The Meadowridge schoolhouse for black students is occupied today as a home. Many of these old schoolhouses have been converted to other uses. In some cases, alterations have changed them considerably and they would not be recognized as schools. Others, such as this one on Meadowridge Road, Elkridge, which is now painted green, are easily identified as former schools. From the author's collection

Agnes Wallace Carter, teacher of Asbury School stands behind her students, in this photograph from about 1918. The community is located on the road to Annapolis Junction, southwest of U.S. 1. School met in a frame building still used as a community hall after the youngsters went to the new Guilford School. Those pictured from the left fron row, are Cosette Carroll (Harding), Helen Arthur, Alvin Hall, Grace Allen, Beatrice Jackson, Conelia Gaither (Mathews), Leonard Moore, and Howard Hall. In the back row, are Elwood Carroll, William Hall, Nellie Thomas (who married William Hall); Glasco Gaither, Carrie Carroll, Helen Gaither (Mathews) Edell Carroll (Johnson), and Florence Carroll. Leola Dorsey and Cosette Harding provided the names. NAACP collection

In the 1950s the May Queen Rally was a popular event at the Asbury Methodist Church, near Annapolis Junction, south of U.S. 1. According to her daughter, Leola Dorsey, the Reverend Aileen Moore, seated on the right, organized this annual event. The Reverend Carter is seated in the center. Participants came from many churches in the area and the lady with the most votes would be announced as the Queen of the Rally. NAACP collection

Savage High School was organized in 1921 as a two-year school with E. C. Ryall as its first principal. At this time there were 335 high school students enrolled in the five county high schools. The student body at the Savage school in 1924 are shown here with their principal, John Yingling. In the front row, from the left, are Albert Downing, Thurston Kingsbury, William Grady, and Jimmy Brot. In row two are Willie Cooney, Elnetta Otterburn, Marian Thompson, Alice Phelps, Louise Ward, Anna Conaway, Jane Rorabaugh, and Louis Smallwood. In row three are Anna Ridgeway, Iola Slater, Katherine Brosene, Catherine Haslup, Catherine Ridgeway, and Elenore Slate. In row four are Elsworth Dixon, Mr. Yingling, Mary Specht, Robert Mathews, Elizabeth Oberlin, and Carl Curtis. Courtesy of Mrs. Marian Thompson Mathews

A school was operated for black children near the present Howard High School at Jonestown by 1900. In 1915 one-half acre of land was purchased by the Community School Club of Jonestown for three hundred dollars. A mortgage to Reuben D. Rogers shows that club officers were William B. Miller, president; Matthew Coates; Moses Jones; Howard Lloyd; and Reno Biggers. Abandoned, the schoolhouse was barely standing in the 1970s and has since disappeared. County natives often asked, when hearing about Jonestown, if the speaker meant black Jonestown or white Jonestown, since another Jonestown community existed north of U.S. 40. It is now called Rockland. From the author's collection

The students at the Fells Lane Elementary School, built in the 1950s, join their teacher, Mrs. Elizabeth Woods, on the steps of the new school for black youngsters. They were all smiles to leave behind the rickety old frame building that stood on the hillside at the foot of Rogers Avenue. It had no playground and outhouses were just outside the front door. The advantages of the new location included indoor toilets, sturdy construction, cleanliness, a play area, and bright colors. By the 1960s the elementary schools began to integrate and Mrs. Woods became the first black teacher at St. John's Elementary School. This Fells Lane School became the police station before it was renamed the Roger Carter Neighborhood Center. Courtesy of Mrs. Elizabeth Wood

161

The Oakland Mills schoolhouse served as the home for the Elwood Wallich family for many years. Here the door has been relocated from the end of the building to the front of the house. Later the Wallichs made other changes, adding dormers to adapt it to the family's needs. This building was torn down for the Maryland 175 and U.S. 29 interchange. Courtesy of Mr. and Mrs. Elwood Wallich

The first consolidated school in the county opened at West Friendship in 1925. Consolidation was not popular when discussed but there was support for it in this community. Although the school was enlarged, in time it was outdated and demolished for the construction of a new elementary school on Maryland 144 near Maryland 32 at the same location as this early one. School busing was provided for the elementary students but high school students were required to pay four dollars a month when they rode. Cooperative Extension Service, Howard County Historical Society

Pindell School had a full house around 1915, and Miss Gillis was a busy teacher directing these youngsters. Four Gore sisters attended that year, as well as four Thompsons, two Gaithers, and three Mills. Bessie Gore Wallich remembers the names of all of her classmates. Seated in front are: Clarence Franklin and Maurice Brown. In the second row, from the left, are Stella Gaither, Irene Gore, Hilda Thompson, Blanche Walters, Theresa Thompson, Leola Gore, Gilbert Murphy, Mary Gaither, Myrtle Mills, Francis Gore, Bessie Gore, Lee Hall, Maurice Thompson, and Cissel Cole. In the back row, are Roche Mills, Jessie Thompson, Bertie Mills, Hester Wessel, Elna Wallich, Queenie Murphy, and Merle Brown. Miss Gillis is in the back center. Courtesy of Mr. and Mrs. Elwood Wallich

The first Clarksville High School building was opened in 1914. This school stood on Maryland 108 on the south side of the road near the fire station. Before being demolished it was used by the county's bureau of highways. The new Clarksville high school was built in 1939 on the opposite side of Maryland 108. That building served as high school and elementary school for many years. Later it became the middle school. The board of education retains the use of the school for special programs. From the author's collection

The students at the Harriet Tubman High School are engrossed in their science studies in this 1956 photograph. The new school opened around 1950, replacing the small and geographically incon- venient Cooksville High School, which was the only black high school prior to the opening of Harriet Tubman. Black youth in the eastern part of the county had to attend high schools outside of the county, if they wanted an education, since Cooksville was small and so far away. NAACP collection

James B. Mathews and Charles D. War-field played important roles in the formation of Union Chapel in 1833. Mathews was one of the original trustees and kept the early church records. Warfield provided the land for the new building. The total cost of construction for this modest house of worship was $1,459.47. In 1886, the chapel was in the Lisbon circuit of the Methodist church, which included Jennings Chapel and Poplar Springs as well. The doors of the chapel were closed in the 1950s and the building fell into disrepair. It has recently been restored and is used for worship by an Episcopal congregation. It is available for weddings, baptisms, and other similar events. From the author's collection

Mount Gregory United Methodist Church stands on Maryland 97 near Cooksville. The buildings to the rear served as part of the county's highway maintenance program before they burned. However, they were built as the Cooksville school in the 1920s as an industrial school for "colored" youths. Later it became the first high school in the county for black students. Harriett Tubman replaced it in the 1950s. An old black cemetery disappeared when an area was blacktopped to make a school yard for the children. Before use by the black community, this property was the site of Warfield's Academy, a private school in the 1840s. The land was sold at a sheriff's sale in 1851 and by 1867 it was deeded for use as a school for black youngsters. From the author's collection

This wood-shingled building was erected in 1868 and served as a Methodist Episcopal church, for a short time. In the next decade it stood empty while Sunday school classes met at Pindell's school-house. By 1888 a congregation returned to worship at this dark gray building, called Zion Chapel, on Laurel Road. In 1918 a new Mt. Zion Church was built by the growing congregation with the building and furniture costing $14,134.29. By 1962 the large modern church at Highland on Maryland 216 was consecrated with Bishop John Wesley Lord in attendance. From the author's collection

GLENWOOD INSTITUTE

Wm. K. Boyle & Son, Printers, Baltimore.

The Glenwood Institute was opened by Lycurgus Mathews after the Civil War. There was a grammar school division that charged eighty-seven dollars for tuition, board and room for one session in 1885. The collegiate department cost ninety-five dollars. In a school pamphlet, the location of the institute was described as being four miles south of Hood's Mills station on the Washington and Westminster Road, (now Maryland 97). It was later operated with J. D. Warfield as the principal. He organized a farmer's group, which sponsored the Glenwood Farmer's Picnic, an annual affair of agricultural events. This building burned in the 1920s on a cold winter day. It was the first trip west for the new Ellicott City gas fire engine. From the author's collection

Members of the Daisy United Methodist Church posed for a photo in the early 1900s. The old log schoolhouse was torn down by 1913 and classes met in the basement of the church building. Hanson Dorsey is on the right. Others in the photo are Emma Harriday, Ida Snowden with her daughters, Mamie and Georgeanna, and Lula Johnson. The congregation has built an addition to the old church and connected it where these members are standing. The church is approached from the opposite end, which faces Daisy Road. Courtesy of Alice "Becky" Thomas

The Daisy School in 1914 was attended by a large class of students who kept the teacher, Miss Lucy Prather, very busy. School classes by then were held in the basement of the Daisy Methodist Church. Earlier they had met in a log cabin. Those in attendance were in the rear, left, Moses H. Dorsey, right, William T. Dorsey. Standing from the left, Elsie Robinson, Catherine Butler, Blanche Thornton, Jean Winston, Rosie Dorsey, Margaret Gaither, Annie Shearn, William Prettyman, James Shearn, Henry Hammond, John Gaither, Augustus Dorsey, and Miss Prather. Kneeling from left, Theodore Duton, Mary Priscilla Dorsey, Mammie Snowden, Carolyn Riggs, Daniel Gaither, Charles Shearn, John Thornton, Channing Dorsey; front row, George Gaither, Raymond Anderson, William Riggs, Georgeanna Snowden, Lilie Dorsey, Sally Stanton, Elizabeth Dorsey, Lula Snowden, and Alice Dorsey. William Dorsey and his sister Alice recalled the names of all their classmates. Courtesy of Alice "Becky" Dorsey

*Howard County sent a float to represent
the county in the opening of the state
bridge over the Severn River in 1924.
Obviously, the county was proud of its
achievements and eager to participate in
the big event. Cooperative Extension
Service, Howard County Historical
Society*

Chapter  8

Entering the Twentieth Century Quietly

Howard County entered the twentieth century without much fanfare. It remained a rural county with good farmers, hard workers, and a satisfaction with the status quo. The outside world seemed to bypass the county. This was a period when government agencies were traveling around the countryside recording the people and events of the times. If it didn't happen on U.S. 1 in Howard County, it wasn't recorded. Other counties, cities, and communities attracted photographers who captured their people, homes, businesses and events. We were simply overlooked.

Newspapers help us to learn what was happening here at home during these quiet years. Real estate transactions were important events. In 1900 the Isaac Granite Quarries at Ellicott City were sold to Albert Weber of Baltimore County. The estate, Wilton, 345 acres in size, was sold for twenty thousand dollars. Formerly it was the home of the state's attorney, Joseph D. McGuire.

Community correspondents reported the events throughout the county. They usually included social gatherings, marriages, births, and deaths. The Clarksville Correspondent in 1900 suggested that the legislature should put a tax on young men from other counties coming to see "our" young ladies. That was undoubtedly the reason there were so many bachelors in Howard County, the writer observed.

In Elkridge, St. Augustine's Church was demolished starting in March 1901, in preparation for the construction of a new church. That same year the railroad was extended from Savage to Guilford, crossing the Middle Patuxent and Little Patuxent rivers.

By 1910, the newspaper reported that C. Russel Hinchman purchased land at Laurel for a race track. The Rover Roller Mills were operated by August Selby and Son. They manufactured Silver Spray flour. That year the night telephone operator in Ellicott City, Miss Bessie Holton, was awarded a medal for helping to avert a disastrous fire. She discovered an electrical fire in the telephone exchange and ran through a snowstorm to sound the alarm via the fire bell. Edward Hammond and William Howard Brown were the county delegates and A. P. Gorman, Jr., was president of the senate. Dorsey and Clark operated the Clarksville Stage, which made regular trips on Monday, Wednesday, and Saturday. The stage left Clarksville at 7:30 a.m. and Ellicott City at 4 p.m. An automobile, the Mitchell, was advertised at eleven hundred dollars for the four-cylinder model with thirty-five horsepower. The six cylinder, seven passenger model was two thousand dollars. Thomas Malony at Dayton sold cream harvesters, buggies, carriages, and runabouts. Ramsburg's Grove in Poplar Springs was the site of a summer tournament and basket picnic. The Simpsonville Roller Mills, operated by the Iglehart Brothers, sold White Dove flour. In Ellicott City, about 1910, Mr. Rody added bowling alleys to his town hall building and the large pin and duck pins proved very popular. The Howard Transport Company operated between Dayton and Ellicott City. It left Dayton at 7:30 p.m., stopped at Highland, Clarksville, Eliok, Columbia, and arrived at the Howard House by 9:00. The reversed evening trip left Ellicott City at 4:00 and arrived in Dayton by 6:00 p.m. It operated on Saturdays and Mondays.

World War I

As the United States entered World War I in 1917, Howard County participated in its own way. One of the biggest events announced in the press was when the old school on the hill, the Patapsco Female Institute, then called "Warwick," would become the Maryland Convalescent Hospital for Soldiers and Sailors. Mrs. Lilly Tyson Elliott loaned the use of her property, which was to be run by the Maryland Women's War Relief. However, this use never materialized.

June 9, 1917 registration for the service brought out 1,183 young men, ages twenty-one to thirty-one, 894 white and 290 "colored." Of this number 518 had dependents, 8 were disabled, 15 declared occupational exemptions leaving 514 eligible for service. The entire list of names was published in the newspaper.

A War Bazaar was planned for the Armory in Baltimore and a committee of six local women was set to take charge of local participation. This Women's Preparedness and Survey Committee included chairman Mrs. William S. Powell, Mrs. Charles Carroll of Homewood, Mrs. William H. Stinson, Mrs. Bladen Lowndes, and Miss Esther A. Brown. There was the solicitation of homemade goods such as preserves and pickles to provide money for relief in Europe.

A typhoid epidemic swept the community. By April of 1917 thirty cases were reported with three deaths. There was considerable discussion and criticism of the public water supply in Ellicott City involving the state health department. By July it was announced that considerable money, over ten thousand dollars, had been spent drilling new wells for the community and that water tested pure.

The big business was the selling of automobiles. The Green Cross Garage sold Chevrolet. The Ellicott City Garage sold the Ford and Studebaker. Burgesses sold the Buick and Dayton Motor Co. sold the Overland. The price range was from $550 to $1,385. Robert Taylor advertised his Ford from $374 to $659 and the Studebaker from $975 to $1,205. Melville Scott bought out the Green Cross Garage from Edward Warfield.

All was not business and war. There were times for entertainment. In the Spring the Chautauqua Lyceum Festival was held for three afternoons and evenings. You could buy a season ticket for $1.25. and hear speakers on educational subjects or see dramatics and magicians, or listen to music. During the summer the communities celebrated with "Dayton Day," "Guilford Day" and "Old Home Day at Ellicott's Mills."

In 1919 an influenza epidemic hit the county. Five children in one family near Guilford died within eleven days of contracting the dread disease. There was discussion of the need for a new high school in Ellicott City. The Hayden and Martin properties were discussed as choices. Nothing happened for another five years and when it did, neither of those sites was selected. Rally days were held by the primary schools at Forty Acres on New Cut Road. There was a big parade followed by athletic competition. 1919 was the first year that the "colored" schools held a rally day at Forty Acres.

Bonds were sold that year to pay off the Victory Loans from the War. They could be purchased at the Ellicott City Courthouse, Grace Parish Hall in Elkridge, St. James Church at Alpha, or Pindell's School at Fulton.

Summer spawned a variety of outdoor events each year. In 1919 the Dayton picnic was held at Brown's Grove, adjacent to the Oddfellow's Hall. A ten-cent charge to the grounds was made. Some of the activities included baseball, stock judging, tractor demonstrations, entertainment, speakers, refreshments, and dancing. The Clarksville picnic was August 6. That month was considered the picnic season, the farmer's vacation month. Guilford and Glenwood also held community picnics. Glenwood held a tractor show at Augustus Riggs' Grove near Cooksville.

The Howard County Grange picnic and basket dinner was held at Riggs' Grove, also including tilting, or jousting, contests. St. Paul's Church in Ellicott City held a lawn fete, supper, and dance at Rock Hill.

In 1924, Isaac Taylor built a new jewelry and music store on the south side of Main Street. His old building on the opposite side of the street was sold to Gendason, who operated Ellicott City's Best Store. The new Taylor store was built at the site of the old post office. Taylor Ridgely was manufacturing wholesome soft drinks under the name of "Budd's Thirst Quenchers." Pound parties were popular; each attendee would bring a pound of a type of refreshment.

E. T. Clark consolidated two of the oldest hardware/farm implement businesses, the one being Joshua Dorsey's and the other known as Talbot and Clark.

Mrs. R. C. Hammond lived at Burleigh Manor. She had to move from her home due to the horrible conditions of the roads, according to the newspaper. She complained that no priest or doctor could come to her assistance. The road was desperately in need of stones. Even her tenant was leaving because he couldn't sell his corn.

The extension service was busy working with the residents during these decades. Meetings were held to instruct citizens on the care of orchards and pruning of the trees. They met at Glenelg, Lisbon, and Pfeiffer's corners. A clean milk drive was promoted at Lisbon, Alpha and Glenelg to reduce the bacteria count by proper cooling of the milk.

Van Lear Black sold Folly Quarter in the Spring of 1924. That summer the fireman's carnival was held in the old depot yard in Ellicott City. It netted twenty-five hundred dollars. The McDonough School Band provided entertainment. In the costume contest, Mrs. G. Ray Helms won first prize as an Indian princess. The baby show had thirty-nine entries and Ruth Lorraine Thompson, daughter of Charles Thompson at Mt. View, won first place.

There were two new cider presses in the county in 1924, one at Ilchester Farms and the other at Hodge's on the Baltimore-Washington Boulevard and Camp Meade-Guilford Road.

It was announced in the local press that President Coolidge was to come through Ellicott City on September 6, 1924, en route to the unveiling of the Lafayette Statue in Baltimore. The President would come through Sandy Spring, Highland, Clarksville, and Ellicott City on his way to Charles Street, Baltimore.

C. Dorsey Hobbs, the treasurer and tax collector, gave notice of where he would be and the hours so people could pay their taxes. He spent fifteen to thirty minutes at locations throughout the county to accommodate the taxpayer.

In September of 1924, the Vineyard Road Pavilion was the site of an Old Time Tournament. The supper, movies, and dance benefited the Fifth District Public Health Auxiliary. In 1925, Prohibition agents seized a 700-gallon still near Elkridge. There were two thousand gallons of mash, sixty-five gallons of distillate, and twelve hundred pounds of sugar.

Patrons from the fifth and sixth districts came to the courthouse to oppose consolidation of their schools. Arlington Farm was sold by its owner, Dorsey Williams, for use as a golf course and polo field. This property became the Allview Golf Course, but the polo field did not materialize.

The Depression was felt in Howard County. There were many unemployed, and the 1930 drought created additional problems. The farmers were ailing from the effects of both. The state passed a law that extended the time to pay the taxes, which provided some assistance.

The newspapers reported the need for additional schools since the county spent so many of its dollars paying other jurisdictions for Howard County students who attended schools out of the county. The superintendent wrote long letters deploring the lack of schools, and the newspaper printed them on the front page.

The newspaper was packed with items that reveal that era's lifestyle. Four pages were devoted in 1931 to the new Easton Funeral Home. There were many pictures, advertisements, and stories about the business. Automobile accidents were serious and frequent. Caplan's spring sale in that year advertised spring dresses from $3.95 to $14.75. Hart, Schaffner and Marx suits were $27.50 and up, while special purchase men's wool suits were $17.50. The Horse show at Doughoregan Manor was an annual spring event, the chief social and outdoor event in the county. It benefited the Howard County Public Health Association. Also, in 1931, the Franciscan novitiate was dedicated and the Allview Golf Course was ready and opened. Elkridge residents, along with their neighbors at Hanover and Harwood, the fastest growing section of the county, approved a water loan. This was the first step to bring public water to that community.

Brendel's Manor Park on Maryland 144 near Folly Quarter Road opened under the new name and was one of the beauty spots in the county. At one special dance two orchestras were available for modern and square dancing at $1.25 a couple. The Park had a large hall, a fine ball field, picnic groves, excellent spring water, a dining room for two hundred, an auditorium with a stage, playground, and an outdoor swimming pool.

The Ellicott City Rotary promoted a clean-up campaign in the county seat. The tax rate was set at $1.63, producing a budget of $335,360.00. The schools received $118,000.00. Gas mains were coming to Ellicott City, the central stone abutment at the B & O viaduct on Main Street was removed, and Chevrolets were priced from $475.00 to $675.00

Howard Countians continued to be interested in agricultural topics. They supported the community athletic teams. They were interested in their politics and were very proud when state politicians spoke at county functions. In 1941 George Slack and Merritt Pumphrey, two 4-H members, were awarded a trip to the Chicago 4-H Congress. The county expressed a strong desire to keep Washington Boulevard as the main road to Washington, D.C., and opposed the state's suggestion that a new road through Anne Arundel County should be built to parallel U.S. 1. After December 7, 1941, the county's energies were consumed by the war effort. There were numerous defense activities. Some of these included the Women's Council of Defense, registration for the draft, active duty for the Guard, collection drives for newspapers, rubber and metal, Red Cross appeal for money, voluntary enlistments, first aid courses, victory book campaigns for the boys, dances to raise money for defense, the selling of defense bonds, the growing of victory gardens, and the commissioners adopting air raid rules and regulations and the regular air raid drills. One of the more unique efforts was the organization of the "Minute Women of Harwood," organized by Mrs. Augusta Kossman. They were trained to handle guns.

After the war, particularly in the late 1940s and into the 1950s, an entirely new way of life—suburbanization—crept into the county. New people found quiet, rural Howard County. First they came from Baltimore. Soon they were arriving from many places and the county would never again be the same.

WHERE FAIRVIEW BUTTER STARTS.

ARTHUR P. GORMAN

FIRST PRIZE MULE TEAM.

"BUCK" AND "BRIGHT THE LOAFER."

FAIRVIEW HOUSE.

ON THE WAY TO THE THRESHER.

VIEWS OF
FAIRVIEW FARM
for
MRS. ARTHUR P. GORMAN
Compliments of William S. Powell.

AN AVERAGE CORN CROP.

STARTING FOR THE MARKET.

When Arthur P. Gorman, Jr., ran for governor in 1911 this was just a little smaller than a full-page ad in the Ellicott City Times *praising Gorman's agricultural interests. Fairview is the name of the former Gorman home on Gorman road at Murray Hill Road. The candidate's grandfather, Peter Gorman, worked for the B & O Railroad and lived in Woodstock until he purchased a former Worthington homestead, three hundred yards west of Fairview. Arthur Pue Gorman, Sr., built the new large frame home after the Civil War. The original burned and was rebuilt and is still standing. Gorman, Sr., was an extremely influential Democrat, serving in the U.S. Senate as well as the Maryland Senate. The younger man lost the race for governor to a Republican, Phillip Goldsborough. Courtesy of Howard County Historical Society*

Benjamin Frederick Bassler selected a romantic setting on his farm to "pop the question" to Gertrude Kline. She must have answered yes because they were married in 1925 and raised eight children. Brother Frank Bassler came along with the family camera shortly after the important event and took a picture of the couple. Their farm stood on Cedar Lane where the college and hospital are now located. Benjamin Frederick was one of ten children of John Gustave Bassler and Dora Bassler who also lived on Cedar Lane. They were members of St. Paul's Luthern Church at Fulton. The immigrant member of the family was John Christian Bassler who was born in Germany, came to America and settled in the vicinity of Pfeiffer's Corner. During this period of time many German immigrants were coming to America, and Howard County became home to many of these families. St. Paul's Lutheran was a German Lutheran church and would hold some services in the native language. Many descendants of this

In the early 1900s friends gathered together in front of the Moxley family home, as seen in the rear. The adults, from the left, were Irvin Stirn, May Moxley, Lillian Stirn, Bertha Linthicum, Jane Moxley, and James Moxley, Sr. The two little boys were, left, Norman and Russell Moxley, with their sister Mildred snuggled with the adults. The family farm was named for the old land grant patent, Mt. Aetna. Later the family would use the name for a business, choosing a different spelling. The house stood near where the Normandy Bowling Lanes were constructed on U.S. 40. Courtesy of Mr. and Mrs. Norman Moxley

family have remained in the county. The family operates a small airfield, which originally was located on Cedar Lane, now on Shepherd's Lane. Courtesy of Elsie Mae and Ben Bassler

The Homemakers' clubs enjoyed the old house tours that were among the groups' special events. Here the ladies are seated in front of Elkhorn Farmhouse, which has not survived. The old Dorsey property stood across Oakland Mills Road, behind the former brick home of Oak Hall. The original house dated into the 1700s but it had been altered many times. After the developer of the new town acquired the property, it burned. Other homes that the group toured that year included Waverly, Troy, and Athol. Of those three homes, all are still standing, but only Athol is in private hands. Waverly is owned by Preservation Mary-

land and has been restored. Troy is owned by the county and is boarded up.

Cooperative Extension Service, Howard County Historical Society

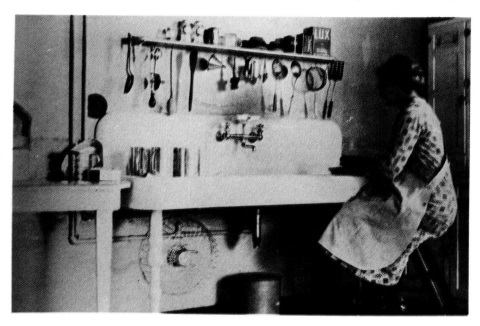

Through the homemakers' clubs, women learned how to better arrange their kitchens to eliminate waste of time and to lessen the number of steps in preparing meals. A contest was held from April 20 to August 20, 1928, in Howard County, with home management agents available to advise the housewives. This improved kitchen shows the "rest and beauty corner," which replaced the bare table with a water bucket that stood in the corner originally. Homemakers' programs were very popular and introduced many subjects and skills to the farm wives. Cooperative Extension Service, Howard County Historical Society

The interior of the Washington Trust Bank, Ellicott City, provided a sturdy, safe facility for the resources of the county residents in the early twentieth century. Carlton R. Sykes is the banker to the left and Louis Getz stands at the right. Commercial & Farmers Bank operates the bank at this location on Main Street today and the interior is considerably different. Courtesy of Frances Sykes Pielert

Billy Barton, an outstanding thorough-bred owned by Howard Bruce of Belmont, is shown jumping at Doughoregan Manor, the location of a horse show in October 1932. Although not identified, the rider may be Mr. Bruce. Billy Barton was an extraordinary thoroughbred and a great pride of the Bruces. In 1926 the horse won the Maryland Hunt Cup and in 1928 ran in the Grand National Steeplechase in England, which he narrowly lost. This champion was buried in full tack on the grounds at Belmont, Elkridge, with a headstone noting his resting place. John Shapiro, then owner of the Laurel Racetrack, engaged sculptor Henry Brenner to cast the likeness of Billy Barton in bronze. The life-size statue of the horse has stood outside the grandstand at Laurel since its unveiling in March 1952. The A. Aubrey Bodine Collection, The Peale Museum, Baltimore, Maryland

Those old narrow roads just were not sufficient, so the state worked to widen them. Work on the Frederick Pike included widening it by the construction of concrete shoulders. Forms were placed three to five inches above the edge of the macadam to reduce the crown of the road. Careful and proper preparation was given to the subgrade and to the concrete mix and the finish. This 1940 photo shows the manual labor. Enoch Pratt Free Library Collection, reproduced by permission

U.S. 1 has been described in stories through the years in less than flattering terms. In the 1920s and 1930s it was known as "Hot Dog Highway" for the colorful stands along it. Tourist cabin motels became popular. In 1937 the newspaper reported that there were seventy-two eating places from the Baltimore city line to the D.C. boundary and 106 trailer camps, cottage colonies, inns, and other tourist accommodations. The twenty-seven miles of the Boulevard had 1,053 billboards. By the early 1950s there were 5,000 billboards on the road from Bel Air to D.C. Souvenir shops, as shown here, are remembered. The county's sign law today would have certainly made some changes in those times. Library of Congress, Prints and Photographs Division

On July 4, 1918 or 1919, Leola Mae and James Franklin Knisley were photographed on an early motorcycle, sidecar and all. This was outside their home on Shirttail Alley in Savage. A cousin and his friend had ridden over from Camp Meade on the vehicle and the Knisleys tried it on for size. Apparently Leola Mae wasn't impressed with the sidecar. Their son Julian shot this picture, put away the old family camera, and ten years later got it out to find it still loaded with film. The only picture that came out on the roll when finally developed was this one. Having worked at the Savage Mill, Mr. Knisley later was a trolley conductor on a line that ran from Laurel into the District. Julian worked many years at the mill and later moved to Bowie. A grandson, Robert Knisley, lives on Waterloo Road. Courtesy of Mrs. Robert Mathews, Sr.

The Green Cross Garage was the early Chevrolet business in Ellicott City. It was owned in 1917 by Edward Warfield. Melville Scott joined as a partner. In 1918 they advertised that work would be done on a strictly cash business. Pictured in 1920 are, from the left, Charles Warfield, brother of the owner; Irene Warfield, their sister and the bookkeeper; Melville Scott, who later started an insurance business; Harry Shipley; Jake Bauman; Jim Ridgley; Sam Yates, Jr.; and Guy Peddicord. This building stands on Hamilton Street behind the post office. At one time the garage could be entered from the Columbia Pike. It is now painted red and is used as storage, but it probably served earlier as livery stables. The river flows under the building. Courtesy of Charles Scott

The Green Cross Garage was busy going over some of the vehicles brought in for service. There were no computers to test the vehicles or elaborate equipment in those early days of automobiles. The skills of the mechanics and their few hand tools were the essential requirements to keep the vehicles operating. In the rear a man is wearing a face mask and appears to be spray painting a fender. Maryland Historical Society

This power plant at Ilchester was purchased by Baltimore Gas and Electric Company in 1913 from the Patapsco Electric and Manufacturing Company. The company obtained about 10,000 KWH daily in 1914. The design of the original dam was unique according to the B G & E News. It was of hollow construction with the water wheels and generator housed within the dam. It was necessary for the new owners to rebuild many parts of the old dam. New head gates and sluice gates were added in 1914. The above picture shows the low water in August 1930 and an employee using a stream of water to clean away the mud. The Peale Museum, Baltimore, Maryland

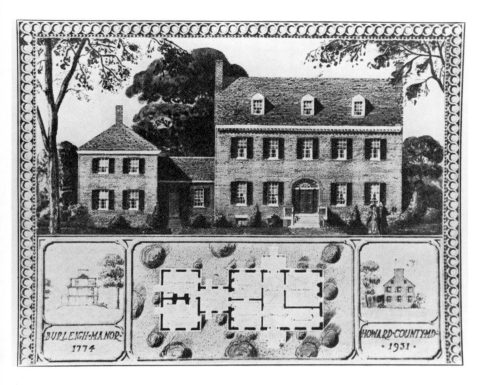

Burleigh Manor was built by Rezin Hammond about 1800, shortly before his death in 1809. Hammond was a bachelor and left the property to a nephew. The old Annapolis Road, which started at the Carrolls, passed by the Hammonds, leading some to observe that this view of the house was the front. It is approached from the opposite side today. There are indications that there may have been less than friendly relations between Carroll and Hammond, politically. The Hammonds were less "gentle" than the Carrolls during the period of the revolutionary war activities. This sketch of the house was made when Burleigh was on the market about 1930 for the price of $29,750, including 606 acres of land. There is a housing development by the same name and the old house is privately owned as a part of the community. Courtesy of Howard County Historical Society

Nearly two hundred members of the Howard County Council of Homemakers gathered for their annual meeting in October 1937 at Brendel's Park, with Mrs. Harvey Hill as president. "Japanese Beetle Control" and "Peace" were two topics that were discussed. The club met their goal of reading seven hundred books for the year and set one thousand as the goal for the following year. A highlight of the program was a talk on "Original Speaking." The Gavotte, an old-fashioned dance, was performed in costume by ten of the club members. Cooperative Extension Service, Howard County Historical Society

All eyes were focused on the entertainment at the Firemen's Carnival in 1934, which appears to have attracted the entire population of the county. These annual affairs helped to provide the funds for the volunteer fire department. The carnivals were held at various locations, the railroad depot yard, the grounds of the Ellicott City School, and the grounds of the new school on Montgomery Road. These fairs were held from 1924 through 1959, excluding the war years. Courtesy of B. Harrison Shipley, Jr.

Woodstock Quarries operated for many years, producing a high grade of granite. Mr. William J. Peach, Jr., was the manager in 1938 when this photo was made for Power Pictorial. Shown is the steam equipment, which was eventually abandoned for modern electric apparatus. The magazine reported that power costs decreased about 50 percent during several full months of operation after the change. It was no longer necessary to fire the steam boiler hours ahead to pump a little water from the quarry. Enoch Pratt Free Library collection, reproduced by permission

The land along the Patapsco River was purchased by the state and operated by the Department of Forestry for recreational uses. Picnicking, camping, swimming, and canoeing attracted many visitors to the park property. These two young men have pitched a tent and are enjoying camping near the Orange Grove area of the park in 1921. Enoch Pratt Free Library collection, reproduced by permission

Votta's was a family business in 1945 when John was busy repairing shoes, a craft he practiced for more than fifty years. Mrs. Votta, Ida, wraps a pair of finished shoes while their son helps from the rear, standing on a stool. The family lived above the store for many years after purchasing the business in the 1930s. Later John became active in county politics and served as sherriff. Courtesy of Mr. and Mrs. John Votta

U.S. 29 intersected with U.S. 40 in the center of Ellicott City during the 1930s, as evidenced by the route markers on the pole to the right. Standard Oil bought the large frame store, Steward's, and tore it down to erect an Esso station. Later the county bought the station to widen the road. Jimmy Brown's later became Paul's Market, continuing the operation of the market with fresh fruits and vegetables along the sidewalk. The large addition where the grocery was located was added in 1900 by the Eckerts, who owned and operated the Howard House, adjacent to the East. The Masons Lodge occupies the upper floors of the 1900 addition. Enoch Pratt Free Library collection, reproduced by permission

Benjamin Mellor, Jr., known as "Dr. Ben," was a prominent Ellicott City businessman. For many years he was a director of the Patapsco National Bank. His title came from his owning and operating the Patapsco Pharmacy. From 1935 to 1946 he was the clerk of the courts. Active in the Howard County Historical Society, he was generous to them and other non-profit organizations. The chair in which he is seated has found its way to the local historical society. Courtesy of Howard County Historical Society

Christmas Gardens are a Baltimore tradition. Setting up trains beneath the family's tree became very popular as villages grew with the train layout. Many model train hobbiests turned their basements into large gardens and invited family and friends to enjoy the creative efforts. Firehouses continued the custom and shared their gardens with the public. In 1933 the Ellicott City station created a Christmas garden, but the tradition did not continue. Looking closely, one can see the dirigible which joined the scene. Because of the Depression, the men had spare time to build the garden. Courtesy of B. Harrison Shipley, Jr.

179

The old millrace across the river from Ellicott City provided a park-like setting for the old Ellicott homes near the flour mill. To the rear are the concrete automobile bridge and the iron trolley bridge. A billboard advertising the Lord Baltimore filling station dominates the landscape. Angelo's Cottage is clearly visible on the hillside on the opposite side of the river. Everything in this scene is gone, except for the castle-like cottage. The millrace was filled in to enlarge the mill parking area, the trees are gone, the trolley bridge is gone, and a new concrete bridge has replaced this one. Courtesy of John Kirkwood

December 7, 1940, was the dedication of the Ellicott City post office on Main Street. Michael Sullivan was the postmaster then. The day's activities started with a turkey dinner served to 150 persons at the firehouse. Both the Rotary and Kiwanis clubs attended as groups. J. Walter Miller, accompanied by Eleanor Dries, entertained at the luncheon. The Dickey Band provided music at the dedication. Many elected officials attended the event. Frame buildings, including Hillsinger's Funeral Home, were torn down for the construction of the new post office. Courtesy of the News American

Glenelg was built as the country estate of Gen. and Mrs. J. Washington Tyson. When the Bladen Lowndes family put the house up for sale about 1940, it was draped with vines of ivy. Tyson built Glenelg in the early 1850s when he moved to Maryland from Philadelphia, where he served as the commissary general of the Army. He died within a decade and his wife remained with the property until she traded it for land in Camden, New Jersey. In 1954, the Glenelg County School opened. Recently a new high school has been added to the campus of this private institution. From the author's collection

William McKinley Matthews, Jr., served in the Navy during World War II. When he returned he settled at Waterloo, in the vicinity of Meadowridge Road. He was employed at the Department of Agriculture and the Department of the Interior. His daughter, Janice Collier, and son, Everett Matthews, are still Howard Countians. Courtesy of Janice Collier and the Howard County branch of the NAACP

German war prisioners helped to harvest the county's crops during the World War II years when manpower was scarce. This 1944 photo shows that the prisoners were brought from Fort Meade daily to Hardman's Tourist Home, Frederick Avenue and St. John's Lane, where the farmers would pick them up. Many of the prisoners could speak English. Arrangements were made by County Agent Warren G. Myers and John E. Yingling. The farmer paid the prevailing wage to the Howard County Farmers Cooperative and the money was turned over to the U.S. Treasury. The prisoners received eighty cents per day in credit or exchange coupons. They could either spend it or retain credit until the end of the war when it was converted into cash. Note that room and bath at the tourist home in 1944 was one dollar. Cooperative Extension Service, Howard County Historical Society

181

Young 4-H club members from the Florence community were proud of their victory garden in 1942. They may still be using their gardening skills learned in the club. One local Victory Corps that received national recognition in 1942 was from the Ellicott City High School. They were featured in school magazines, Student Life and Scholastic. Helen and Martha Thurman, John Werking, and Mason Swartz were pictured in the publications. Katherine Brown and Mary Ruth Mumford co-authored articles about the school's Victory Corps. Cooperative Extension Service, Howard County Historical Society

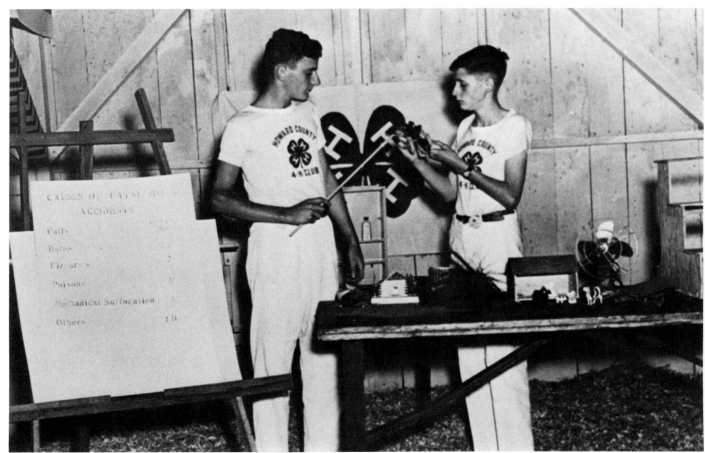

Nearly seventy years ago 4-H activities were started for Howard County young people. By 1926, eighty-five girls and seventy-seven boys belonged to 4-H school clubs. World War II saw an increase in 4-H activities and victory gardens and other peace related activities. In 1946 James Pfefferkorn and Reginald Arrington presented a home safety demonstration at the state fair, concerning causes of fatal homes accidents. Members of 4-H have opportunities to compete on local, state and national levels. Cooperative Extension Service, Howard County Historical Society

Jane Gaither of Clarksville, daughter of Mr. and Mrs. Alvin Gaither, won first prize in the National Ayrshire Essay Contest in 1941. Her subject was "Why My Dad Should Own Purebreds and Why They should be Ayrshires." She received a purebred bull and an all-expenses-paid trip to the National Dairy Show in Memphis. Jane is now Mrs. Hugh Hill of Clarksville. Cooperative Extension Service, Howard County Historical Society

William H. "Bud" Hill, Jr., shows his junior champion bull in 1946 at the Howard County Fair. The ruins of the St. Charles College in the rear place the site of the Fair as Brendel's Manor Park. This was the first annual Howard County Fair under the supervision of a fair committee. By 1953 the association purchased property at West Friendship where the annual event takes place each August. Cooperative Extension Service, Howard County Historical Society

Paving the Clarksville-Dayton road in 1947 was a major undertaking for the State Roads Commission. Dirt roads were common in the county. By this time, machinery was available. In the early days the road work was done by laborers. Later this would become Maryland 32, and is the Ten Oaks Road today. Enoch Pratt Free Library collection, reproduced by permission

Raymond Zeltman showed his grand champion trio of Hampshire barrows at the Baltimore Livestock Show in 1946. He remembers that they went to the Esskay Company and were put to good use. Mr. Zeltman grew up on Waterloo Road near Pfeiffers Corner. Later he moved to Mt. Airy and was in the dairy business for many years. Very recently he sold his cows under a federal buy-out program to reduce the quantity of milk production and is now crop farming. The county agricultural extension agent helped the young 4-Hers with their projects. Warren G. Myers served in that capacity, starting in 1937. Cooperative Extension Service, Howard County Historical Society

Four young men in the 4-H organization and a 4-H leader were awarded trips to the National 4-H Club Congress in Chicago in 1946. Shown from the left, are William "Buddy" Hill from Daisy who won for dairy production. Next, is Truman Kelley, who excelled in tractor care and maintenance. Beatrice Cissel Pfefferkorn started the Alpha club in 1926 and served many, many years as a leader in 4-H. Jacob K. Thompson, Jr., won the meat animal award. Joseph Thompson, Jr., of Fulton received the award for the most outstanding 4-H member. Cooperative Extension Service, Howard County Historical Society

Elwood Wallich and Bessie Gore grew up as neighbors near Cedar Lane and Owen Brown roads. It's not surprising that they married and that his brother Stanley married her sister Louise. Elwood and Bessie are pictured here in the 1940s outside their home at Oakland Mills, the former schoolhouse. Mr. Wallich's warm, outgoing personality was shared by his customers during the many years that he worked at Taylors in Ellicott City.
Courtesy of Mr. and Mrs. Elwood Wallich

Channing Dorsey of Daisy wore the garb of the Odd Fellows Order to which he belonged at Poplar Springs. Many black communities had such social and beneficial organizations. They joined together to provide insurance coverage for their members. Many of them had lodge buildings near the church in the community. One such building, the Joshua Hall in Glenwood, stood on the west side of Maryland 97 and burned in late 1986.
Courtesy of Alice ''Becky'' Thomas

Channing and Mary Dorsey relax on Easter Day in April 1944 in front of their home on Duvall Road. Mr. Dorsey built the log home for his family about 1902. Now covered with shingles and enlarged, the home is the residence of their daughter, Alice "Becky" Thomas. The Dorseys are buried in their family plot not far from the home along with Mr. Dorsey's parents, Hanson and Alice Dorsey. Alice Dorsey was a slave with the Crapster family and Hanson Dorsey was with the Edwin Warfield family. Their son Channing was named for an evange-list who traveled through the countryside and stopped for a visit with the Crapsters. The Reverend William T. Crapster directed the Lisbon Academy in the 1870s. "Becky" Thomas has preserved some of the family history. She moved back to help take care of her father many years ago. She was working as a young woman for the Hess family in Pikesville as the "upstairs" maid. Her chores

included working with the children and serving the meals. She met her husband while he was chauffeuring in Baltimore. Courtesy of Alice "Becky" Thomas

Young Robert H. Wehland was just beginning in the dairy business with his father George at their farm on Waterloo Road in 1949. His new eight-can milk cooler kept the milk from his Ayrshire herd fresh until pickup from the Mary-land Milk Cooperative. In addition to farming, George Wehland operated a feed and farm supply store, Southern States, along with a grocery at that farm location. A gas station is on the site today and the road is now Maryland 108. Robert moved to Carroll County to con-tinue his dairy farming. He and his twin sister, Helen, graduated from Ellicott City High School on Montgomery Road. Helen continued in the grocery business when she married Ken Tyler. They operated Tyler's store on Montgomery Road for forty years. The Peale, Museum, Baltimore, Maryland

The team waits patiently while S. Dallas Slack prepared the grain drill to sow wheat or barley and to lay fertilizer at the same time. This 1949 photo was taken at Slack's Corner, where the family's farm was located. A housing development grows nearby today. Methods and equipment for this task did not change much in nearly one hundred years as the farmer preferred the horse team to the tractor for ease of performing this task. Mr. Slack became a judge of the orphans' court and his son, George, was the county's register of wills for many years. The Peale Museum, Baltimore, Maryland

William F. Rex operated the ESSO station for about twenty years, starting in 1947 on Montgomery Road near the Columbia Pike. This was a typical filling station of that era. Later, the property was sold and has operated as Bill's Ranch Exxon after an entirely new facility was built. Courtesy of Mrs. Emma Lacey and Betty Gerwig

Wheatfields was the typical county farm in the 1950s when owned by the Widdups. It lies south of Montgomery Road (Maryland 103) between U.S. 29 and Maryland 104. It was originally the Clark family home. Today the surrounding fields are sprouting housing developments instead of wheat or corn. Brampton Hills is one community in the vicinity. These two thousand acres between Maryland 103 and Maryland 108 at one time belonged to Dr. Arthur Pue, Sr., who built himself a house about 1800. Later the Pue home belonged to Samuel Wethered who called it Santa Fe. Today the home is called Mont Joy by its owners. The Clarks bought a parcel from Dr. Pue's heirs in the 1850s and built their house, which still survives amidst the trees. The eastern border of the original Pue property was a road that once was Waterloo Road, later Maryland 175 and is today a short roadway numbered 104. Enoch Pratt Free Library collection, reproduced by permission

Russell Zepp is the third generation in his family to farm along Highland Road near Dayton. His grandfather bought the property in 1868. In 1936 when he bought the place from his father, he had electricity brought to the farm. Soon he had electric milking machines to help with the work load. In 1955 Mr. Zepp purchased a barn cleaner and is shown inspecting the new motor. The equipment would clean the manure from the floor of the barn daily and bring it out onto the conveyor and into the manure spreader. No longer a dairy farmer, he now raises beef cattle. As a boy he recalls driving the beef herd into Union Stockyard in Baltimore, right down Main Street of Ellicott City. The Peale Museum, Baltimore, Maryland

The fire department volunteers and the Rescue Squad provided an additional county service when this vehicle was purchased from the federal government in 1958 by Civil Defense and the Volunteer Fire Department, according to B. H. Shipley, Jr., fire department historian. The Civil Defense director was Herbert C. Brown, former superintendent of schools. These men Rescue Squad volunteers, Everett McIntyre; H. S. Cushing; E. T. Clark, Jr.; A. Parks Johnson; Harold Dean Cassidy; and James R. Baugher were associated with the Clark Hardware and Coal Yard, where the vehicle was first housed. The rescue work involved providing manpower and tools at the scene of auto accidents and other critical events. Photo by Jim Lally, courtesy of the News American

If you haven't seen The Goddess *on late-night TV, you should watch for the very next showing. It didn't take much in the mid 1950s to turn Main Street Ellicott City into the 1936 era for the filming of the Paddy Chevesky movie. It was one of the biggest events in the county seat over its 200-year history. Kim Stanley came to town and appeared in scenes with local citizens, including Mrs. Caleb Rogers and Lloyd Taylor. Courtesy of Howard County Historical Society*

Operated by the Harrison family, the Enchanted Forest amusement park on U.S. 40 has enchanted hundreds of thousands of youngsters and oldsters since its opening in 1955. A smiling Humpty Dumpty allows Miss Anne Bell, a Miss Maryland contestant, to adjust his beanie as the August 15 opening date approached, along with the threat of Hurricane Connie. Although the park opened as scheduled, the hurricane arrived before the opening date and destroyed thousands of dollars of nursery plantings, which had to be replaced. The amusement park was not greeted warmly by the county in its initial years. This provincial attitude was reflected in the local newspaper, which announced the opening of the park with a short inside story. Courtesy of the News American

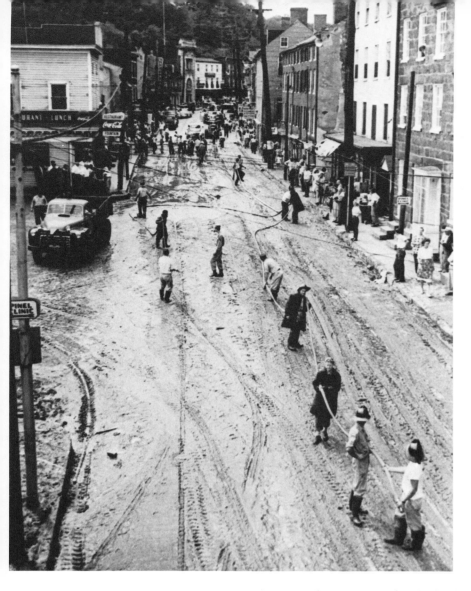

The Tiber River played tricks on the old town of Ellicott City in the mid 1950s when she came over her banks and deposited a layer of mud on Main Street. The result was reminiscent of the old country roads. Once again it was the fire department to the rescue as they manned the hoses and undertook the effort of cleaning up the mess. The sidewalk superintendents kept busy offering advice. Courtesy of B. Harrison Shipley, Jr.

For thirty-five years the Dorsey Speedway stood along Maryland 176 off U.S. 1 for those who enjoyed the sport of auto racing. Jack Coburn, Dawes Wolf, and Ken Whitaker cleared fifty-seven acres of abandoned farm land to build a racetrack in 1950. An abandoned still operation was part of the rubbish removed. One race was run on the first track. A second track and grandstand replaced it immediately and served until the 1960s. In 1957, Carl Meyer and John Mears formed Dorsey Speedway, Inc., when they purchased the property. Jack Coburn became general manager for a period of time and remained with the track operations until it closed in 1985.

The earliest officials at Dorsey Speedway were, from the left, Bruce Ehlers, Chick Little, Jack Coburn, and Carl Meyer. Courtesy of Jack Coburn

Normandy Bowling alleys broke ground for construction in 1960. This was just the beginning of many, many new projects that would alter rural Howard County. Politicians who attended in the front row were, from the left, Dan Murray, Arthur Pickett, James Clark, Charles Scott, and Frank Shipley. Others in the rear, second from left, Norman Moxley, Charles Scrivenor, Philip Thompson, Robert Moxley, Jean Moxley, Dessie and Jim Moxley, Evelyn Moxley, and Eldridge Moxley. Not long afterward, the construction would begin on the opposite side of the roadway for the Normandy Shopping Center. Courtesy of Jim Moxley

Chapter  9

New Ways, New People, New Town

Population growth in the county remained remarkably stable for decades, with a growth of fewer than 100 persons a year. But suddenly, the decade between 1940 and 1950 saw a 34 percent increase from 17,175 to 23,119.

This growth of new citizens to the county in the mid-century brought radical changes to Howard's status quo. As Robert Watson wrote in the "Columbia Forum," a section of the *Central Maryland News,* January 9, 1975, "These people were professionals, doctors, managers, lawyers, accountants, engineers. They were well educated and had good incomes...(they) intensely disliked any suggestions by the 'old timers' that they were not 'really Howard Countians' and scoffed at the attitude, which was exaggerated, that 'you have to live here ten generations before the 'original Howard Countians' recognize you'...Both old and new residents viewed high density development as an evil, but the newcomers were more intense about it than the old: ...I moved out here to get away from that."

A growing population brought other changes. In the 1950s the Enchanted Forest, a nursery rhyme park, opened on the new state highway, Route 40. A Welcome Wagon arrived to greet newcomers and introduce them to the businesses of the county. The county police force grew in 1958 to ten members. The police (yes, the police) also enforced the building code and assisted the zoning commissioner with building inspections. The Second District was the fastest growing area with Savage and Elkridge close behind. Kindercraft was formed at Clarksville by Mrs. David Reeder. In time she would spearhead the drive for public kindergartens and later serve on the Board of Education. The county purchased its first ambulance from the Higinbothom Funeral Home. It had a two-way radio, warning signals and lights and emergency equipment. The price of twenty-five hundred dollars included insurance and gas and oil for one year. The county took donations to pay for it.

These new citizens helped to implement improvements in the county. For a long time there was a need for a new public library. One had existed and was located in various places, including a church basement, Main Street store, and the locker plant at St. John's Lane. Finally the new central library opened in the early 1960s on land donated by Charles Miller. Today that is the enlarged and renovated Miller branch of the Howard County library system. Two new shopping centers, the Golden Triangle and Normandy, opened on U.S. 40 about the same time. Businesses started to move off Main Street, Ellicott City and the impact was felt by the local merchants in the old town.

The YMCA arrived in the community in the early 1960s. They promoted a variety of activities for both the youth and the adults. One of the organizations that the Y sponsored was the Tom Thumb Square Dance Club, which remains active within the county but no longer carries an affiliation with the Y. The League of Women Voters was formed and plays an ongoing role in the county. Later the American Association of University Women founded a chapter offering additional opportunity for community participation to the professional women in the county.

The *Central Maryland News* came into circulation and operated for more than twenty years as a newspaper espousing the Republican philosophy. Charter government was proposed and debated in the early 1960s before approval in 1966. The Howard County Citizens Association was formed with representatives from the many new housing developments and played an active role in shaping the early growth through the 1950s, 1960s and into the 1970s.

The Parent-Teacher Associations developed and provided another vehicle for community participation. Parents became very involved in the activities and programs of the county schools, volunteering many hours of service to the schools. New businesses were welcomed. Westvaco brought their research facility to the county, joining Johns Hopkins and W. R. Grace as new laboratories for research.

The Town and Country Apartments were first started on Rogers Avenue, near Normandy Shopping Center. And a new branch of the post office was opened at the Normandy Shopping Center, being relocated in 1986 to its own facility on Ridge Road.

Thus when the proposal of a new town came before the county commissioners, Howard was already a county experiencing change.

Columbia

Some say it's the best thing that ever happened to Howard County. A few still don't want to mention the word. Most everyone admits that it was inevitable. Development and growth would come to this prime land attractively located between Washington, D.C., and Baltimore, Maryland. It was a matter of how and when. When James Rouse chose the location for his new town of Columbia, it was with much planning and deliberation. The acquisition of the land was a complicated sequence of purchases that appeared unrelated but were generally kept within their goal of $1,500 to $2,000 per acre. Three large property owners who were called "The Three Bears," Isodore Gudelsky, Henry Seiling and partners George and Irving Dasher, provided an important key to the purchase puzzle. In time their land and many other farms were combined into the fourteen thousand plus acres that would become the new town of Columbia, Maryland. Although called a "town," Columbia, like all other communities in Howard County, is not incorporated.

The projected population for the new town has been 110,000. This was to have a tremendous impact on a county population of 36,000 in 1960. Fortunately, according to Thomas G. Harris, Jr., long-time planning director for the county, Howard County had adopted a general plan in 1960. A first in the Baltimore region, the plan was based on the comprehensive plan for sewer and water. It included renewal for the areas of highway and public transportation; parks, recreation and agriculture; commercial; industrial; and residential. Subdivision regulations and a zoning map and regulations were revised to go with the plan.

When the new town proposal was brought to the county officials, it created great interest. The imaginative development team of the potential builders of the new town spent over a year meeting, talking, presenting, and selling their ideas to the people of the county.

The announcement of the proposed plan came in October 1963 and approval was granted in August 1965. By 1967, the first residents of Columbia, Maryland moved into their homes.

Today (1987) the new town of Columbia is twenty years old and half-complete. Its history is a story in itself and when it observes its silver anniversary shortly, I feel certain that the new town's history will be well presented. There are too many important happenings to try to recall them all. There is no reason for us to criticize or justify the development of Columbia in Howard County, Maryland. These comments have been going on for more than twenty years. An obvious conclusion is that planned growth is far superior to unplanned growth. In a county as small as Howard, the land is even more precious.

An example of taking a hard look at the new town was the appointment of the Columbia Commission in 1970. The commission was charged by the county council to look at the issues raised by the growth of the new town. These matters included the new town regulations, roadways, public utilities, open space, tax revenues, and educational facilities. They presented a detailed report with suggestions.

By 1972, in just five years of growth, twenty-one thousand people lived in Columbia. That's more than the county's population had grown to in all its years before 1940, when the population stood slightly over seventeen thousand.

The Columbia Medical Plan, then operated by Johns

Hopkins Hospital, was a pioneer proposition that led to the opening of the county's first hospital. The Columbia Combined Ministry brought all religious faiths together to develop a new type facility for worship, called inter-faith centers. A major shopping center, the Columbia Mall opened in 1971 and the absence of shoppers was obvious until the population expanded. One of the greatest changes that affected families with school children was the new concept in education that had developed in connection with the new town. Open space schools in which students work in large, communal settings, were built in the county. The debate on that innovation in education continues.

Villages are the center of the community in the new town. Within the villages are neighborhoods. The first villages to open were Wilde Lake, Harpers Choice, and Oakland Mills. Each village was to have its own schools, community center, and shops. The tenth and final village is in the planning and will be developed near Clarksville along Maryland 32, south of Maryland 108.

A community college was planned early and opened in the 1970s. Newspapers were plentiful in the early days of Columbia. They came and went over the years. Finally, the *Columbia Flier* survived to be the sole distributor of totally local news. It even bought out the *Howard County Times* and combined it into one newspaper staff.

Organizations are numerous in Columbia. There is a chapter of nearly every kind of club or civic group. There is opportunity to participate in all spheres of interest. There are village boards that govern activities within the village and are represented on larger governing boards. The boards have provided stepping stones into county and state politics.

A general decline in the economy during 1974 and 1975 slowed down the growth of the new town. After a financial restructuring, Columbia got a second wind and continues to grow toward its ultimate size. The final completion date is projected into the 1990s.

Fortunately the history of one's county does not end. Howard is now experiencing those events that will soon be recorded as the final years of the twentieth century. For more than three hundred years, people have lived in upper Anne Arundel County, now Howard County. The Indians roamed here centuries before that. There are old family names associated with the earliest days, Shipley, Dorsey, Warfield, Worthington, Ridgely, and Owings, to name a few. But there were newcomers too through the centuries who worked hard to succeed in these fine farmlands. The struggles of the late twentieth century may be different from those of the seventeenth century, but the future of the county is based on the abilities, the character, the diligence, and the caring, of those women, men, and children who call this county home. Holding onto and preserving the history of our past three centuries will provide a firm basis for those who will come in the centuries ahead. We anticipate an exciting future for our great county and are grateful for the contributions of all its past citizens.

Ellicott City's second fire station became the police station on Main Street. In 1963 there was a personnel dispute between the police chief and a long-time police officer. Pickets arrived at the station to express their support for the officer. This building is near Talbott's Lumber Yard. Courtesy of the News American

The Seventeenth Annual Voice of Democracy contest was held December 20, 1963, at the VFW hall. The winner was Jacquelin Linda O'Neill, a senior at Howard High School. This was the first time that a Howard County school participated. From the left are Frank Lupanshunski, Howard High faculty, Omar Jones, principal; Miss O'Neill; Charles Kreatchman, VFW; and Senator James Clark. Courtesy of the Central Maryland News

A new addition to the county courthouse received its finishing touch from the Board of County Commissioners in 1962. Charles M. Scott, Norman E. Moxley, and Arthur K. Pickett participate. At this time a new access road was built that came from Rogers Avenue and led to the back of the property. The new parking lot was also constructed. The cost of the entire project, building addition, access road and parking lot was $450,000. The courthouse is presently undergoing a nine-million-dollar renovation. Courtesy of the News American

Jean Hannon, left, was the central committee chairman of the "Paint Ellicott City Campaign" in 1961. She discussed plans for the old mill town with Eugene Wheeler, director of the Howard County Planning Commission. In the background, Virginia "Ginger" Clark, a co-chairman of the event, practiced for the event on the building between the railroad tracks and the river. This recently-restored building had many uses as the Bridge Market, Radcliff's Hardware and Coal Yard, the Church of God, Clark's, and Appalachian Outfitters, before the 1972 flood. Photo by Fred G. Kraft, Jr., courtesy of the News American

Elkridge National Bank broke ground for the new $250,000 building in August 1964, with Charles E. Wilford, Jr., president, at the controls. Looking on were Charles E. Miller, chairman of the Howard County Commissioners and Walter A. Henley, director of industrial relations for the county. The colonial style brick building is located at Montgomery Road and U.S. 1. The Central Maryland News *reported that the bank's assets had increased by 800 percent over the past two and a half years, necessitating larger facilities. Courtesy of the* Central Maryland News

Glen Fulmer, left, helped collect signatures to place on the November 1964 ballot the opportunity for Howard County citizens to vote for or against drafting a charter to change the form of government from county commission to county executive and council. They needed only 828 signatures, 5 percent of the registered voters. Three of the nominees for the Charter Board, a five-member committee to draft a charter should the question pass were Seymour Barondes, Anita Iribe, and Charles Wehland. The question was opposed by the county Democrats for that year and was defeated. In 1966 the question passed. Courtesy of the Central Maryland News

A 1966 celebration in Savage took place on the Bollman Bridge and marked the acceptance of the bridge by the county commissioners. A landmark plaque was presented by E. L. Durkee of the American Society of Civil Engineers who noted that Bollman had built bridges in Mexico, Cuba, and Chile. He also stated that the series of spans at Harper's Ferry was one of Bollman's most notable achievements. At the event were two of Bollman's great-granddaughters, Miss Hilda K. Bollman, foreground and Mrs. Katherine Eggleston (barely visible). A great-grandson of John Savage, for whom the town was named, Hugh Murray Savage, of Scarsdale, New York, right rear, attended. Others included Dr. Frank Shipley and Judge Frederick W. Brune, president of the Maryland Historical Society, in the front row. Charles Miller, Howard Crist, and Senator James Clark are also visible. Photo by William Clayton, the News Leader, Laurel, courtesy of the Smithsonian Institution

The purchase of these 1,039 acres of land marked the first sale of property that would become the new town of Columbia. Situated along Cedar Lane, Robert A. Moxley had assembled the parcel of land for a client who turned it down. James Rouse, Howard Research and Development, a client of Dukehart realty, paid just under six hundred dollars per acre for this first parcel after contacting Moxley and expressing an interest. The assembling of the many parcels of land involved the formation of six corporations to help conceal the long-range plan in order to keep down the purchase prices and make the project financially possible. Courtesy of Jim Moxley

Four persons key to the opening of the new town of Columbia were, from the left, developer James Rouse and Commissioners Hubert Black, Charles Miller, and David Force. They are discussing the model of Columbia, which was the first display available to county residents and prospective owners at the first exhibit building east of U.S. 29 near Allview Estates. Courtesy of the Rouse Company, from the author's collection

The groundbreaking for Hittman Corporation, Columbia's first industry, was an important occasion in May 1967. In attendance, second from left, were Congressman Charles "Mac" Mathias, developer James Rouse, Fred Hittman, president of the company, County Commissioner Harry Murphy, and Governor Spiro T. Agnew. Hittman is still in operation in the Oakland Ridge Industrial Center off Maryland 108. Office of Public Information, Howard County

The opening of the Merriweather Post Pavilion in Columbia came on July 14, 1967. Among the dignitaries attending the gala festivities were the vice president president of the United States, Hubert Humphrey, Mrs. Marjorie Merriweather Post, flanked on the left by developer James Rouse and the right by Howard Mitchell, director of the National Symphony. Featured along with the National Symphony at the Pavilion's first concert was pianist Van Cliburn. The Pavilion was built with an acoustical shell designed by Christopher Joffe, one of the foremost sound consultants in the country. The outdoor facility is the site of summer performances of popular groups and individuals. In the early days, the National Symphony and the Baltimore Symphony performed regularly at the Pavilion. Courtesy of the Rouse Company, from the author's collection

Jim Roberts, from the Ellicott City station, delivered mail to early Columbia residents. These mail boxes are grouped where the residents receive their daily delivery, providing a more pleasingly aesthetic appearance than individual posts and boxes. Photo by Jim Lally, courtesy of the News American

Faculty sponsor, Miss Leah Mather, introduced the student council officers at the Ellicott City Elementary School in November 1967. They are, from the left, Joel Nupp, vice president; John Slack, second vice-president; Kathy Teal, recording secretary; Norma Foster, president; Sharon Harrison, corresponding secretary; and Jeffery White, treasurer. One goal of the council was to promote good citizenship. Principal of the school was Charles Eckes. Miss Mather is now Mrs. Leah Farmer, principal at Thunder Hill Elementary School. Ellicott City Elementary School is closed. Courtesy of the News American

200

When Richard Kinlein was sworn in as Howard County's state's attorney in 1966, he received a certificate from the circuit court judges, left, T. Hunt Mayfield and James Macgill. Judge Macgill served as the only judge until county growth necessitated an additional appointment. Judge Macgill bears the same name as his ancestor, the Reverend James Macgill who arrived to serve Christ Episcopal Church on Oakland Mills Road in the 1730s. Office of Public Information, Howard County

Columbia's first post office was located in a stone house near Wilde Lake. Raising the flag at that location were, from the left, Senator James Clark, Willard Rouse, Commissioner Charles Miller, John Shallcross, and John Slayton. Courtesy of the Rouse Company, from the author's collection

County Street ran from Main Street and connected with Fells Lane. In time the entire street was called Fells Lane. Homes were built through the area before the Civil War. In time the Sewing Room, a building that held a small industry of manufacturing clothes, was operating on the street. Gradually, the houses deteriorated and were considered unsafe. The county bought them, relocated the residents to Hilltop and demolished the old houses. Today the area is the parking lot behind the fire station. The first house on the left was said to have been the location of the first jail in the 1840s. There were bars on the basement windows and the conditions of this first jail were so inhuman that a new stone building was built behind the new courthouse in 1851, later joined to the 1878 jail and still in use by the county. Courtesy of the News American

Dust settled along the former Fells Lane in 1970 when the homes were demolished, the area leveled and later paved to become a parking lot to the rear of the fire station on Main Street Ellicott City. In later years, the housing had deteriorated and was owned by the county. These families moved into new Hilltop housing. Discussions were held for years about replacing the housing before a fire in February 1965 took the lives of five persons living in the sub-standard buildings. Although the lower part of Fells Lane was demolished, many older homes remain on the upper end of the road, including the brick home of Ezra Fells, one of the last Quakers who lived in Ellicott Mills. Courtesy of the News American

Residents displaced by the demolition of the houses on Fells Lane moved into Hilltop housing in 1970. Raymond Jones, left, plays with his half-brother Quentin Jackson near their new home. Ellicott Mills Drive was opened as a new roadway to access Hilltop. The county prides itself on building the housing totally with county funds. Photo by James Kelmartin, courtesy of the News American

The Howard Vocational-Technical Center opened September 1968 with programs to educate and train the county youth for employment. Dorothy Luyster and Brenda Sirk, in that opening year, learned the fine art of hair styling, including the popular "teasing." Other skills the center teaches include food service, horticulture, automotive repairs, data processing, printing, and building maintenance. *Courtesy of the* News American

Mini-skirted Carol Blankenship, left, and Grace Huster joined a paint campaign in 1969 to continue a face-lift for the county seat. Their shop the Wig-wam, was located west of Caplan's Department Store. There have been many tenants since that time. A fire in the late 1970s damaged the rear of the building considerably, but it remains as a Main Street store. Photo by James Kelmartin, courtesy of the New American

The first county council elected to a four-year term was sworn in December 1970 in the council chambers. They met on the lowest level of the courthouse. At the left, C. Merritt Pumphrey, clerk of the court, swears in Edward L. Cochran, James M. Holway, William S. Hanna, Ridgley Jones, and Charles E. Miller. Later Cochran became the second county executive. Photo by John Stadler, courtesy of the News American

In June 1967 the Board of Commissioners cited the best performing squad in the police department, led by Corporal W. A. Boone. They are, from the left, K. F. Beezley, H. R. Ferguson, T. E. McConnell, M. A. Chiuchiolo, E. E. Geisler, R. N. Neubauer, and Boone. At this time the uniform was dark blue, with boots and helmets. At the same time, Officer Goldman was cited for highest scores in physical fitness and George Davis for scholastic achievement. The group is shown on the steps of the police station when it was located on Fells Lane in the former black elementary school. Courtesy of the News American

Recognizing "Indian Guide Week" is County Executive Omar Jones, seated; YMCA Director John Turner, center; and Chief Ken Koppenhoefer, and his son Kyle or "Little Hawkeye." They were members of the Indian Guide program in the early 1970s. A popular Y program of fathers and sons, the Indian Guides were joined by a program of Indian princesses for fathers and daughters. Turner was the second Y director for Howard County. From the author's collection

The Howard County YMCA proudly purchased property on Montgomery Road in 1963. Prior to this move, activities were directed from offices in Ellicott City and on U.S. 40 Although this frame house has been demolished, it provided offices and an acitvity center before the larger facility was built to the rear of the house. A small outdoor pool augmented the services provided at the house. David Bergman was the first full-time director of the Y. Jean Holmes, editor of the Times, was the first chairperson of the Y Board, according to Burt Mobley, long-time supporter of the local branch of the YMCA. Courtesy of the News American

All Maryland lakes are man-made. Columbia's are no exception. Wilde Lake was born from a meadow and this dam construction was essential. The bulldozers moved the dirt required for the formation of a lake. In the distance is the Wilde Lake barn, which was later restored and designated a Historic Landmark of Agricultural engineering. The barn was noted for the trench silos, which the Oakland estate owner Francis Mooris developed in 1876. The silos preserved silage, which was made by trampling the cut corn stalks and covering the trench with boards covered with straw and tightly packed clay. The lakes provide active and passive recreational pursuits. Columbia's first birthday celebration was held lakeside near the barn. Courtesy of the Rouse Company, from the author's collection

A bubble building was constructed by Antioch College and was inspected by student Phil Hawkey. This was a smaller model of a larger experimental structure, which was a part of the environmental studies where students learned by participating. The experiment was to determine the feasibility of using such a structure for offices and classrooms. This pilot was found to have serious problems, according to Morris Keeton, former vice president and provost of Antioch College in Yellow Springs, Ohio. Stephen Plumber was the dean of the Washington-Baltimore campus of the college. According to Mr. Keeton, structures using this concept are now in use in the United States. Photo by Vernon Price, courtesy of the News American

As the new town of Columbia started to grow, the main road, U.S. 29, also grew from a two-lane to a four-lane highway. This early downtown view shows Lake Kittamaquandi with the American Cities building standing in view. The location for the mall had been cleared but was not yet under construction. Courtesy of the Rouse Company, from the author's collection

Large crowds attend the popular groups who perform at the Merriweather Post Pavilion. At a 1970 performance of The Who, twenty thousand teens flocked to the show. Local police officers as well as pavilion security guards helped to keep order on such occasions. The National Symphony and the Baltimore Symphony were performers at the Pavilion in the early years. Photo by Gordon E. D. Snyder, Courtesy of the News American

Backstage at the 1972 American Association of University Women's Historic Fashion show are, from the left, Mary Agnes Lewis, co-chairperson; Becky Turner; Betty Balthis; and Ann Elsasser waiting to model their gowns. The show brought together outfits worn over the centuries by local women, including riding clothes, mourning pieces, garden dresses, bridal gowns, undergarments, and young girl's clothes. From the author's collection

Yogi, the popular mascot during the 1970s at the Ellicott City Main Street Fire Station, posed with Dave Tumblin in 1972. Yogi was so well-loved in the community that when he received a broken leg, after being hit by an automobile, his many admirers showered him with letters and gifts. Mr. Tumblin was a volunteer when the picture was made but soon after became a career firefighter with the county. *Photo by Vernon Price, courtesy of the* News American

"Freshets" were a common occurrence throughout the centuries along the Patapsco River. However, Hurricane Agnes in 1972 produced nearly record flooding at the Thomas Viaduct in Elkridge. This repeated flooding has carried away history and greatly altered the river's environs. During normal times, the Patapsco is barely visible at this location. The Liberty Dam has reduced the flow of the river in the valley between Howard and its bordering counties. Some of these changes included the disappearance of the swimming holes and the attraction of fishing. From the author's collection

A drug store without a druggist, Eddie's had a soda fountain and a cozy atmosphere. It was built as a part of the Ellicott Theater when that new building was constructed around 1940. Townspeople in Ellicott City knew it was not unusual to find Judge Macgill having lunch at Eddie's. The store closed in the early 1970s—one of the last small town stores operating in Ellicott City. Today a beauty shop greets clients at this location. Courtesy of the News American

Marriott's Great America theme park touched off months of controversy when the corporation filed a petition for entertainment center zoning on a parcel of land encompassed by Maryland 32, I-95, and Broken Land Parkway. This proposed sketch shows the components of the park. When discussions ended and the zoning board voted, the change was refused and the idea of a theme park slipped into the past. Courtesy of the News American

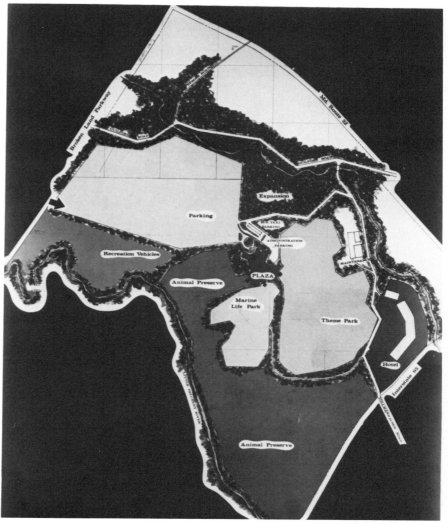

Kim Walker, center, and Kevin Smith receive assistance from Mrs. Thelma Wooley, an instructor at the creative writing center of the Waterloo Elemen-

tary School in 1971. Mrs. Wooley is still a classroom teacher at the Waterloo school, helping youngsters to better express themselves in creative ways. The

school has since been renovated and enlarged to meet the demands of the growing community. Photo by Gene Boyars, courtesy of the News American

Joining into the 1976 Bicentennial spirit were members of the Mt. Hebron Presbyterian Church. They presented a reader's theater production of the development of the Presbyterian church in America, authored by H. Jones Baker III. Baker was then a recent graduate of Catholic University with an MFA in playwriting and he continues his interest in that dramatic medium. The readers, from the front left, are Sandy Koukola, Jean Williams, Helen Carey, Patricia Baughman, and Laura Carey. In the second row are Tony Koukola, Howard Baughman, Richard Anderson, Richard Hemphill, and Charles Oakes. The Baker family farmed the Mt. Hebron Church property for nearly fifty years and are the developers of the homes in that area. From the author's collection

For three generations the Stirns farmed on Maryland 99 (Old Frederick Road) near Rogers Avenue. In 1972, it was Donald Stirn's farm and his son-in-law Richard Boswell was raking the hay to feed the livestock over the winter. In addition to farming the land, the Boswells operated school buses. The Stirns have sold the farm, but it is still being worked actively. The Boswells live down the road and are no longer in the farming business. Photo by Vernon Price, courtesy of the News American

Marlene Harris, Dennis Margrown, and Therese Colder raised a fifteen-star flag on March 5, 1973, at the Ellicott City Middle School on Montgomery Road. The flag was presented to the school by members of the Yingling-Ridgely VFW Post No. 7472. This school served as the Ellicott City High School, starting in the late 1930s and was enlarged. Currently it is the Waterloo Middle School. Photo by John Stadler, courtesy of the News American

Elk Ridge Farm was the name that Booker Clark used for his property outside Ellicott City, along Montgomery Road. Local residents remember with amazement that such an elaborate home could be built during the days of the Depression. Later it operated as Schaeffer's Convalescent Home. It is no longer standing, and a residential and retail development will be builit at this location. From the author's collection

County Executive Omar J. Jones cut the ribbon to open the Bicentennial Headquarters in Ellicott City, August 29, 1972, to celebrate the founding of Ellicott Mills. Also present from the left were Sherwood Balderson, president of the celebration; Monica Rothe, headquarters chairperson; and Pete Ruff and Bert Anderson, co-chairmen of the celebration.

Bicentennial activities were held in the fall with parades, parties, luncheons, walking tours, contests, etc., to observe the occasion. A highlight was the comeback that the town made to hold such a celebration. In June that year Hurricane Agnes sent the rivers on a rampage that wrecked bridges, buildings, and businesses, but not the morale of the celebration planners. A renaissance initiated in the 1960s continued transforming the old town into a quaint village. Courtesy of the News American

There is a fascination for the Patapsco River and the stories that it could tell. This 1972 picture shows the new concrete bridge that replaced the sixty-year-old bridge, which Hurricane Agnes destroyed. You can barely see the granite supports for the old trolley bridge. The stone building tucked beside the railroad tracks stood abandoned for over a dozen years after the flood before it was restored by local attorney Robert Brown. The frame sheds to the rear were torn down by the county to create a much needed parking lot. The dam was gone. It's difficult to imagine the factory buildings called the Granite Company. They stood on the east side of the river before 1868. Remains of the old concrete bridge sank into the river bed to continue to remind passersby of what was there in the past. Courtesy of the News American

U.S. 1 has brought many surprises through the years. It was enough to turn many heads when cement-hulled boats were built along the highway in the 1970s. The white frame house was a stark contrast to the unusual business located so far from a body of water. None of this scene remains, further proving that the old boulevard is constantly changing. From the author's collection

213

Outdoor pumps and privies were still being used into the 1970s in Ellicott City. Although public utilities were available by then, not all properties were supplied with these modern conveniences. Michael Wright of New Cut Road draws the family's water, a task that became extremely unpleasant when winter arrived. Photo by Vernon Price, courtesy of the News American

Tyler's store on Maryland 108 near Worthington opened in 1946 and closed in 1984 to make room for a new development. After nearly forty years of operation it was difficult for Kenny Tyler and his wife Helen to close. Before the Tylers opened their store, a bar had operated once at this location. Tyler's was a convenience store before the large chains appeared throughout the community. Helen was not a stranger to the store business since her father had operated one on Waterloo Road, now Maryland 108. Ken Tyler and Helen Wehland had graduated from Ellicott City High School. In 1971 their customers helped them celebrate their twenty-fifth anniversary at the store, showering them with flowers and other tributes recognizing their importance to the community. At the time of closing, they were serving the third generation of some early customers. Courtesy of Kenny and Helen Tyler

The River Hill Game Preserve sits off Guilford Road awaiting the inevitable development of Columbia's final village. An old house, which belonged in the Owings family, still stands, reflected in the pond. This Owings family gave its name to the Owingsville that later became Simpsonville and is marked now by a few ruins at Cedar Lane and Guilford Road. Photo by Vernon Price, courtesy of the News American

Oakland may be the most impressive historic site in the new town of Columbia. This south view of the rear of the building shows the large porch that was removed when the Ryans owned the property prior to 1940. According to Mike Trostel, historic architect, the building was constructed in 1820 by Charles Sterrett. He added Ridgely to his name to enable him to inherit his uncle's estate. Enoch Pratt Free Library collection, reproduced by permission

Owen Brown was one of the many ordinary people who were born, raised, worked and died in their home county. He lived in this house on a road that bears his name. His family believes that he would be surprised to learn that a village in a new town was named for him. At one time Owen Brown operated the store and was the postmaster at Elioak, a community on the Clarksville Pike (Maryland 108) at Manor Lane. Although it's easy to identify and remember the wealthy and socially and politically prominent people in history, it's also important to recall that a majority of the people were more ordinary and did not achieve any degree of fame. From the author's collection

The Children's Zoo was a popular stop for the young ones in Columbia's early years. Mary Lonas, assistant manager at the zoo, playfully scratches one of her charges, a lion club, in the fall of 1976. The animals were supplied from the Catcotin Zoo. Now closed, the Children's Zoo was located off the Little Patuxent Parkway, near the Pavilion. Courtesy of the News American

A notable event occurred in 1984 when this log cabin was moved, intact, from Gorman Road to the Rockburn Branch park. A two-part two-story cabin, which appears to have been built in the nineteenth century, it was donated by the Newburn Development Company and the county government helped to fund and arrange the move. It will be restored and used on county property known as Clover Hill and on a part of the Rockburn Branch park. From the author's collection

As recently as November 1984, the cry of "fire!" brought terror to Ellicott City, her residents, businesspeople, and friends. Five of the town's most successsful businesses were burned out that night. Leidigs' Bakery, Chez Fernand, The Old Clock Shop, Marino's Art Shop and Gallery, and the Iron Rail all were destroyed. Once again the businesses struggled back and new, fire-proof buildings with appropriate historic facades now fill the voids. Courtesy of the News American

217

It was a time for great celebration when the bike-footpath bridge over U.S. 29 finally opened in 1984. A large crowd came to cut the ribbon and release the balloons. This connection joined East Columbia and West Columbia through the path system. In the front of the picture from the left are Pam Mack, Columbia Association; Ruth Keeton, Howard County councilmember; Edward Jeffrey; J. Hugh Nichols, county executive; and Alvin Thompson, chairman of Recreation and Parks Board. Office of Public Information, Howard County

Another significant Columbia groundbreaking was the turning of the shovels at Beaverkill Road in Harper's Choice for the Florence Bain Senior Center. Councilmember Elizabeth Bobo, senior activist Florence Bain, and county executive J. Hugh Nichols wielded the traditional shovels at the ceremony. The senior center opened in 1983. Office of Public Information, Howard County

It was an election year in August 1982 when Governor Harry Hughes visited the county's waste water treatment plant at Savage. Three county employees, Bob DePaola, Gary Stonesifer, and Jim Roberts were there to shake his hand. The governor won re-election. Office of Public Information, Howard County

It was no accident when Amoss' tavern burned in the fall of 1986. The property had stood empty for some time and a developer was ready to begin work on his land. The fire department made plans to come in and use it as a practice drill. The tavern became famous for the fact that it had remained segregated and served the different races in two separate rooms of the tiny structure. It had no running water, so the beverage was served in its original container. The restrooms were in the form of outhouses. The clientele was strictly local residents and the bar was never desegregated. It is believed that Charlie Amoss moved the old West Friendship schoolhouse to this location and converted it to the tavern. Nothing remains at that curve in the road going west from Maryland 32 to identify the old watering hole. From the author's collection

Blueprints and a Caterpillar bulldozer were present for the spring 1985 groundbreaking of the Owen Brown Business Center. Douglas McGregor, general manager for Howard Research and Development; Hillsman Wilson and Leonard Gerber of McCormick Properties; and J. Hugh Nichols, county executive, were in attendance. Westinghouse Electric is occupying the property located on Berger Road in the Guilford Industrial Park. Office of Public Information, Howard County

Rising like "Brigadoon" from the meadows, the Town Center of Columbia exhibits the features of a growing city. At the far left is the large hotel, the Columbia Inn, which overlooks Lake

Providing a contrast to the new town of Columbia is Ellicott City, the old town. A favorite view from the Columbia Pike captures the gold domed courthouse and the spire of the former Presbyterian church, now the home of the Howard County Historical Society. A stability is reflected in the old town, which helps one to understand how this county seat has survived more than two hundred years in the valley of the Patapsco River. Photo by Leigh Wachter

Kittamaqundi. Continuing mid-photo from the left are the Rouse Company building, the American City building, the Equitable office building and the Columbia Mall. Newer office buildings in the background and the foreground are also important components of the city. This photo was taken from the senior high-rise structure, Vantage Place. Keith Weller, Patuxent Publishing Corporation

Bibliography

Bedini, Silvio. *The Life of Benjamin Banneker.* New York: Charles Scribner's, 1972.

Brooks, Neal A., and Rockel, Eric G. *A History of Baltimore County.* Towson, Md.: Friends of the Towson Library, 1979.

Evans, Charles Worthington; Tyson, Martha Ellicott; and Bartlett, G. Hunter. *American Family History.* Cockeysville, Md.: Fox, Ellicott, Evans Fund, 1976.

Fox, William Lloyd, and Walsh, Richard, eds. *Maryland: A History 1632–1974.* Baltimore: Maryland Historical Society, 1974.

Gardner, G. Page, "Study of Public Education in Howard County, Maryland." University of Maryland Master Thesis, 1926.

Harwood, Herbert H., Jr. *Impossible Challenge, The Baltimore and Ohio Railroad in Maryland.* Baltimore: Barnard, Roberts, & Co., Inc., 1979.

Holland, Celia M. *Ellicott City, Maryland, Mill Town, U.S.A.* Chicago. Adams Press, 1970.

Hopkins, G. M. *Atlas of Howard County Maryland, 1878.* Reprint. Ellicott City, Md.: Howard County Bicentennial Commission, Inc., 1975.

McGrain, John. "Grist Mills in Baltimore County, Md." Baltimore County Public Library, 1980.

McGrain, John. "Oella—Its Thread of History." Oella Community Improvement Association, 1976.

Van Devanter, Ann C., ed. *Anywhere So Long as There Be Freedom.* Baltimore Museum of Art, 1975.

Warfield, J. D. *Founders of Anne Arundel and Howard Counties, Md. reprinted.* Baltimore: Regional Publishing Co., 1973.

Index

A

Alberton Mills, 50, 51, 100
Algonquian, 19
Alhambra, 12
Allview Golf course, 169
American Association of University Women, 208
Amoss, Charlie, 219
Amoss, Oliver, 91
Anderson, Isaac, 66
Angelo's Cottage, 122, 127, 128
Annapolis and Elk Ridge Railroad, 109
Annapolis Junction, 100
Antioch College, 207
Arcadia, 74
Asbury, Francis, 146
Asbury School, 160
Avalon Mills, 58

B

Baltimore and Ohio Railroad, 28, 51, 120, 124
Banneker, Benjamin, 44, 45, 46
Bassler, Benjamin, 171
Belmont, 26, 32
Belvidere, 9
Billy Barton (horse), 173
Bodine, A. Aubrey, 24, 41
Bollman Bridge, 59, 198
Bollman, Wendel, 59-61
Brendel's Park, 72, 169, 177, 183
Brinker, John, 37
Brown, George D., 34
Brown, Owen, 216
Brown, Ruth, 85
Brown, Samuel, 85
Brown, Thomas, 85
Bruce, Howard, 173
Buetefisch, Henry, 131
Burgess, George, 139
Burgess, Samuel W., 138
Burgess, Thomas, 66
Burleigh Manor, 177

C

Calvert, Cecil, 16
Calvert, George, 16
Campmeeting grounds, 64
Carr, Willie, 93
Carroll, Charles of Carrollton, 7, 44, 62, 63, 66, 69, 72
Carroll, John Lee, 10, 13, 15, 71
Caton, Richard, 64
Chatham, 10, 12, 93
Chesapeake Bay, 19, 25, 26
Chew, Harriet, 8
Chew, Peggy, 8
Christmas Gardens, 179

Churches
    Christ Episcopal Church, 144, 147
    Daisy United Methodist, 165
    Emory Methodist, 154
    First Presbyterian, 154
    Gaines AME, 154
    Gary Memorial Methodist Church, 52
    Mount Gregory United Methodist, 164
    Mount Hebron Presbyterian, 211
    St. Augustine Catholic, 37, 147, 167
    St. James Methodist, 146
    St. Johns Episcopal, 12, 74
    St. Paul's Catholic, 127, 155
    St. Peter's Episcopal, 127, 155
Civil War, 35, 66, 109
Claremont, 12
Clark, James, 83
Clark, John L., 83
Clay, Henry, 65
Clarksville, 100, 109, 167
Clarksville High School, 163, 168
Clover Hill, 217
Cobb, Joe, Mrs., 34
Columbia, 194
Cooksville, 100, 101, 112, 113
County Council, 204
Crapster, William T., 186
Crowner, Liza Jane, 68

D

Daisy, 114, 115
Daniels, C. R., 50, 51, 52, 53
Darnell, Mary, 64
Davis, William, 84
Davis and Hemphill, 36
Dayton, 100
Dickey, W. J., 54
Dobbin, George W., 34, 80
Donaldson, Thomas, 10, 28, 80
Donut Corporation of America, 142
Dorsey, Albert, 113
Dorsey, Caleb, 66, 74
Dorsey, Caleb, Dr., 18, 22, 23
Dorsey, Caleb, Jr., 26, 31, 32
Dorsey, Channing, 185, 186
Dorsey, Charles Worthington, 12
Dorsey, Edward, 13, 32
Dorsey, Helen, 66
Dorsey, Larkin, 73
Dorsey, Mary Tolley, 11
Dorsey, Sallie, 11
Dorsey, Reuben M., 66, 73, 74
Dorsey, Thomas Beale, 10, 74, 76
Dorsey, Thomas, 26, 68
Dorsey, W. Baker, 66
Dorsey, William H. G., 75, 80

Dorsey Speedway, 191
Doughoregan Manor, 12, 13, 18, 22, 23, 25, 63, 64, 70-72
Dunloggin Dairy Farm, 12, 93

E

Eastons, 125
Education, 148
Elkhorn Farmhouse, 172
Elkridge, 25, 30, 38, 40, 66, 100
Elkridge Assembly Rooms, 28
Elkridge Baseball team, 39
Elkridge County Club, 38, 39
Elkridge Furnace, 25, 27
Elkridge High School, 29
Elkridge Landing, 12, 24, 27, 31, 99
Elkridge National Park, 197
Elkridge Preparatory Meeting, 49
Ellicott, Andrew, 43, 47
Ellicott, Andrew, Major, 45, 48
Ellicott, Benjamin, 45, 46, 48
Ellicott, Elizabeth, 47, 49, 146
Ellicott, George, 44, 47, 102, 146
Ellicott, George, Jr., 54, 125, 129
Ellicott, John, 42, 44, 46, 128
Ellicott, Jonathan, 44, 47, 127
Ellicott, Joseph, 45, 46, 48, 93
Ellicott, Judith, 48
Ellicott Mills, 12, 42, 44, 49, 65, 66, 100, 123, 128
Elmonte, 12
Elysville, 50, 53, 99, 100
Enchanted Forest, 190

F

Fairfields, 83
Fairview, 171
Fairy Knowe, 28, 33
Fells Lane, 161, 202
Fire equipment, 130, 140, 195
Fireman's Carnival, 177
Fleming, Aubrey, 119
Fleming, Clara, 119
Fleming, John J., 90
Font Hill, 93, 94
Fort, William, 125
Four-H clubs, 182
Fulton, 101
Furnace Avenue, 38

G

Gaither, Charles D., 81
Gaither, Dennis, 66
Gaither, Greenbury, 86
Gaither, Jane, 183
Gaither's Chance, 85, 86
Gambrill mill, 142

Gary, 53
Gary, Alberta, 50
Gary, James A., 50
Glenelg, 10, 100, 181
Glenwood, 77, 100, 113, 168
Glenwood Institute, 113, 165
Glenwood Community Brass Band, 116
Gold rush, 80
Granite Manufacturing Co., 49
Goddard, Mary Katherine, 27
Goddard, William, 27
Goddess, 190
Gorman, Arthur Pue, Jr., 170
Gorman, Arthur Pue, Sr., 14, 96
Granite factory, 128
Great Falls Iron Works, 27, 31
Green Cross Garage, 168, 175
Griffith, Joshua, 26
Griffith, Dennis, 21, 46, 99
Guilford, 50, 168

H

Hairbarium, 84
Hammond, Rezin, 65, 177
Hammond, Philip, 26
Hanover, 26
Harriday, Dena, 114
Harriday, Isaiah, 114
Hayden, Edwin Parson, 140
Hazelhurst, Henry R., 129, 130
Henrietta Maria, 16
Highland, 110, 168
Hill, William H., Jr., 183, 184
Hilton, 21, 100
Hipsley, Freeborn, 66
Hockley Mill, 26, 35
Hodges, William, Dr., 132
Homemaker's club, 177
Howard, George, 8, 10, 11, 13, 15
Howard House, 134, 135, 137
Howard, John Eager, 8-10, 64
Howard Vocational Technical Center, 203
Hugg-Thomas Park, 96
Hunt, Beulah, 86, 93, 94
Hurricane Agnes, 125

I

Ilchester, 54, 56, 94, 98, 100, 102, 103, 176
Indians, 18, 19
Irving, Washington, 55

J

Jones, Omar, 205, 213
Jonestown, 100, 161

222

K

Kennedy, John Pendleton, 55
Knisley, James, 174
Knisley, Leola Mae, 174

L

Latrobe, Benjamin H., Jr., 28
Latrobe, John H. B., 24, 33, 73
Lawn, The, 34
Lawson, Alexander, 27
Lawrence, Dawson, 85
Ligon, T. Watkins, 10, 11, 15
Lilburn, 129
Lindens, 95
Lisbon, 10, 66, 100, 121
Long Corner, 64, 100, 117
Long Reach, 22
Longwood, 77, 78
Lord Baltimore, 18

M

McCubbin, James, 12
MacGill, Patrick, 26
Macgill, James, 144, 147, 201
Marriott's Great America, 210
Marriottsville, 100
Mathews, James B., 113
Matthews, William McKinley, Jr., 181
Mayfield, W. F., 133
Mayfield, T. Hunt, 201
Mellor, Benjamin, Jr., 179
Merriweather Post Pavilion, 199, 208
Middle Patuxent Archeological Group, 19
Moore, Mordecai, 26
Mount Hebron, 74
Mount Ida, 127
Moxley, Ezekiel, 97, 125
Moxley, Charles, 97
Moxley, Mark, 97, 125
Moxley, Norman, 97, 171, 196
Moxley, Robert, 198
Moxley, Russell, 97, 171

N

Nanticokes, 19
New Town Hall, 10, 122
Normandy Bowling Alleys, 192
Norwood, Edward, 27
Norwood, Samuel, 27

O

Oakdale, 4, 14, 88
Oakland, 82, 215
Oakland Mills, 50, 100
Oak Lawn Seminary, 140
Oella, 54
Oldfield, Hamilton, 139

Oliver Viaduct, 138
One Spot, 108
Orange Grove Mill, 57
Owings, Levin, 87
Owings, T. B., Dr., 126
Owingsville, 100, 112

P

Patapsco Female Institute, 12, 81, 122, 158
Patapsco Manufacturing Company, 55
Patapsco Flour Mill, 128
Patapsco River, 26, 51, 120, 128, 178
Patapsco Park, 57, 178
Patteron Viaduct, 54
Phelp, Almira Hart Lincoln, 124, 158
Peach, Josephine O., 111
Peach, Warner W., Sr., 111
Peach, William, Jr., 178
Pfefferkorn, Beatrice, 184
Pfefferkorn, James, 182
Piscataway, 20
Pickett, Charles D., 118
Pickett, Arthur, 196
Pindell School, 162, 164
Pine Orchard, 100, 111
Police Department, 205
Poplar Spring, 11, 21, 90, 100, 117-119, 168
Post Office, Columbia, 201
Post Office, Ellicott City, 180
Pue, Arthur, Jr., 76

Q

Quaker School, 135

R

Red House Tavern, 21, 78
Rescue Squad, 189
Rex, William, 188
Ridgely, Charles Sterrett, 10
Ridgely, Prudence Gough, 11, 13
River Hill Game Preserve, 215
Rock Hill, 124, 126, 156
Rockland Farm, 86, 87
Roxbury Mills, 101, 114
Rouse, James, 11, 198

S

Santa Heim, 104
Saplin Range, 87
Saint Charles College, 12, 72
Saint Clement's Hall, 159
Saint Mary's College, 103
Savage, 59, 60, 65, 100, 104-106, 108
Savage High School, 161
Savage Manufacturing Company, 58

Savage, John, 58, 107
Schofield, John, 66
Schools
    Primary, 148-150
    Private, 151
    Ellicott City, 156, 157, 200, 212
Scott, Charles, 196
Scott, Melville, 175
Senior Center, Florence Bain, 218
Shepherd, Rev. J. Avery, 159
Shipley, B. H., 140
Simpsonville, 112, 168
Slack, S. Dallas, 187
Smith, Capt. John, 26
Spurrier's Tavern, 21, 67
Starkwether, Nathan, 12, 75, 76
Starr, Scott, 138, 143
Stewart, Claudius, 65
Stirn, Donald, 212
Stockett, Thomas G., Dr., 81
Stockwood, 81
Stowe, Thomas, 27
Susquahannocks, 19
Sykes, Carlton R., 95, 172
Sykes, Claude, 95
Sykes, Guy Carlton, 95
Sykes, Mordecai Gist, 95
Sykes, Rachel Gist, 95
Sykes, Sylvanus, 95

T

Talbott, Georgia, 86
Talbott, Edward, 86, 159
Talbott, Richard, 159
Temperance Hall, 27
Thistle Mills, 56, 101, 147
Thomas Garage, 112
Thomas Viaduct, 28, 35, 41, 58, 60, 209
Thompson, Harvey, 138
Tilghman's Store, 38
Tittsworth, Edyth, 141
Toll gate, 91
Tom Thumb, 73
Tongue Row, 143
Triadelphia, 116
Trinity School, 103
Trolley, 136
Troy, 68
Tyson, Martha Ellicott, 44, 47, 123, 145
Tubman, Harriet, High School, 163
Tyler's Store, 214

U

Union Chapel, 164
Union Mills, 54
Upper Anne Arundel County, 21, 23

Upper Mills, 45, 48
U.S. Route One, 40, 41, 174, 213

V

Viaduct House, 36
Viaduct Manufacturing Company, 36
Votta's Band, 92
Votta, Frank, 92
Votta, Ida, 178
Votta, John, 178

W

Wallich, Elwood, 162, 185
Watersville, 90
Warfield, Albert G., Jr., 89
Warfield, Albert G., Sr., 4, 14
Warfield, Charles Alexander, 77, 78
Warfield, Edward, 175
Warfield, Edwin, 4, 10, 14, 88, 97, 117
Warfield, Gustavus, 66, 78
Warfield, Mary Thomas, 77
Warfield's Academy, 164
Washington Trust Bank, 172
Washington Turnpike, 37
Waters, 101
Waterloo Elementary School, 211
Watkins, William W., 10, 66
Waveland, 73
Waverly, 11, 13
Weber's Quarry, 135
Wehland, George, 186
Wehland, Helen, 186
Wehland, Herman, 89
Wehland, Robert, 186
Welling, Henry, 65
Welling, William, 66, 79
West Friendship, 100, 162
Wheatfields, 83, 188
Wilde Lake, 206
Williams, Amos, 58
Willow Grove jail, 131
Wilton, 12, 75
Woodbine, 101, 120, 121
Woodlawn, 76
Woodstock, 100, 110
Woodstock Quarries, 178
World War I, 168
World War II, 181
Worthington, Thomas, 65

Y

Yates, Robert, 133
YMCA, 205, 206

Z

Zeltman, Raymond, 184
Zepp, Russell, 189

About the Author

A resident of Howard County, Maryland, for twenty-five years, Joetta Cramm has taught local history through Howard Community College for more than ten years. Her interest in local history was piqued during the 1972 Bicentennial celebration of the founding of Ellicott City. At this time the American Association of University Women, Ellicott City branch, of which she was then president, developed a walking tour of the old town. Since then she has spoken to schools, scouts, civic organizations, businesses, and historical organizations sharing her slides of the county. She has researched a number of private homes, tracing them back to the original patent. Ms. Cramm has led tours of the county for a variety of groups, including the Smithsonian Associates and the county Department of Recreation and Parks.

Ms. Cramm serves as a legislative assistant to the Howard County Council, following many years of community and volunteer activities in the county. Born and raised in East Moline, Illinois, she graduated from Western Illinois University and taught in Illinois and South Dakota before moving to Maryland. She has traveled extensively and enjoys gardening when time permits.

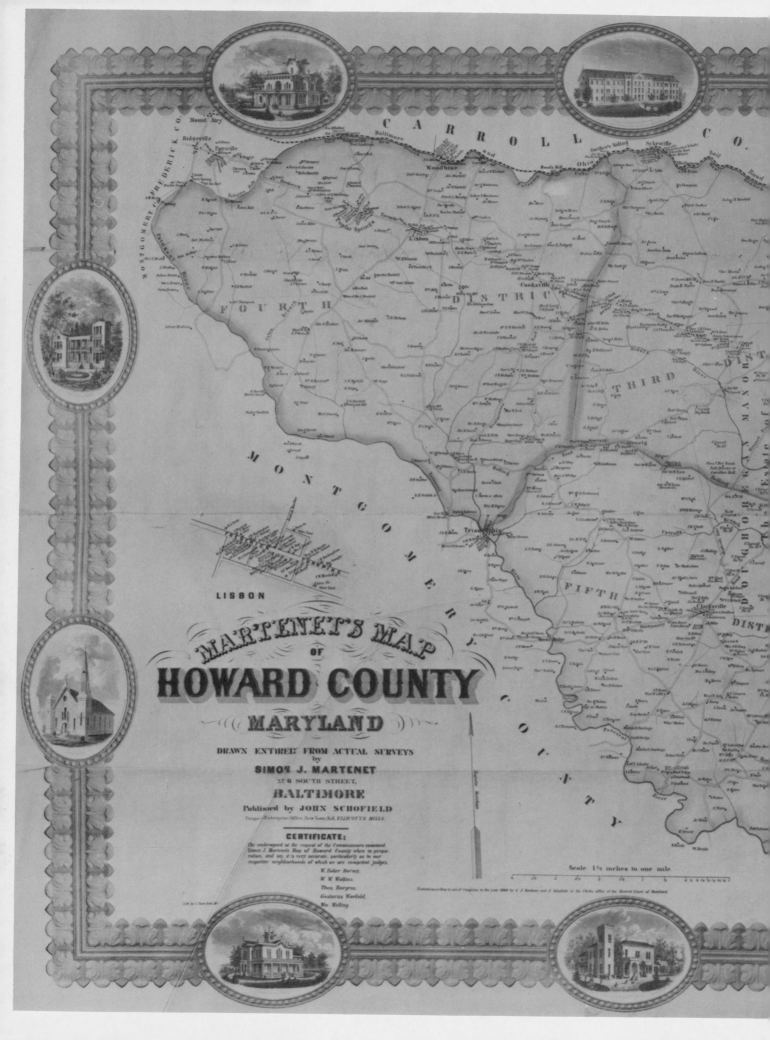

LISBON

MARTENET'S MAP
OF
HOWARD COUNTY
MARYLAND

DRAWN ENTIRELY FROM ACTUAL SURVEYS
by
SIMON J. MARTENET
No 6 SOUTH STREET,
BALTIMORE
Published by JOHN SCHOFIELD

CERTIFICATE:

The undersigned at the request of the Commissioners examined
Simon J. Martenet's Map of Howard County when in preparation, and say it is very accurate, particularly as to our
respective neighborhoods of which we are competent judges.

W. Baker Dorsey.
W. W. Watkins.
Thos. Burgess.
Gustavus Warfield.
Wm. Welling.

Scale 1½ inches to one mile.